D1708106

LANGUAGES IN CONTACT

LANGUAGES IN CONTACT

CONTACT

FINDINGS AND PROBLEMS

by

URIEL WEINREICH

With a Preface by

ANDRÉ MARTINET

Seventh Printing

1970

MOUTON

THE HAGUE · PARIS

Originally published as Number 1 in the series "Publications of the Linguistic Circle of New York" (New York, 1953).

Second Printing 1963
Third Printing 1964
Fourth Printing 1966
Fifth Printing 1967
Sixth Printing 1968

To My Parents

and to Bina

Preface

There was a time when the progress of research required that each community should be considered linguistically self-contained and homogeneous. Whether this autarcic situation was believed to be a fact or was conceived of as a working hypothesis need not detain us here. It certainly was a useful assumption. By making investigators blind to a large number of actual complexities, it has enabled scholars, from the founding fathers of our science down to the functionalists and structuralists of today, to abstract a number of fundamental problems. to present for them solutions perfectly valid in the frame of the hypothesis, and generally to achieve, perhaps for the first time, some rigor in a research involving man's psychic activity.

Linguists will always have to revert at times to this pragmatic assumption. But we shall now have to stress the fact that a linguistic community is *never* homogeneous and hardly ever self-contained. Dialectologists have pointed to the permeability of linguistic cells, and linguistic changes have been shown to spread like waves through space. But it remains to be emphasized that linguistic diversity begins next door, nay, at home and within one and the same man. It is not enough to point out that each individual is a battle-field for conflicting linguistic types and habits, and, at the same time, a permanent source of linguistic interference. What we heedlessly and somewhat rashly call 'a language' is the aggregate of millions of such microcosms many of which evince such aberrant linguistic comportment that the question arises whether they should not be grouped into other 'languages'. What further complicates the picture, and may, at the same time, contribute to clarify it, is the feeling of linguistic allegiance which will largely determine the responses of every individual. This, even more than sheer intercourse, is the cement that holds each one of our 'languages' together: It is different allegiance which makes two separate languages of Czech and Slovak more than the actual material differences between the two literary languages.

One might be tempted to define bilingualism as divided linguistic allegiance. Divided allegiance is what strikes the unilingual person as startling, abnormal, almost uncanny in bilingualism. Neither the layman nor the dialectologist will use the term 'bilingualism' in the case of country folks using alternately some form of a standard language and their own patois because there should be no linguistic allegiance to the latter. Yet the concept of linguistic allegiance is too vague to be of any help in deciding, in doubtful cases, whether or not we should diagnose a bilingual situation. Furthermore, nothing would be gained for the linguist by thus restricting the use of 'bilingualism' if this might induce the language contact specialist to exclude from his field a vast number of sociolinguistic situations that deserve careful consideration. The clash, in the same individual, of two languages of comparable social and cultural value, both spoken by millions of cultured unilinguals, may be psychologically most spectacular, but unless we have to do with a literary genius, the permanent linguistic traces of such a clash will be nil. The coexistence, in a number of humble peasants, of two at times conflicting sets of linguistic habits, the one a prestigious language, the other a despised patois, may have important repercussions on the linguistic history of that part of the world. Linguistic allegiance is a fact, an important fact, but we should not let it decide when language contact begins.

We all, more or less, adapt our speech to circumstances and differentiate it from one interlocutor to another. Now this unceasing process of adaptation would seem to differ basically from what happens when we shift from one language to another, as from English to Russian. In the former case we, all the time, make use of the same system; what changes from one moment to the next, is our choice among the lexical riches and expressive resources which the language, always the same, puts at our disposal. In the latter case we leave aside one totally homogeneous system and shunt off to another totally homogeneous one. This is at least what we assume would take place in an ideal bilingual situation. But to what extent is this situation actually realized? By the side of a few linguistic virtuosos who, by dint of constant cultivation, manage to keep their two, or more, linguistic mediums neatly distinct, wouldn't careful observation reveal in the overwhelming majority of cases some traces at least of structural merger? On the other hand couldn't we imagine all sorts of intermediate cases between every successive two among the following ones; a unilingual who shifts from style to style; a substandard speaker who can, if need be, trim his speech into something close to standard; a patois speaker who can gradually improve his language from homely and slipshod to what we might call his best linguistic behavior, for all practical purposes the standard language; another patois speaker who will treat his vernacular and the standard as two clearly different registers with largely deviating structures? Mutual understanding cannot be used as a criterion of unilinguality because it is no great problem for Danes and Norwegians, Czechs and Slovaks to converse, each man speaking his own language. Mutual understanding is a highly relative concept. Who knows all of 'his' language? It will often be easier to understand the foreigner enquiring about the station than to follow the discussion of two local technicians. Two speakers who, when first brought together, had found their respective dialects mutually unintelligible, may in a few hours or a few days discover the clues to unimpeded intercourse. If cooperation is a pressing necessity every one will soon learn enough of the other man's language to establish communication even if the two mediums in contact have no genetic ties or synchronic resemblances of any sort. If the will to communicate is wholly or mainly on one side, a bilingual situation will soon develop on that side.

Contact breeds imitation and imitation breeds linguistic convergence. Linguistic divergence results from secession, estrangement, loosening of contact. In spite of the efforts of a few great scholars, like Hugo Schuchardt, linguistic research has so far favored the study of divergence at the expense of convergence. It is time the right balance should be restored. Linguistic convergence may be observed and studied in all places and at all times, but its study becomes par-

ticularly rewarding when it results from the contact of two clearly distinct structures. It is a scientific exploration of contemporary bilingual patterns that will
enable us to define exactly what shall be meant by such terms as substratum,
superstratum, and adstratum, and to what extent we have a right to apply them
to a given historical situation. We needed a detailed survey of all the problems
involved in and connected with bilingualism by a scholar well informed of current linguistic trends and with a wide personal experience of bilingual situations.
Here it is.

ANDRÉ MARTINET

A NOTE ON THE REPRINTED EDITION
(OF 1963)

Ever since the original edition of 1953 went out of print, the author has
been eager to prepare a thoroughly revised version of the book, in which he
could incorporate what he has learned about language contact in the ensuing
years: from the criticisms of reviewers, colleagues, and students; from his
readings, both in older sources previously missed and in current literature;
and from his own and his students' investigations of various aspects of
bilingualism and linguistic interference. However, academic duties and urgent
research commitments prevent the immediate completion of this major task;
in the meantime, the demand for copies of the original edition appears to be
undiminished. Consequently, it was with great satisfaction that the author
accepted the proposal of Mouton to reissue the original edition in a photo-
mechanical offprint and to keep it available while the revised version of the
book is in the works.

U. W.

Acknowledgments

I am profoundly grateful to Professor André Martinet for his guidance and help from the earliest to the final stages of this work. It was under his supervision that the master's thesis and the doctoral dissertation on which the book is based were written. I therefore thought it fitting to adopt as the title of this study the name of a course which he introduced at Columbia University. I also thank Professor Roman Jakobson, now at Harvard University, for his encouragement at the outset of the project, and Professor Joseph H. Greenberg at Columbia for his helpful criticism on each part of the dissertation.

The American Council of Learned Societies was responsible for making possible my field work in Switzerland under a Research Fellowship in 1949–50. I thank the Council and Mr. William Ainsworth Parker, its Secretary on Fellowships, for their generous and sympathetic interest in my training and research. Thanks for its aid in the publication of the book are also due to Columbia University, where I have had the privilege of occupying the Atran Chair in Yiddish Language, Literature, and Culture since 1952.

The teachers, friends, and informants in Switzerland who helped me so whole-heartedly in my field work are too many to enumerate. I should like to record my indebtedness at least to the following: Rudolf Hotzenköcherle, Professor of German; the late Jakob Jud, Professor of Romance Linguistics; Eugen Dieth, Professor of Phonetics and Director of the Phonetic Laboratory; Richard Weiss, Professor of Folklore; and Manfred Szadrowsky, Professor of Germanic Linguistics (all at Zurich University); furthermore, to the Schweizerische Gesellschaft für Volkskunde in Basle for permission to examine the unpublished material of the Swiss Atlas of Folk Culture; to the Ligia Romontscha in Chur for its constant assistance (especially to Mr. Stiaffan Loringett, its president, and to Dr. Jon Pult); to Dr. Andrea Schorta, editor of the Grison Romansh Dictionary; to Professors Ramun Vieli and Rudolf O. Tönjachen of the Grison Cantonal School; to my friends Gion Barandùn in Feldis and Margritta Salis in Thusis; and to Dr. G. Gangale of Copenhagen University.

I also thank Professors Einar Haugen of the University of Wisconsin, A. Debrunner of the University of Berne, Ralph Beals and George C. Barker of the University of California, Paul H. Christophersen of Ibadan College, Nigeria, James Rahder of Yale University, and Hywella Saer of the University College of Wales for their bibliographical suggestions; Professors John Lotz and Carl F. Bayerschmidt of Columbia University, Max Weinreich of the City College of New York, Carl F. Voegelin of Indiana University, and Dr. Robert Billigmeier of Standford University for constructive criticism of various chapters.

Above all, I am grateful to my wife, Beatrice S. Weinreich, for her able and substantial help at every stage of the project. Without her participation in it, and without her encouragement in moments of dismay, I could not have brought the book to its present form.

U. W.

Contents

TRANSCRIPTION NOTE

For the presentation of phonemic and phonetic forms, the International Phonetic Alphabet has been utilized. However, because of typographical limitations, small capitals have been used to indicate lax, voiceless stops; thus, [D] = I.P.A. [d]. Also, for retroflex *r*, the sign [ṛ] had to be employed. Where the pronunciation is not relevant, forms are cited in conventional orthography. Forms belonging to languages that do not use the Latin alphabet are cited in a transliteration which includes the following graphs: š = [ʃ], č = [tʃ], ž = [ʒ], *j* = consonantal *i*, *x* = [x]; ' = palatalization. Stress is indicated in the transliteration by an acute accent over the stressed vowel, e.g. Russian *nogá*, *nóžka*.

As for the transliteration of bibliographical titles, see note on p. 123.

1 The Problem of Approach

1.1 Contact and Interference

In the present study, two or more languages will be said to be IN CONTACT if they are used alternately by the same persons. The language-using individuals are thus the locus of the contact.

The practice of alternately using two languages will be called BILINGUALISM, and the persons involved, BILINGUAL.[1] Those instances of deviation from the norms of either language which occur in the speech of bilinguals as a result of their familiarity with more than one language, i.e. as a result of language contact, will be referred to as INTERFERENCE phenomena. It is these phenomena of speech, and their impact on the norms of either language exposed to contact, that invite the interest of the linguist.

The term interference implies the rearrangement of patterns that result from the introduction of foreign elements into the more highly structured domains of language, such as the bulk of the phonemic system, a large part of the morphology and syntax, and some areas of the vocabulary (kinship, color, weather, etc.). It would be an oversimplification to speak here of borrowing, or mere additions to an inventory. As Vogt puts it (**599,** 35),[2] "every enrichment or impoverishment of a system involves necessarily the reorganization of all the old distinctive oppositions of the system. To admit that a given element is simply added to the system which receives it without consequences for this system would ruin the very concept of system." In the more loosely patterned domains of a language—some of the syntax, or vocabulary of an incidental nature—"borrowing" might more properly be spoken of when the transfer of an element as such is to be stressed. But even there the possibility of ensuing rearrangements in the patterns, or interference, cannot be excluded.

1.2 Difference Between Languages

Language contact and bilingualism will be considered here in the broadest sense, without qualifications as to the degree of difference between the two languages. For the purposes of the present study, it is immaterial whether the two systems are "languages," "dialects of the same language," or "varieties of the same dialect." The greater the difference between the systems, i.e. the more numerous the mutually exclusive forms and patterns in each, the greater is the learning problem and the potential area of interference. But the mechanisms of interference, abstracted from the amount of interference, would appear to be the same whether the contact is between Chinese and French or between two sub-

---

[1] Unless otherwise specified, all remarks about bilingualism apply as well to multilingualism, the practice of using alternately three or more languages.

[2] Bold-face numbers in parentheses refer to the bibliography (pp. 123 ff.); light-face numbers indicate pages in the cited works.

varieties of English used by neighboring families.[3] And while control of two such similar systems is not ordinarily called bilingualism, the term in its technical sense might easily be extended to cover these cases of contact as well.

From the point of view of the bilingual, the origin of a similarity between two languages—whether it is the result of a common heritage or a convergent development—is irrelevant. A particular type of relationship, however, which occurs frequently among genetically related systems is that which can be stated as an automatic conversion formula. Thus, in central Romansh, most [awŋ] occurrences of one village correspond to [aŋ] sequences of another and to [œŋ] sequences of a third. Insofar as such conversions are regular, they diminish the interdialectal gap and simplify the problems of the bilingual; to the extent that they are irregular, they present pitfalls. By following regular conversion patterns, many a Frenchmen has been tempted to use *inconvenient* as a noun in English, after the model of the French noun /ēkōveniã/.[4]

Great or small, the differences and similarities between the languages in contact must be exhaustively stated for every domain—phonic, grammatical, and lexical—as a prerequisite to an analysis of interference.[5] It might even be fruitful to draw up general canons of differential description.[6] These should probably include, among others, a picture of the degree of *apriori* structural homogeneity of the languages in contact and the precedents for borrowing in each.

Some investigators have explored the possibilities of expressing the difference between two languages in a brief formula. One method has been to measure the proportion of common vocabulary;[7] another approach is based on experimental measurements of mutual intelligibility of dialects.[8] It remains to be shown, however, how the resulting numerical coefficients can be utilized in a bird's-eye survey of a given contact situation.

[3] Since the identity of two very similar varieties of a language often depends on the identity of two or more specific interlocutors, the concept of "idiolect," used by some linguists to designate a single person's total set of speech habits at any one time, could not be applied to the present discussion.

[4] Graur (175) cites his experience of rendering Rumanian *loc viran* 'waste place' in French as /ljœ virã/, according to well-known conversion patterns, only to discover that Rumanian *viran* is of Turkish origin, and unknown in French. Among Yiddish speakers, such mock German forms as *leváne* (after Yiddish *levóne* 'moon' on the pattern of *Tag:tog*) are a standard joke.

[5] M. E. Smith, author of one of the most ambitious experiments on interference to date (531), contents herself with a four-page outline of the differences between eleven languages as unlike as English, Cantonese, and Tagalog. Obviously generalizations of this type cannot serve the linguist.

[6] The problem was investigated by Seidel (505), who gave an exemplary differential treatment of two languages (Rumanian and Russian), but reserved judgment concerning general canons.

[7] See Reed and Spicer (438), where previous literature is listed. Cf. also Dodd's "index of familiarity" (125) and Swadesh's r-coefficient (557).

[8] Voegelin and Harris (598). The technique might be utilized in investigating cases of non-reciprocal intelligibility, such as is reported to exist between speakers of Swedish and Danish: The latter are said to understand the former readily, but not vice versa.

1.3 Psychological and Socio-Cultural Setting of Language Contact

The forms of mutual interference of languages that are in contact are stated in terms of descriptive linguistics. Even the causes of specific interference phenomena can, in most cases, be determined by linguistic methods: If the phonic or grammatical systems of two languages are compared and their differences delineated, one ordinarily has a list of the potential forms of interference in the given contact situation. Lexical borrowing, too, can often be explained by investigating the points on which a given vocabulary is inadequate in the cultural environment in which the contact occurs. But not all potential forms of interference actually materialize. The precise effect of bilingualism on a person's speech varies with a great many other factors, some of which might be called extra-linguistic because they lie beyond the structural differences of the languages or even their lexical inadequacies. A full account of interference in a language-contact situation, including the diffusion, persistence, and evanescence of a particular interference phenomenon, is possible only if the extra-linguistic factors are considered.

Among the non-structural factors, some are inherent in the bilingual person's relation to the languages he brings into contact, for example:

a. The speaker's facility of verbal expression in general and his ability to keep two languages apart;

b. Relative proficiency in each language;[9]

c. Specialization in the use of each language by topics and interlocutors;

d. Manner of learning each language;

e. Attitudes toward each language, whether idiosyncratic or stereotyped.

Nor are extra-linguistic factors restricted to bilinguals as individuals. The impact of interference phenomena on the norms of a language may be greater if the contact occurs through groups of bilinguals. When dealing with bilinguals in groups, it is therefore useful to determine which, if any, of the above factors are characteristic of the group as a whole. In addition, there are certain other features of bilingual groups which are relevant to a study of interference, such as the following:

f. Size of bilingual group and its socio-cultural homogeneity or differentiation; breakdown into subgroups using one or the other language as their mother-tongue; demographic facts; social and political relations between these subgroups;

g. Prevalence of bilingual individuals with given characteristics of speech behavior (in terms of points *a-e* above) in the several subgroups;

h. Stereotyped attitudes toward each language ("prestige"); indigenous or immigrant status of the languages concerned;

---

[9] Many writers have attempted to define bilingualism by a minimum degree of proficiency in both languages; cf. Hall (189), 16f. But, as Bloomfield has pointed out (55, 56), the distinction is relative. It is more convenient to treat the factor of proficiency as one of the many variables.

i. Attitudes toward the culture of each language community;

j. Attitudes toward bilingualism as such;

k. Tolerance or intolerance with regard to mixing languages and to incorrect speech in each language;

l. Relation between the bilingual group and each of the two language communities of which it is a marginal segment.

It is thus in a broad psychological and socio-cultural setting that language contact can best be understood; what is needed is "a more exact treatment of the conditions under which . . . an influence [of one language on another] is possible and the ways it would work."[10] This involves reference to data not available from ordinary linguistic descriptions and requires the utilization of extra-linguistic techniques. On an interdisciplinary basis research into language contact achieves increased depth and validity. The present study, which springs primarily from linguistic interests, seeks also to explore the limits of the linguistic approach and some of the paths that lead beyond those limits. More precisely, it attempts to show to what extent interference is determined by the structure of two languages in contact as against non-linguistic factors in the socio-cultural context of the language contact.

Purely linguistic studies of languages in contact must be coordinated with extra-linguistic studies on bilingualism and related phenomena. Geographers and ethnographers have described bilingual populations; sociologists have examined the functioning of coexisting languages in a community; jurists have studied the legal status accorded to minority languages in various states; the inquiries of educators interested in bilingual children and in foreign-language teaching have stimulated psychologists to analyze the effects of bilingualism on personality. All these studies are described in a vast, scattered literature. But divergent as they are in purpose and scope, they are all essentially complementary in understanding a phenomenon of so many dimensions. The psychiatrist who, in generalizing about language disturbances of bilinguals, fails to make linguistically sound observations on his subjects' speech behavior undermines his conclusions in advance. Similarly, the linguist who makes theories about language influence but neglects to account for the socio-cultural setting of the language contact leaves his study suspended, as it were, in mid-air; "talk of substrata and superstrata must remain stratospheric unless we can found it solidly on the behavior of living observable speakers."[11]

Of course, the linguist is entitled to abstract language from considerations of a psychological or sociological nature. As a matter of fact, he SHOULD pose purely linguistic problems about bilingualism. He may then see the cause of the susceptibility of a language to foreign influence in its structural weaknesses; he may trace the treatment of foreign material in conformity with the structure of the borrowing language. But the extent, direction, and nature of interference of one language with another can be explained even more thoroughly in terms of the speech behavior of bilingual individuals, which in turn is conditioned by social

[10] Leopold (**304**), I, xiii.

[11] Haugen (**202**), 271.

relations in the community in which they live. In other words, more complete findings can be expected from coordinated efforts of all the disciplines interested in the problems. It is also the author's belief that the great advantages of this interdisciplinary approach to language contact are not necessarily dependent on the particular descriptive methods which have been applied in this work to the linguistic aspects of the problem.

Obviously the present study does not aim at exhausting the subject. Selected problems have been delineated, and the actual cases of contact and the interference forms that have been cited were selected out of a multitude of others for their illustrative value. Any student working in the field could furnish additional examples from his own experience.

1.4 Language Contact and Culture Contact

Language contact is considered by some anthropologists as but one aspect of culture contact, and language interference as a facet of cultural diffusion and acculturation. However, despite the flourishing of anthropological interest in contact problems, particularly in the United States since World War I, studies of language contact and culture contact have not enjoyed extensive coordination, and the relation between the two fields has not been properly defined. While each discipline is entitled to its own methodology, there are certain inescapable parallels in the two domains.

In linguistic interference, the problem of major interest is the interplay of structural and non-structural factors that promote or impede such interference. The structural factors are those which stem from the organization of linguistic forms into a definite system, different for every language and to a considerable degree independent of non-linguistic experience and behavior. The non-structural factors are derived from the contact of the system with the outer world, from given individuals' familiarity with the system, and from the symbolic value which the system as a whole is capable of acquiring and the emotions it can evoke. In present-day linguistics, the effectiveness of structural factors is taken more or less for granted.[12] But in culture-contact studies, too, the role of the organization of culture elements has been stressed time and again. The following passages are typical.

Obviously, the results of transmission . . . cannot be considered as mere additional acquisitions.[13]

Culture change normally involves not only the addition of a new element or elements to the culture, but also the elimination of certain previously existing elements and the modification and reorganization of the others.[14]

That a cultural practice is invested with emotion is an important thing about it, but is not decisive for its stability or lability. What decides between continuance or change seems to be whether or not a practice has

---

[12] For a survey of structuralist theory in linguistics, see Martinet (345).
[13] Thurnwald (572), 561.
[14] Linton (312), 469.

become involved in an ORGANIZED SYSTEM of ideas and sentiments: how
much it is interwoven with other items of culture into a larger pattern. If
it is thus connected . . . it has good expectations of persisting, since large
systems tend to endure. But a trait that is only loosely connected and
essentially free-floating can be superseded very quickly.[15]

Such statements reflect an emphasis in acculturation study which resembles
the structuralist approach to linguistic interference. To be sure, structuralism
in non-linguistic aspects of cultural science is not stressed to the same degree as
in linguistics, nor is it certain that it could or should be carried that far. But
anthropologists seem to be growing more and more aware of the structuring of
culture elements as a force affecting their transfer, and on this point they naturally look for guidance to linguistics, "the oldest of the sciences dealing with
culture," whose descriptive techniques have gained "an objectivity and a precision far beyond that produced by other sciences of culture."[16] More specifically, anthropologists investigating acculturation are urged to include linguistic
evidence, developed by the linguist, as indices of the total acculturative process;
in the words of one distinguished student of acculturation, its linguistic aspects
"offer unexplored potentialities" to the anthropologist.[17] Linguists on their part
need the help of anthropology to describe and analyze those factors governing
linguistic interference which, though lying beyond the structure of the languages in contact, do fall within the realm of culture. Finally, linguists and
anthropologists together, working from the premise that the individual is the
ultimate locus of contact, must turn to psychologists for their contribution to
the understanding of language and culture contact.[18]

While no systematic synthesis of linguistic and anthropological points of view
has been attempted in this study, certain areas of potentially fruitful comparison, especially on the matter of structural causation, have been brought into
the discussion.

[15] Kroeber (287), 402. Emphasis supplied.
[16] Hoijer (225), 337.
[17] Beals (33), 635.
[18] Cf. the psychological studies of acculturation by Thurnwald (572) and, notably,
Hallowell (192), who writes (pp. 174f.): "In the last analysis, it is individuals who respond
to and influence one another. . . . Individuals are the dynamic centers of the process of
interaction."

2 Mechanisms and Structural Causes of Interference

2.1 Theoretical Preliminaries

2.11 Interlingual Identification of Expression and Content Units

A structuralist theory of communication which distinguishes between speech and language (or *parole* and *langue*, message and code, process and system, behavior and norm) necessarily assumes that "every speech event belongs to a definite language."[1] Only on this assumption is it possible to conceive of an utterance containing some elements which belong to another language than the rest. Because it is usually known, to either the speaker or the describer or both, to which language an utterance as a whole belongs,[2] the non-belonging elements can be separated as "borrowed" or TRANSFERRED. This is one manifestation of linguistic interference.

But there is also a type of interference, extremely common in language contact, which does not involve an outright transfer of elements at all. It can affect both expression and content, and is analyzed most effectively in structural terms if it is assumed that the basic units of expression and content—the phonemes and semantemes—are defined within each language by oppositions to other phonemes and semantemes of that language. For example, /p/ in Russian, or $_R$/p/, is defined, among others, by its distinctive feature of non-palatality (in opposition to $_R$/p'/), while the definition of /p/ in English, or $_E$/p/, involves no such restriction. From the point of view of the languages, therefore, $_R$/p/ and $_E$/p/ cannot be "the same." However, the physical resemblance of [p] in certain renditions of both phonemes in speech—for example, in $_R$/t'ip/ 'type' and $_E$/tip/ 'tip', both pronounced with similar [-p]—tempts the bilingual to identify the two phonemes astride the limits of the languages. Even syllables and whole words in two languages are occasionally equated by dint of their "identical" or "similar" phonemic shapes; a Yiddish-speaking immigrant in the United States, for example, reported that to him English *cold* and his dialectal Yiddish /kɔlt/ 'cold' were, phonemically, "the same word."

Interlingual identifications can also be made between grammatical relationships and procedures other than segmental morphemes, such as word order. By comparing English and Russian sentences of the order SUBJECT + VERB + OBJECT, a bilingual may identify the English order with the Russian, even though its function in English is denotative, in Russian largely stylistic.

Finally, interlingual identifications of units occur on the plane of content. In English, a certain area of meaning is included in, and divided by, the semantemes

---

[1] Lotz (**325**), 712. See also Jakobson, Fant, and Halle (**245**, 11) and Fano (**144, 696**) on the principle of "switching code."

[2] On the possible loss of this awareness, see p. 63.

7

'foot' and 'leg'. Russian has no identical opposition; instead, it divides approximately the same content into three semantemes: 'nóžka' (furniture leg), 'nogá' (entire animal leg), and 'fut' (12-inch length). Thus, the semantemes in each language are differently defined. In a contact situation, however, the material similarity between some of the referents of, say, $_E$'foot' and $_R$'nogá' suggests to the bilingual an interlingual identification of the two.[3]

While in theory, then, the basic units—phonemes, features of order, selection, dependence, etc., and semantemes—of two languages are not commensurable, in practice classificatory overlappings of physical sound and of semantic reality are of course extremely common. The bilinguals' interlingual identifications only increase this overlapping; hence the particularly extensive parallelisms between languages which have been in long and intensive contact.

Inasmuch as a language is a system of oppositions, a partial identification of the systems is to the bilingual a reduction of his linguistic burden. And it is these natural identifications which are at the root of many forms of interference. The identification of English $_E$/p/ and Russian $_R$/p/ may lead the bilingual to pronounce *pull* in the Russian manner, i.e. [pul], rather than [pʰʊl]. The identification of the semantemes $_R$'nogá' and $_E$'foot' may lead him to say *I have long feet*, meaning 'legs'. Identification of the word-order patterns may cause him to violate English order by constructing a sentence of the type SUBJECT + OBJECT + VERB, e.g. *I him see*, which is perfectly admissible in Russian.

In the subsequent sections of this chapter, interference resulting from such inter-language identifications is discussed in detail.

2.12 Coexistence of Merging of Systems

It is of some theoretical interest to inquire whether, for a bilingual, the two phonemic or semantic systems in contact merge into a single system. In the phonemic domain, for example, the English-Russian bilingual has a stock of morphemes in which [t-], [t'-], and [tʰ-] all occur in identical environments.[4] As Swadesh has suggested (**556**, 65), "the two sets of sounds . . ., from the standpoint of phonemic theory, can be regarded as a single system"—a system with three voiceless dental stops. Another interpretation, however, seems preferable. Since the bilingual is ordinarily aware of the language to which his utterance "belongs,"[5] we may characterize the utterance by the feature of "Russianness" or "Englishness," extending over its entire length. Aspiration of the voiceless dental stop would then be an automatic concomitant feature of Englishness, non-aspiration (of non-palatals) a concomitant of Russianness (inasmuch as the bilingual does in fact correctly produce and suppress aspiration). The sounds [t-] and [tʰ-] could not now be found in identical environments, and a complemen-

---

[3] The preceding analysis can be conveniently phrased in glossematic terminology: While the forms of expression and content in each language are incomparable and incommensurable, certain overlappings in the substance of the expression and the content suggest their cross-identification to the bilingual.

[4] E.g. $_R$/ti/ 'you', $_R$/t'ip/ 'type', $_E$/tʰip/ 'tip'.

[5] On contrary cases, see §2.54.

tary distribution would be established. This restatement of the facts in terms of two coexistent systems, rather than a merged single system, probably corresponds more closely to the actual experience of the bilingual.[6]

Similar considerations apply on the plane of content. An English-French bilingual may, for example, have in his verbs a compound system of oppositions consisting of the following "tense" semantemes: $_E$'preterite', $_F$'definite past', $_F$'indefinite past', $_F$'imperfect', $_E$'non-past', $_F$'present', $_{EF}$'future'.[7] Again, it would be more convenient and probably more valid to keep the semantic systems separate, as are their phonemic expressions. In utterances marked by overall French-ness, the oppositions 'definite past'-'indefinite past'-'imperfect'-'present'-'future' would be admitted, while the triad 'preterite'-'non-past'-'future' would be restricted to utterances distinguished by their Englishness.[8]

There is need for experimental investigation of the possibility that some bilinguals interpret at least parts of the linguistic systems as merged rather than coexistent. The purely linguistic evidence so far has not been conclusive.

2.13 The Nature of the Sign in Language Contact

The problem of coexistence vs. merging also affects the nature of the sign, which, in Saussurean terms, combines a unit of expression and one of content.

Once an interlingual identification has occurred between semantemes of two languages in contact, it becomes possible for the bilingual to interpret two signs whose semantemes, or signifieds, he has identified as a compound sign with a single signified and two signifiers, one in each language. Instead of treating the English *book* and Russian *kníga* as two separate signs (A),[9] he could regard them as a compound sign (B):

$$(A) \quad \begin{array}{cc} \text{'book'} & \text{'kníga'} \\ | & | \\ \text{/buk/} & \text{/'kn'iga/} \end{array} \qquad (B) \quad \begin{array}{c} \text{'book'} \equiv \text{'kníga'} \\ \diagup \quad \diagdown \\ \text{/buk/} \quad \text{/'kn'iga/} \end{array}$$

Several writers have gone so far as to distinguish two types of bilingualism according to the two interpretations of the sign. Ščerba reports (**477**) that the bilingual Sorbians have only one language with two modes of expression; in other words, they possess one set of signifieds with two signifiers each, as in B

---

[6] This applies to interference in the SPEECH of bilinguals, which should be distinguished from the language as a system, even if influenced (see §2.14 below). In describing the more or less established "borrowings" in a LANGUAGE, a single phonemic system is often to be preferred; cf. Wonderly's conclusions about Spanish loanwords in Zoque (**650**) and Fries and Pike's theoretical discussion (**154, 31** and *passim*).

[7] The corresponding forms of *eat* and *manger*, for instance, are *ate, mangea, a mangé, mangeait, eats, mange, will eat=mangera*.

[8] We need not exclude the possibility that different bilinguals experience a merging of systems in various degrees (on individual differences, cf. §3.22). The question of merging vs. unmerged coexistence is a problem *par excellence* in speech-language relations. In studying it, psychological reasoning therefore cannot be excluded.

[9] It may be overlooked, for the purposes of the present discussion, that *kn'ig-a*, and possibly even *book+0*, can themselves be regarded as compounds of at least two signs each.

above.[10] Elsewhere (476) he classifies this as "pure" bilingualism, reserving the term "mixed" presumably for type A. Loewe (317) calls B a "two-member system of the same language."[11]

It would appear offhand that a person's or group's bilingualism need not be entirely of type A or B, since some signs of the languages may be compounded while others are not. No direct attempt has been made to date to determine experimentally the extent to which a given bilingual interprets signs as interlingual compounds (B), but a possible method for such an investigation emerges from the association techniques employed by H. Saer (462) in her experiments on Welsh-English bilingual children.[12] In those tests, children were requested to give their immediate verbal reactions to a series of Welsh and English stimulus words scattered at random. Both Welsh and English responses were permitted, regardless of the language of the stimulus word. The response and the elapsed time from the stimulus were recorded. A special type of answer turned out to be the "translation response," in which a subject responded with the English equivalent of the Welsh stimulus word and vice versa. This was an indication of a preoccupation with translating on the child's part—and a hint of the compounding of signs. By varying the domains from which the stimulus words were drawn, testing responses to equivalent semantemes in English and Welsh, and by other refinements of the technique, Saer opened exciting prospects for further experimentation.

One more interpretation of the sign by bilinguals needs to be considered, an interpretation which is likely to apply when a new language is learned with the help of another (by the so-called "indirect method"). The referents of the signs in the language being learned may then be not actual "things," but "equivalent" signs of the language already known. Thus, to an English speaker learning Russian, the signified of the form /ˈknˈiga/ may at first be not the object, but the English word *book*, thus:[13]

$$(C) \quad \left\{ \begin{array}{c} \text{'book'} \\ \text{/buk/} \end{array} \right\}$$
$$\text{/ˈknˈiga/}$$

Type C would seem to correspond to Roberts' "subordinative" bilingualism (450), while A would be the "coordinative" type. In this vein, too, Schuchardt (497, 424) distinguishes between *Sprachen können* (A) and *Sprachen kennen* (C).

[10] "I had occasion to observe closely a bilingual population. . . . I can state that each word of these bilingual persons carries three images: the semantic image, the sounds of the corresponding German word, and the sounds of the corresponding Sorbian word, all forming a unit like the word of any other language" (477, 12f.). Cf. also Capidan (91), 76.

[11] The distinction between "organic" and "inorganic" bilingualism, based on specialization of functions (see p. 81 below), is apparently but another facet of the same dichotomy.

[12] Described in greater detail by Bovet (73), 5ff. While Miss Saer's problem was formulated somewhat differently, her technique promises to be applicable in many additional ways.

[13] In the semiotic terminology of C. Morris, this would now be a "metasign" (377, 179–80).

How the transition from C to A occurs in language learning, and whether some speakers acquire fluency in a language while continuing to interpret all its signs by reference to signs in their first language, also merits investigation as a problem in psycholinguistics.[14]

2.14 Interference in Speech and in Language

In speech, interference is like sand carried by a stream; in language, it is the sedimented sand deposited on the bottom of a lake. The two phases of interference should be distinguished.[15] In speech, it occurs anew in the utterances of the bilingual speaker as a result of his personal knowledge of the other tongue. In language, we find interference phenomena which, having frequently occurred in the speech of bilinguals, have become habitualized and established. Their use is no longer dependent on bilingualism. When a speaker of language X uses a form of foreign origin not as an on-the-spot borrowing from language Y, but because he has heard it used by others in X-utterances, then this borrowed element can be considered, from the descriptive viewpoint, to have become a part of LANGUAGE X. For example, when a bilingual, a native speaker of a variety of Romansh, instead of using /ˈforbıʃ/ 'shears', inserts Schwyzertütsch /ˈʃeːri/ into an otherwise Romansh sentence, this is an act of borrowing in which he participates, a case of interference in his speech. At the time of his utterance, it is a "nonce-borrowing." But when this same bilingual utters the word /ˈtsıtım/ 'newspaper' (<Schwyzertütsch /ˈtsiting/) instead of /ɹaˈzɛta/, this is another matter, for /ˈtsıtım/ has generally replaced /ɹaˈzɛta/ and is an established element in this variety of Romansh. Even unilingual Romansh children learn to say /ˈtsıtım/ for 'newspaper' as they learn to speak. For the individual speaker today, it is an inherited loanword which he may or may not recognize as such.

This theoretical distinction is necessary if we wish to understand what language contact means to an individual who experiences it,[16] for what the historical linguist finds to be an effect of interference from another language (e.g. /ˈtsıtım/) may not be one to the user of the language; the consumer of imported goods only rarely has the same awareness of their origin as the importer or the investi-

[14] Again the Saer technique, outlined above, may be useful. Administering a Saer-type test to some Swiss bilingual children, this author found that while German stimulus words generally produced other German words as the first associations, the responses to Romansh stimuli consisted largely of German translations to the Romansh words. This is at least a hint that German mediates in the use of Romansh by the subjects.

[15] The only one to have drawn the theoretical distinction seems to be Roberts (**450**, 31f.), who arbitrarily calls the generative process "fusion" and the accomplished result "mixture." In anthropology, Linton (**312**, 474) distinguishes in the introduction of a new culture element "(1) its initial acceptance by innovators, (2) its dissemination to other members of the society, and (3) the modifications by which it is finally adjusted to the pre-existing culture matrix."

[16] Anthropologists have faced a similar problem with regard to acculturation. In Hallowell's words (**191**, 105), "so far much more attention has been paid to *what* has happened [as a result of contact] than to the acculturation process itself." It was for the purpose of making a distinction not unlike the one between speech and language that Malinowski (**336**) devised the concept of the "zero point" in culture contact; cf. Beals (**33**), 632.

gator. The questions which the linguist asks about the speech phase of interference are, accordingly, different from those about language. In speech, factors
of perception of the other tongue and of motivation of borrowing are paramount;
in language, it is the phonic, grammatical, semantic, and stylistic integration of
foreign elements that is of interest.

2.15 Methods of Studying Speech Interference

The methods of studying interference are not the same in the two phases.
The study of borrowed elements established in a language is simpler because they
can be elicited through repeated questioning of an informant when the field
worker has him to himself; written texts can also be utilized with good results.
The observation of interference in the act of speech is much more precarious.
Since it is best noted in the conversation between two informants, the observer
is faced with a peculiar difficulty: On the one hand, he wants to let the informants
speak as freely as possible; yet, on the other hand, he must interrupt them to
obtain clarifications on usage and motivation.[17]

Various aspects of bilingual speech behavior have been emphasized. The
majority of studies have stressed the language-learning phase. This group
includes the classic study by Ronjat (**451**), the works by Pavlovitch (**399**),
Emrich (**136**), Bateman (**25**), Čouka (**108**), Kenyères (**264**), Tits (**574**), and
M. E. Smith (**529**), and is crowned by the four-volume book of Werner F.
Leopold (**304**). The study of language forgetting has received less stress than it
deserves; Leopold (**304**) gives some data on word mortality at a very early age,
while Cornioley's observations (**106**) are all too sketchy. The studies of normal
bilinguals in various degrees of unconsciousness are stimulating but have yet to
produce anything of value; Epstein (**138**), Velikovsky (**592**), Braun (**77**), and
Hoche (**222**) have made remarks on bilingual dreams,[18] and the case of a hypno-
tized bilingual has also been reported on.[19] Pathologic speech behavior is recognized to be a highly valuable source of insight, as demonstrated by Minkowski
(**366**), Leischner (**301**), and Goldstein (**172**); all these studies suffer, however,
from the lack of linguistic advice. Stengel and Zelmanowicz's evidence on
morphologic mixture (**548**) would also be more valuable if it were linguistically
sound. Another aspect of speech mixture that may eventually be utilized is that
of bilingual folklore[20] and the literary production of bilinguals.[21]

The methods used in the collection of data have been various. Highly significant material has been obtained by linguists through introspective observation;

[17] Pap's inquiries into naïve speakers' identification of Portuguese and English words
(**395**, 90f.) represent the study of interference in the speech process at its best. Usually
writers on borrowed elements in language have to treat such identifications hypothetically
and a posteriori.

[18] The general possibility of utilizing dream material for linguistic study has been demonstrated by Pound (**417**).

[19] Epstein (**138**), 85f.

[20] Cf. Haas (**186**), Redlich (**433, 434**), and Weinreich (**620**), where additional literature
is cited.

[21] Cf. Harten-Hoencke (**197**).

the studies by Lowie (**326**), Blocher (**53**), and Epstein (**138**) belong to this group.[22] The self-observation of trained linguists can yield data which are probably unobtainable in any other way. The observation of bilingual children over extended periods was the basis for the report by the Sterns (**549,** 379–84) and the above-named studies by Cornioley (**106**), Emrich (**136**), Kenyères (**264**), Leopold (**304**), Pavlovitch (**399**), Ronjat (**451**), and Tits (**574**). Smith (**531**) and Saer (**462**) have tried group testing techniques. The recorded speech of bilinguals in guided conversations was used, apparently for the first time, by this author (**624**). Finally, the method of clinical case work has been applied by neurologists, although not yet by linguists.

[22] The evidence offered by Haas (**186**) and Bunsen (**85**) is less instructive.

2.2   *Phonic Interference*

2.21 Types of Interference in Phonemic Systems

The problem of phonic interference concerns the manner in which a speaker perceives and reproduces the sounds of one language, which might be designated secondary. in terms of another, to be called primary.[1] Interference arises when a bilingual identifies a phoneme of the secondary system with one in the primary system and, in reproducing it, subjects it to the phonetic rules of the primary language.

Phenomena of this type were described traditionally under the heading of "sound substitution."[2] With the development of phonemic theory, investigators advanced from a mere description of the "mispronounced" sounds to the search for exact and verifiable causes of mispronunciation inherent in the speakers' primary systems.[3] Since the actual sounds produced by the bilingual lie, as it were, in the structural no man's land between two phonemic systems, their interpretation in functional, i.e. phonemic, terms is subject to special difficulties. The present chapter is intended to survey selected problems of interpretation. As an illustration, there follows, in outline, a description of an actual case of language contact in Switzerland, studied by this author in 1951.[4]

The chart on the opposite page represents the sound systems of two languages in the Domleschg valley, canton of Grisons: Schwyzertütsch, an Alemannic dialect, as spoken in the village of Thusis; and a variety of Romansh peculiar to the village of Feldis (Romansh: Vieuldan), about eight miles to the north. The hundreds of bilingual persons in Feldis and in intermediate villages provide the language contact.

The upper half of the chart lists the phonemes (the proof of phonemicization is dispensed with); some of the ways in which the phonemes behave are given below. Boxed in are those phonemes in each system which have no counterparts in the other: Romansh /ɲ, ɟ, c, ʎ, ʒ/; and Schwyzertütsch /pf, kʰ, y, ø/, and the full set of long vowels. Romansh /ɪ, ɛ, a/ resemble Schwyzertütsch /e, æ, ɑ/ as to their place in the system, but in unilinguals' speech the Schwyzertütsch sounds are respectively lower and further back.

---

[1] This pair of non-committal terms (rather than "mother-tongue" and its opposite) has been selected because the primary language is not always the native one; cf. §3.33.

[2] E.g. Paul (**397**), 394f.; Bloomfield (**55**), 445ff.

[3] The anticipator of phonemics, Jost Winteler, dealt with interference in functional terms as early as 1876 (**646**, 36). Boas' analysis of 1889 (**56**) was also closely akin in spirit to present-day phonemic interpretations. Russian linguists, notably Polivanov (**413**), Seliščev (**509, 510**), Bogoroditzkij (**63, 64, 65**), and Georgevskij (**166**) have systematically applied phonemic techniques to the clarification of language-contact problems. Troubetzkoy (**582**, 54–6) devoted a brief but important chapter to sound interference. American linguists, too, have subjected the speech of bilinguals to phonemic analysis. Oftedal's study of Amer. English filtered through the Norwegian sound system (**387**) may be cited as one of the best recent publications, while Berger's still unpublished monograph (**40**) is perhaps the most thorough description of a case of phonemic interference that has been attempted.

[4] Details in doctoral dissertation (**624**, 405ff.)

Romansh	Schwyzertütsch
(*Feldis*)	(*Thusis*)

Romansh (*Feldis*):

m   n   ɲ
b   d   ɟ   g
p   t   c   k
     ts   tʃ
f   s   ʃ   h
v   z   ʒ
    l   ʎ
    r

j   w
i   u
ɪ   o
ɛ   a

/ˈ/ Stress

/n/ has the allophone [ŋ] before /k, g/, and after /w/.

/p, t, c, k, f, s, ʃ/ are distinguished from /b, d, ɟ, g, v, z, ʒ/, respectively, by voicing the latter series.

Vowels are rendered long in word-final position and before all phonemes except /p, t, c, k, f, ts, tʃ/, but not before any consonant in gemination:
/ˈkwatar/ = [ˈkwatar]
/ˈkwadar/ = [ˈkwa·dar].

Hissing and hushing fricatives are affricated after /l, ʎ, n/.

Stress is distinctive, but can only be final or penultimate.

Schwyzertütsch (*Thusis*):

m   n   G
ʙ   ᴅ   (k)
p   t
pᶠ   ts   tʃ   kʰ
f   s   ʃ   ħ
v   z
    l
    r

j
i   y   u   i·   y·   u·
e   ø   o   e·   ø·   o·
æ   ɑ   æ·   ɑ·

/ˈ/ Stress

/n/ has the allophone [ŋ] before /k, g/.

/p, t, k, f, s/ are distinguished from /ʙ, ᴅ, G, v, z/, respectively, by the tenseness of the former series.

In checked position vowels are usually rendered more open than elsewhere: /ort/ = [ɔrt].

/ħ/ intervocalically has some pharyngeal friction.

Stress is demarcative; it is free in words, but is usually fixed on the first syllable of the root morpheme.

There are two ways in which this contact can be experienced by bilinguals. The Schwyzertütsch system can be interpreted with reference to the Romansh system, or else the Schwyzertütsch system can function as primary and the Romansh one as secondary.[5] Both cases will now be examined for sources of difficulty.

CASE A: PRIMARY SYSTEM—Romansh; SECONDARY SYSTEM—Schwyzertütsch.

(1) The phoneme $_S$/pᶠ/ is strange to the primary Romansh system, but it can be interpreted as $_R$/p + f/, and therefore presents little difficulty.

[5] Romansh and Schwyzertütsch forms are distinguished, wherever necessary, by preceding subscripts R and S, e.g. $_R$/pawn/, $_S$/ʙro·t/.

(2) By the same token, $_s$/kʰ/ could be interpreted as $_R$/k + h/; however, $_s$/kʰ/ is a very frequent phoneme in Schwyzertütsch, while $_s$/k/ is quite rare. Because of this highly uneven distribution in the vocabulary, the Romansh speaker will tend to confound $_s$/kʰ/ with the more familiar $_{s, R}$/k/ and to render unaspirated [k] where Schwyzertütsch requires /kʰ/. The relatively low functional yield of the opposition[6] precludes corrective responses from those to whom Schwyzertütsch is primary. Lack of aspiration where it is required is therefore one of the main features of a Romansh "accent" in Schwyzertütsch.

(3) The identification of the Schwyzertütsch lax with the Romansh voiced series of consonants is likely, but it is not fatal since, in Romansh, voice is automatically accompanied by laxness, while unvoiced consonants are regularly tense. If the Romansh speaker should say [drai], with voice, for /ᴅrɑi/ 'three', the Schwyzertütsch listener will not mistake his phonemic intent. On the other hand, the naïve Romansh speaker may not perceive the difference between $_s$/t/ and $_s$/ᴅ/, pronouncing them both [t]; e.g. [tɛnkʋ] for $_s$/ᴅɛnkɑ/ 'to think'. The danger of misunderstanding is reduced by the low burdening of the opposition tense : lax.

(4) The mid series /y, ø/, or the distinction of lip rounding that separates these phonemes from /i, e/, respectively, is lacking in the Romansh system. Cases of unrounding may therefore be expected, like [ˈepʋr] for [ˈøpʋr] = $_s$/ˈøpɑr/ 'somebody'.

(5) $_s$/e/ and $_R$/ɛ/ are likely to be confused, since phonetically $_s$/e/ is rather open; for example, $_s$/henᴅ/ = [henᴅ] 'hands' may be interpreted by the Romansh listener as *$_R$/hɛnt/, with /ɛ/.

(6) The automatic affrication of $_s$/s/ and $_s$/ʃ/ after /n, l, ʎ/ is to be expected on the Romansh model, e.g. [hɑlts] for $_s$/hɑls/ 'throat'.

(7) The distinction of vowel length presents peculiar difficulties because of the fact that in Romansh, vowels are rendered automatically long before /s, ʃ/, all voiced consonants, and in word-final position. A form like [ˈzi·ʙʋ] 'to strain', phonemically $_s$/ˈzi·ʙɑ/, could be interpreted in terms of the primary Romansh phonemics as *$_R$/ziʙɑ/, with plain /i/; for, preceding /b/, this vowel is automatically rendered long. The same would apply to [ˈzæ·ɢʋ] 'to say', phonemically $_s$/ˈzæ·ɢɑ/, which would sound almost the same in terms of Romansh *$_R$/ˈzega/. A form like [ˈvi·lʋ] = $_s$/ˈvi·lɑ/ 'moments (plural, oblique case)' would correspond to *$_R$/vila/, since Romansh vowels are also long before /l/. On the other hand, a form like [ˈfili] = $_s$/ˈfili/ 'many' could be interpreted as *$_R$/filli/, since gemination would then account for the short consonant. But words like [ˈziʙʋ] = $_s$/ˈziʙɑ/ 'seven', [ˈbæzʋ] = $_s$/ˈbæzɑ/ 'broom', or [ˈa·pʋr] = $_s$/ˈa·pɑr/ 'free of snow' do not fit into the Romansh pattern in any way.[7] The user of Romansh as a primary system would be inclined, therefore, to pronounce incorrectly [ˈzi·bʋ], [ˈbæ·zʋ], [ˈapʋr]. The consequent forced lengthening of vowels in certain positions and their

---

[6] That is, the small number of pairs in which it is distinctive. On the concept of functional yield, see Martinet (**343**), 8ff., 31f.

[7] The geminate interpretation applicable to $_s$/ˈfili/ would not work, since $_R$/b, z/ do not occur in gemination.

shortening in certain others is another major feature of a Romansh "accent" in Schwyzertütsch.

(8) Any words that are stressed on syllables other than the last or next to last are strange to the primary Romansh pattern. Hence, in cases of suffixation the behavior of the Schwyzertütsch stress is quite alienating, e.g. in the words for 'silver':

	Romansh	*Schwyzertütsch*
NOUN	arɟian	ˈzilʙɑr
ADJECTIVE	arɟan-ˈtiɲ	ˈzilʙɑr-iɢ

To summarize: The basic features of a Romansh "accent" in Schwyzertütsch can be predicted to be the confusion of /k/ and /kʰ/, the unrounding of /y, ø/, and the lengthening or shortening of vowels according to their environment. There would also be needless voicing of lax consonants; affrication of some fricatives; pronunciation of /e/ too low, /æ/ too high, /ɑ/ too far in front; finally, insufficient pharyngeal friction might be given to /ħ/, which is more like pure breath in Romansh.

CASE B: PRIMARY SYSTEM—Schwyzertütsch; SECONDARY SYSTEM—Romansh.

(1) The whole series of Romansh palatal consonants is difficult. Various substitutions are attempted, e.g. [tʃ] for ʀ/c/, [lj] or [j] for ʀ/ʎ/, etc. Of all the palatals, ʀ/ɲ/ is in practice mastered most easily—perhaps because it is frequent in word-final position, where the interpretation */-nj/ is unlikely in view of the fact that such a cluster is unknown in the primary, Schwyzertütsch system.

(2) ʀ/ʒ/ is a foreign phoneme, but can be interpreted as the lax equivalent of /ʃ/. Unvoicing is likely, but—

(3) The problem of voice is quite general. Schwyzertütsch speakers tend to interpret the oppositions ʀ/b, d, . . . /—ʀ/p, t, . . . / in terms of laxity, as in their primary language. They therefore reproduce the voiced series usually as lax, voiceless [ʙ, ᴅ, ɢ], etc.—except for slight occasional voicing in intervocalic position. Incomplete or absent voicing is the main feature of a Schwyzertütsch "accent" in Romansh.

(4) The rendition of ʀ/n/ as [ŋ] after ʀ/w/ is difficult; a form like [pawŋ] 'bread' is likely to be simplified to [pawn].

(5) The rendition of ʀ/s, ʃ/ as affricates after ʀ/n, l, ʎ/ is no source of difficulty, since Schwyzertütsch has /ts/ and /tʃ/ phonemes. Thus ʀ/ruˈmawnʃ/ = [ruˈmawŋtʃ] 'Romansh' can be interpreted as *ₛ/ruˈmauntʃ/ (except for the [ŋ]).

(6) The Schwyzertütsch system contains enough vowels to deal with most Romansh situations. The long allophones can easily be reproduced, even if they receive an unnecessary phonemic interpretation: [ˈlaˑdɐ] 'wide', which in Romansh is simply /ˈlada/, is reinterpreted as *ₛ/ˈlaˑda/, with length. Sometimes the distinction is "misplaced" without harm to the immediate results: Romansh [ˈmɛsˑɐ] 'Mass' is interpreted as *ₛ/ˈmesa/, with a short vowel, while in Romansh the form is phonemically /ˈmɛssa/, with geminated consonant. No difficulty corresponding to that of Case A (7) exists.

(7) The distinction between the Romansh phonemes $_R$/i/ and $_R$/ɪ/ is difficult. In the primary system, Schwyzertütsch, these sounds are allophones of $_s$/i/ whose selection is determined by the checked or free nature of the syllable. The two are therefore easily confounded. For example, $_R$/kun|tɪ/ 'knife' is likely to be mispronounced [kun|ti·].

(8) The stress of any one Romansh word can be learned easily enough, but the morphological functions of stress in the secondary system are quite baffling to this type of bilingual. Such distinctions as $_R$/|maʎa/ 'eats' and $_R$/ma|ʎa/ 'to eat' are unknown in Schwyzertütsch. Wrongly stressed infinitives are to be expected, and have actually been recorded by the author. Iambically and anapestically stressed words, such as $_R$/la|dɪm/ 'dung', $_R$/ladɪ|mɛ/ 'dunghill', though rare, are not entirely unknown in Schwyzertütsch (cf. $_s$/kʰɑn|to·n/ 'canton', $_s$/pɑ|rɑ·t/ 'ready', etc.), and do not seem to offer any difficulty.

To summarize: The basic features of a Schwyzertütsch "accent" in Romansh are the substitution of more familiar phonemes and clusters for the palatals, the unvoicing of the voiced series of stops and fricatives, the rendition of [-wn] for [-wŋ], the confusion of /i/ and /ɪ/, and the misplacement of the stress. There might also be excessive voicing or pharyngeal friction in the pronunciation of /h/, and the substitution of [a] for /ɑ/ and [æ] or [e] for /ɛ/.

Examining the phenomena of interference in rendering a secondary phonic system, as illustrated by the preceding example, from a phonemic point of view, four basic types can be discerned:

(1) UNDER-DIFFERENTIATION OF PHONEMES occurs when two sounds of the secondary system whose counterparts are not distinguished in the primary system are confused. In the cited case, the Romansh speaker's confusion of $_s$/y/ and $_s$/i/, or the Schwyzertütsch speaker's confusion of $_R$/i/ and $_R$/ɪ/, are examples of under-differentiation.

(2) OVER-DIFFERENTIATION OF PHONEMES involves the imposition of phonemic distinctions from the primary system on the sounds of the secondary system, where they are not required. The process can be inferred from a comparison of the sound systems in contact even if it is not always noticeable. In the contact of Romansh and Schwyzertütsch, the interpretation of $_R$/|lada/ 'wide' as *$_s$/|la·dɑ/, with extraneous phonemic length, is a case in point. In a description of Lettish-German contact, Mitzka (368) similarly attributes the "clear, careful" pronunciation of German by Baltic Germans to their possession of a distinction between palatal and non-palatal consonants; in other words, German [k] and [k'] are over-differentiated and interpreted as separate phonemes, one dorsal, the other palatal, as in Lettish.

(3) REINTERPRETATION OF DISTINCTIONS occurs when the bilingual distinguishes phonemes of the secondary system by features which in that system are merely concomitant or redundant, but which are relevant in his primary system. For example, the Romansh word [|mɛs·ɐ] 'Mass', which is phonemically $_R$/|mɛssa/, can be interpreted almost as Schwyzertütsch *$_s$/|mesɑ/; the distinctive length, or geminateness, of [s·], meaningless in this type of Schwyzertütsch (where -ss- does not occur), is overlooked, while the shortness of the vowel,

which in Romansh is a concomitant of its position before a geminate, is made distinctive in the Schwyzertütsch reinterpretation. Similarly, Schwyzertütsch [ˈfil·i] 'many', phonemically $_s$/ˈfili/, can be interpreted as *$_R$/ˈfilli/. The length of [l·], which in Schwyzertütsch is a concomitant of its position after a short vowel, is seen as distinctive, while the properly distinctive brevity of the [i] is disregarded, since Romansh does not treat vowel length as relevant.

(4) Actual PHONE SUBSTITUTION, in the narrow sense of the term, applies to phonemes that are identically defined in two languages but whose normal pronunciation differs. In the situation described, Romansh /ɛ/ and Schwyzertütsch /æ/ are both defined as front vowels of maximum openness (apart from the shortness of $_s$/æ/), yet the Schwyzertütsch phoneme is pronounced more open. The phonemes $_R$/b/ and $_s$/в/ are both defined by their oppositions to tense (voiceless), spirant, and nasal homorganic consonants, yet $_R$/b/ is always voiced,[8] $_s$/в/ only occasionally. The pronunciation of $_s$/ˈlæ·вɑ/ 'to live' as [ˈlɛ·вɐ] by a native Romansh speaker illustrates two cases of phone substitution in a single word.[9]

It ought to be stressed that the above classification emerges not from the raw data directly, but from their phonemic analysis. Viewed impressionistically, the facts cited as types (2) and (3) might not warrant being termed interference at all. The phonetic substance may still fall within the range defined for the rendition of the phonemes of the secondary language, even if certain redundant features are interpreted by the speaker as relevant. The criteria of classification were determined by the standards governing the phonemic description of unilingual speech, on the one hand, and the demands of diachronic phonemic theory, for which the analysis of interference phenomena is of great significance (cf. §5.1), on the other.

It may be noted that of the four types of interference, the first three form a group apart from the fourth.[10] The former concern features relevant in one or both languages; the latter, which has been called phone substitution, covers features which are, from the point of view of synchronic function, redundant but which are apt to become relevant if the phonemic system changes.

Some cases of phonic interference are no doubt too complicated to be identified with a single one of the four basic types. In particular, the complicating possibility of HYPERCORRECTNESS, which may operate both in listening and in speech, and which is subject to experimental testing,[11] must always be allowed for.

[8] Except in word-final position: $_R$/nɪv/ = [nɪ·f].

[9] Since phone substitution, as defined here, is a type of interference in which the identity of other phonemes is not disturbed, it can more easily affect phonemes with few correlations, like /r/ or /h/ in many languages, than those with multi-dimensional correlations in the phonemic pattern. Cf. the grammatical parallels discussed on pp. 37f.

[10] The first three types are parallel to the three varieties of phonemic change distinguished by Jakobson (243): "dephonemicization," "phonemicization," and "transphonemicization."

[11] In an experiment on hypercorrectness, Marckwardt (338) found that Spanish speakers reported more mishearings of English final /-n/ as [ŋ] than any other errors in nasals. This can be explained by the bilingual's excessive caution against under-differentiating /n/ and /ŋ/, a phonemic distinction which Spanish does not possess.

Yet the kind of analysis which was applied here makes it possible not only to state the forms of phonic interference in functional terms, but frequently also to determine their structural causes.[12] And it can be applied with equal validity to that special type of contact that occurs when a linguist observes the sounds of a new language. Like the layman, the linguist can be the victim of his primary sound system; his native phonemics can be an important source of error, particularly if his description is of the subphonemic, impressionistic type still practiced by dialectologists.[13]

There is one type of study in which the decisive role that phonemic structure plays in sound interference emerges with especial clarity. This is the comparison of the interference of one primary sound system with several secondary systems, or of several primary systems with the same secondary one. In a multiple analysis of this sort, many isolated phonetic details become meaningful in a structural framework (see §5.2).[14] Reed, Lado, and Shen (437) were able, for example, to predict with remarkable accuracy the interference phenomena of Spanish, Chinese, and Portuguese with the English sound system. The significance of this approach for language teaching needs no pleading. But even for theoretical purposes, the many unsolved problems in this domain cry for structural solutions. For example, neither French nor Russian have /ð, θ/ phonemes, but in contact with English, French speakers tend to render $_E$/ð, θ/ as [z, s], while Russian speakers generally pronounce [d, t]. In other words, the French perceive the continuance of $_E$/ð, θ/ which distinguishes them from /d, t/ as most relevant, while the Russians consider the mellowness of /ð, θ/ which distinguishes them from /dz, ts/ as decisive. The reaction is so constant that it must be attributable to the phonemic systems in contact,[15] and the possibilities of structural explanation are most promising.[16]

[12] The structural causes of interference are all too often overlooked. Larry (296), for example, made a statistical count of mispronunciations of English vowels by naïve speakers of other languages in Hawaii, but in her study the correlation of errors with the phonemic structures of the several native languages goes all but unmentioned.

[13] Bjerrum (46) has presented a valuable account of the field linguist's difficulties on this score.

[14] Even non-linguistic presentations, like the Hermans' manual of foreign accents in English for actors (214), are useful as a point of departure for comparative investigations.

[15] This is the explanation suggested by Jakobson. For an opinion to the contrary, see Berger (40), 48–50.

[16] Anthropologists have to deal with cultural factors in the structuralization of perception which correspond to a certain extent to the way in which the continuum of sound is organized into phonemic systems. "We have departed a long way," says Hallowell (190, 165), "from the notion . . . that we literally see with our eyes and hear with our ears." As Herskovits puts it (219, 56), "the force of the early enculturative experience is such that each innovation, when presented to an individual, is projected against an already existing apperceptive mass. . . . It is out of this process that the phenomenon of REINTERPRETATION emerges, whereby the newly perceived cultural stimulus . . . sets up the new cultural patterns that will never be the same as those existing under an earlier cultural gestalt." Not in all domains of culture could one find exactly the same four types of interference as between phonemic systems, but in music and pictorial art, at least, very similar problems emerge. Cf. the discussion of the interference of "European" and "African" musical systems by Waterman (608).

2.22 Double Interference: Perception of Foreign Accents

When a lay unilingual hears his language spoken with a foreign "accent," his perception and interpretation of the accent is itself subject to the interference of his native phonic system.[17] A bilingual attempting to speak language S, for example, renders the sounds of S by reference to the system of language P, which to him is primary; the unilingual speaker-listener of S then interprets this distorted speech by reference to the S system as the primary one. In the Swiss contact situation described above, the native speaker of Schwyzertütsch will tend to render $_R$/dat/ 'gives' as [ɒɑt], substituting [ɒ] for [d] and [ɑ] for [a]. One feature of the initial consonant—the laxness—will be there, but the unilingual Romansh listener will miss the crucial voicing. Assuming that he will resubstitute, in hearing, /a/ for [ɑ], he will have the impression of hearing [tat]—a phonemically different word. In the proper context, of course, the form will be understood correctly, but there is still little precise knowledge as to what constitutes a "proper" context. It is to be hoped that the problem of understanding imperfect speech distorted by a foreign sound system, which is of interest to linguistics and psycholinguistics,[18] will not be neglected by the phoneticians and communication engineers studying the problems of understanding.[19]

Not all types of interference, of course, are equally liable to cause misunderstanding, even in the same context. PHONE SUBSTITUTION as defined above, that is, the non-customary pronunciation of an identifiable phoneme, is possibly the type of interference least detrimental to intelligibility. Thus, the foreigner's use of an apical [r] in languages where uvular [ʀ] or retroflex [ɽ] is standard will hardly result in misunderstanding. The foreigner's OVER-DIFFERENTIATION is also immaterial to the listener; the unilingual Russian listener cannot notice that an Italian is treating the allophones [e], as in $_R$[p'et'] 'to sing', and [ɛ], as in $_R$[n'ɛt] 'no', as separate phonemes. On the other hand, the under-differentiation of phonemes invariably leads to a unilingual listener's disorientation, even if it is a minor one and is offset by the context.

While lay unilingual listeners usually perceive phone substitution accurately and remain unaware of over-differentiation altogether, their conception of what a foreign "accent," or interference pattern, consists of as far as the other two types of phonic interference are concerned is often quite distorted. The foreigner who UNDER-DIFFERENTIATES, i.e. substitutes a single phoneme for two phonemes, nevertheless renders that single phoneme in different ways according to allophonic rules of his own language which remain unknown to his unilingual listener. In REINTERPRETING phonemic distinctions according to his own system of relevant features, the foreigner produces sounds which are sometimes recognizable to the unilingual listener as the correct phonemes, but sometimes are not, as the first example in the present section ($_R$/dat/ → $_S$[ɒɑt] = */tat/) shows.

The spurious conception of the foreign way of speaking is thus structurally determined by the unilingual's phonemics; because of constant reinforcement, it

---

[17] It was Hugo Schuchardt (496) who formulated this problem of double interference.

[18] Cf. Ščerba (476); Martinet (343), 4; Miller (363), 79.

[19] Cf. Straus (552), 710.

easily becomes stereotyped. Linguistically uninitiated Frenchmen, for example, believe that Alsatians, in speaking French, regularly interchange voiced and unvoiced consonants. In reality, Alsatians treat the French consonants according to their native, dialectal German system: A single series is pronounced with voice intervocalically and voiceless elsewhere. Hence, ꜰ/pari/ and ꜰ/abe/, rendered as [ʙari, abe], may be interpreted as "correct," but ꜰ/bɛt/ may be pronounced [ʙɛt] and ꜰ/epe/ as [eʙe] and be heard as "incorrect." The non-phonemic, allophonic distinction [ʙ] — [b] ɪs not formulable in terms of the French system and will therefore remain unnoticed; the impression is one of randomness, or even of a negative correlation, a regularity of incorrectness. A similar situation prevails when speakers of a Yiddish dialect in which [h] is not phonemic pronounce English words. The layman's impression is that /h/ is dropped where it belongs and introduced where it does not. Actually, in this Yiddish dialect [h] is a regular non-phonemic glide between any two vowels. Therefore, ᴇ/his armz/ and ᴇ/tuw hedz/ will be rendered correctly, but ᴇ/tuw armz/ will sound [tu· harmz], while ᴇ/hiz hed/ will appear as [hiz ed]. In both examples, the bilingual's under-differentiation is noticed but his phone substitution is incorrectly classified.

For every point of difference between two phonic systems, there is interference, no matter which system is primary; but the interference may be of different types. For example, if language A distinguishes long and short vowels, while language B is indifferent to vowel length, there will be over-differentiation in contacts where A is primary and under-differentiation where B is primary. However, because not all types of interference are perceived with equal readiness, unilingual listeners may be struck by features of a B-accent different from the ones that the B-listener finds characteristic of an A-accent. Thus, native Romansh speakers noticeably confuse ꜱ/kʰ/ and ꜱ/k/ in speaking Schwyzertütsch, but native Schwyzertütsch speakers do not appear to have difficulty with the single Romansh voiceless dorsal stop; over-differentiation in the latter case is covert. This point may be significant when reciprocal influences of languages on one another are studied.

2.23 Structural Factors Favoring or Inhibiting Phonic Interference

The contrastive analysis of the phonemes of two languages and the way they are used yields a list of the forms of expected phonic interference in a particular contact situation. When the sounds are viewed as part of a phonic SYSTEM, certain additional factors emerge which favor or inhibit faulty sound reproduction.

One factor which obviates certain errors in foreign-language speech is the existence of suitable "holes in the pattern" or "empty cases"[20] in the primary phonemic system into which strange phonemes of the secondary system can be pigeonholed. In the case of Swiss language contact that has been cited, the phoneme /ʒ/ of the Romansh system is as strange to Schwyzertütsch as /ʎ, ɟ/,

---

[20] Cf. Martinet (**343**), 19ff.

etc. But a glance at the system of Schwyzertütsch (see p. 15) shows that there is a ready place for /ʒ/, or at least for its unvoiced equivalent, in Schwyzertütsch. One who uses Schwyzertütsch as a primary language need not master a single new articulatory distinction to pronounce this sound in Romansh; he simply applies the tongue curving of $_s$/ʃ/, the friction of $_s$/z, v, . . . /, and the laxness of $_s$/z, ʙ, . . . / (or voicing, if he can manage it). The phonemic pattern as a whole is thus more amenable to the correct rendition of /ʒ/ than to that, say, of /ʎ/, for the palatality of which Schwyzertütsch has no model. The interference of Schwyzertütsch with the former of the two phonemes is consequently alleviated by structural factors.

Up to this point, phonemes have been considered as members of sound systems. But SEQUENCES of phonemes which occur in the vocabulary of a language constitute an additional field of interference. The existence or absence of similar sequences in the primary language may, respectively, eliminate or instigate malfunction in the secondary language. Thus, counterparts of Schwyzertütsch /i, n, g/ exist in Romansh, yet the sequence $_s$/-ing/ in /ˈtsiting/ 'newspaper' was replaced by a more familiar $_R$/-ɪm/ when the word was borrowed as /ˈtsɪtɪm/ into Romansh. Similarly, bilingual speakers of Schwyzertütsch who had mastered the foreign palatal phoneme $_R$/c/ were heard by this author nevertheless to pronounce $_R$/ˈgratsca/ 'thanks' as [ˈgratsɐcɐ], with epenthetic [-ɐ-] to simplify the cluster of an unfamiliar type.

Another way in which the distribution of phonemes in the vocabulary regulates interference is by the functional yield of phonemic oppositions.[21] Because of his primary sound system, the native speakers of Schwyzertütsch can theoretically be predicted to confuse Romansh /i/ and /ɪ/ (cf. p. 18 above). However, it so happens that the functional yield of the opposition /i/-/ɪ/ is most heavy; many common words are distinguished by the difference between these two phonemes, including such pairs as $_R$/ci/ 'who' and $_R$/cɪ/ 'what', occurring in syntactically identical positions. The frequency of situations in which the distinction is critical tends to inhibit potential under-differentiation. By contrast, the distinction between $_s$/kʰ/ and $_s$/k/ (cf. p. 16), or between $_s$/y/ and $_s$/i/, is not heavily burdened. As a matter of fact, neighboring varieties of Schwyzertütsch with essentially similar vocabularies function without the /y/-/i/ distinction. There is no comparable limitation on the under-differentiation of these two phonemes by speakers of Romansh as the primary language.

2.24 Diffusion of Phonic Interference Phenomena

In studying the spread of sound changes induced by foreign influence, it would be worthwhile investigating whether the results of the several types of interference are diffused in the same manner or with equal ease. The evidence is very scant, but it may not be inappropriate to raise a few theoretical points.

Clearly, the type of interference which was termed phone substitution stands out as a case apart. It was defined as causing no immediate disturbance in the

---

[21] *Ibid.*, 8ff.

secondary phonemic pattern and was shown to be, at the same time, the type of interference most accurately perceived by the unilingual listener. Thus, phone substitution is not only a recognizable signal of the presence of a foreign pattern, but it can also be practiced with relative impunity from the point of view of the secondary sound system. These two characteristics make it the favorite type of interference for diffusion in the secondary language community. If the attributes of fashionableness become associated with a new manner of rendering a phoneme, it will be all the more likely to spread. New manners of rendering phonemes are almost as easily diffused from one language to another as within one language community, for a common manner of rendering phonemes in both languages is not dependent on an extensive common vocabulary; it can be applied in entirely unrelated words.[22]

That a bilingual should render phonemes of two languages in the same way if he identifies them is only natural from the point of view of economy: The practice of the same phonetic habits in both languages is an efficient way of easing one's burden of linguistic devices (cf. p. 7). As a matter of fact, it requires a relatively high degree of cultural sophistication in both languages for a speaker to afford the structural luxury of maintaining separate subphonemic habits in each. For example, if a Swiss bilingual identifies Romansh /h/ and Schwyzertütsch /ħ/, he is likely to pronounce them alike, even though unilinguals in Schwyzertütsch use more pharyngeal friction in their pronunciation of the sound.[23] If he does not pronounce them alike, other than structural forces must be at play.

Of course, phone substitution, beginning innocuously, may eventually cause a change in the phonemic system of the language that has been affected. The substitution of a uvular [ʀ] for an apical [r], for example, may in some languages interfere with /x/ and /γ/ sounds and cause a displacement of a series of phonemes.[24] In Sapir's terms, "we may suppose that individual variations arising at linguistic borderlands—whether by the unconscious suggestive influence of foreign speech or the actual transfer of foreign sounds into the speech of bilingual individuals—have been gradually incorporated into the phonetic drift of a language" (472, 213f.). This shows, incidentally, that a sound system which is known to have been influenced by a foreign one need not be expected to represent an exact replica of the influencing system.

The study of the spreading of subphonemic innovations across language borders can be handled as an extension of a dialectological type of research in which, it must be realized, cultural criteria rather than the exigencies of linguistic structure may play the determining role. The Swiss bilingual in whose primary, Romansh system the /h/ phoneme has no voice or no pharyngeal friction will be disposed by force of habit to render an identical [h] in speaking Schwyzertütsch;

[22] Troubetzkoy (583), 348. Martinet has illustrated this vividly by an example from patois-French contact in a Savoy village (341, 7). Cf. also Haudricourt and Martinet (198).

[23] For similar reasons, Wolff (648) found that, in teaching English to native Spanish speakers, "familiar" phonemes with unfamiliar allophones presented much greater difficulty than brand new phonemes.

[24] Cf. Martinet (343), 5ff.

only the demands of a puristic Schwyzertütsch pronunciation could persuade
him to break his habit and to use a "native-like" voiced h or fricative [ɦ]; for
nothing in the structure of the secondary language demands it. If, in the contact
situation, [h] does come to be substituted for voiced h or [ɦ], then it is rather a
matter of fashion and of a "cultural slope," as it were, whether the new phonetic
variant spreads from the language divide into the bulk of the unilingual
hinterland.

At this point the domain of strictly structural linguistics seems to end.
Whether the purity of Schwyzertütsch does indeed possess enough symbolic
value in the given contact situation to prevent the substitution of [h] for [ɦ]
by Romansh bilinguals, or whether the bilingual fringe is so looked up to in the
Schwyzertütsch language community as a whole that unilingual speakers might
adopt from that fringe an [h]-pronunciation of the /ɦ/ phoneme, cannot be determined from such data as are available in an ordinary linguistic description.
Additional information of a psychological or a socio-cultural nature must be
examined and techniques other than descriptive linguistic ones must be drawn
upon for help (see chap. 4).

As for the diffusion of the results of those types of interference which involve
immediate disturbances of the phonemic system, they would seem to be subject
to structural conditions and to be largely independent of cultural considerations.
To be sure, a phonemic rearrangement is sometimes associated with social
status. The merger of /l/ and /l'/ in Czech, for example, is attributed to the
fashionable speech of the cities which was strongly tinged with a German accent;[25]
similarly, the merger of /ʃ, tʃ/ with /s, ts/ in urban Croatian is said to stem from
the foreign accent of native speakers of Venetian Italian.[26] In most other cases,
on the contrary, phonemic rearrangements spread without symbolizing social
status,[27] or even as tokens of less respectable speech (e.g. the progressive merger
of /ɯ/ and /i/ in Welsh[28]). One might therefore say, with Jakobson (**244**, 54),
that a language "accepts foreign structural elements only when they correspond
to its tendencies of development." Since such latent internal tendencies, however,
by definition exist even without the intervention of foreign influence, the language
contact and the resulting interference could be considered to have, at best, a
trigger effect, releasing or accelerating developments which mature independently.
If latent tendencies (or drifts, as Sapir called them), could heretofore be discovered only *a posteriori*, it is to be hoped that new methods in diachronic
phonemics will make it possible to pin them down even before they are manifested. When that stage is reached, the relevance of interference studies to
historical linguistics will become even greater than it is.

[25] Jakobson (**244**), 54.
[26] Seliščev (**511**), 721.
[27] As Jakobson put it (**244**, 54), "the influence which one language exerts on the phonemic
structure of another—contrary to current opinion—does not necessarily presuppose the
political, social, or cultural preponderance of the people speaking the first language."
[28] Sommerfelt (**533**), 96.

2.25 Phonic Treatment of Transferred Morphemes

The preceding discussion dealt with speech events belonging to one language, S, using connected vocabulary of that language, but the sounds of another language, P, with a different phonic system. If the subscript indicates the phonemic system, while the letters between the slashes designate the vocabulary to which the morphemes belong, the following situation was involved:

$$_P/\ldots S\,S\,S\,S\ldots/.$$

If, on the other hand, a morpheme belonging to the vocabulary of S is transferred into P-speech,[29] it is also subject to the interference of the phonic system of P. Of course, individual transferred morphemes are handled not only by bilinguals, but by unilinguals as well; they may be "inherited" loans in whose transfer the speaker did not personally participate (cf. §2.14).

Fundamentally, the problem is whether the borrowed S-morpheme is integrated into the phonic pattern of P, or whether it is rendered in terms of original S-sounds; in other words, which of the following will occur:

$$(1) \quad _P/\ldots P\,P\,P\,S\,P\,P\,P\,P\ldots/,\text{ or}$$
$$(2) \quad _P/\ldots P\,P\,P/\ _S/S/\ _P/P\,P\,P\,P\ldots/.$$

For example, if a Yiddish speaker uses the English morpheme $_E/{}^|\text{wɒ}\int\text{iŋtən}/$ in a Yiddish utterance, he may choose to (1) integrate it phonemically into $_Y/{}^|\text{vɑ}\int\text{ington}/;$ (2) make an effort to retain, as far as possible, the English sounds.[30] The English forms $/\text{æ}^|\text{lʌmnaj},\ \text{æ}^|\text{lʌmnij}/$ represent, respectively, the masculine and feminine if they occur as phonemically integrated loanwords $(/\text{aj}/ = \text{-}i,$ $/\text{ij}/ = \text{-}æ)$, but just the opposite if an attempt is made to retain the Latin sounds (then $/\text{aj}/ = \text{-}æ$ and $/\text{ij}/ = \text{-}i)$.

On what basis is the choice made? It has been argued that if the speaker is bilingual, he attempts to reproduce the borrowed morpheme with its original

---

[29] Lexical borrowing is discussed more fully in §2.4.

[30] Pap points out (**395**, 101–2) that the difference between phonically adapted and unadapted loanwords is "rather relative than absolute, being a matter of degree." From the listener's point of view, indeed; since the attempt to integrate the loanword or to render it the foreign way is not always successful, the heard result usually lies somewhere in between. From the speaker's point of view, however, a definite choice of procedure is involved, namely, to adapt the loanword phonically or to retain its original phonic form as best he can. It is important to distinguish the speaker's selection of the procedure from the result of his efforts.

While the formulas cited above refer to the usual conception of loanwords, the following situation should also be considered:

$$_P/\ldots S\,S\,S\,P\,S\,S\,S\ldots/.$$

In this case, the bilingual inserts a word from his primary vocabulary into speech in the secondary language, as when a Frenchman speaking English uses the words *tiens!* or *garage.* In a nonce-borrowing like *tiens!*, the pronunciation of the inserted P-word involves a relaxation rather than an intensification of effort; but for "inherited," non-individual loans like *garage*, even greater effort must be exerted by the Frenchman to pronounce Amer. [gə${}^|$ra·ʒ] or British [${}^|$gærədʒ] than for any traditionally English word.

sounds; if he is unilingual, he is more likely "to force the loanwords to conform to the native phonetic and phonemic pattern."[31] Thus, the unilingual Menomini renders *automobile* as /atamo·pen/; the bilingual says /atamo·pil/.[32] Similarly, the author has observed Yiddish speakers who, in the old country, said /ˈvɑʃington/ but who, after learning English in the United States, began saying /ˈwɒʃiŋtən/ even in Yiddish utterances. Haugen (**203**, 216f., 222) in this respect classes unilinguals together with people that became bilingual as adults, who all make phonic adaptations of loanwords, as distinct from childhood bilinguals, who retain foreign phonemes in borrowed words; for example, Norwegian adult immigrants to the United States, in speaking Norwegian, render *lake* as /lek/, while their bilingual children pronounce it more properly as /lejk/.

A further possible determinant of the selection which has not received sufficient attention is the speaker's attitude toward the source language (*S*) of the borrowed morpheme. If that language enjoys great cultural or social prestige in the *P*-language community, the pronunciation of loanwords in a phonic form close to the original *S* may serve as a mark of education or status. Thus, whether one pronounces *salon* as /sɑˈlõ/ or /sæˈlɒn/ may, in certain English-speaking circles, be important socially, regardless of whether the speaker is bilingual or not. Such circumstances spawn hypercorrect forms, like English /tejtejtej/ for *tête-à-tête*. Conversely, the disavowal of the foreign language's prestige generates artificial mock forms, like Amer. English /fizikjuw/ for *physique* /fiˈzijk/.

The exertion of effort to retain the original sounds is probably governed by individual and socio-cultural factors very similar to those which regulate the total amount of interference (see chap. 4). It would be worthwhile to study the differences in the amount of effort exerted, say, by the speakers of English in the reproduction of·original phonemes when borrowing from languages with high socio-cultural status, e.g. French, or of low status, e.g. American Indian languages.[33]

As a consequence of the introduction of numerous loanwords in a fully or even partly unassimilated phonic form, changes may take place in the sounds of the recipient language. Not only are new sequence patterns established through borrowing, such as word-initial *v-* and *z-* in English, final *-ng* in French, word-initial *dl-* in Yiddish, and the like, but new relevant distinctions and new phonemes may be created: /g/ as distinct from /k/ in Czech,[34] /ʎ, ɲ/ as distinct from /l, n/ in Yiddish, /o/ as distinct from /uo/ in Lettish, /f/ as distinct from /xv/ in dialectal Russian,[35] /t/ as distinct from /d/ in Mazateco,[36] and so forth.

The phonic fate of isolated loanwords is the result of the same mechanisms of

---

[31] Fries and Pike (**154**), 40; cf. Haugen (**203**), 216; Møller (**374**), 9.

[32] Bloomfield (**55**), 447f.

[33] The view that prestige contributes to the faithfulness of phonemic reproduction in loanwords is reflected in the strange Soviet efforts to declare the laws of vowel harmony "inapplicable" to recent Russian loanwords in Yakut and other languages in order to emphasize the socio-cultural status of Russian; cf. Mordinov (**375**), 84.

[34] Mathesius (**347**) is the source for the English and Czech examples.

[35] Avanesov (**13**), 125f.

[36] Fries and Pike (**154**), 30. See Garvin (**157, 13**) on Zoque.

interference as those that govern connected speech in a secondary language
(§2.21–3). But a bilingual's connected utterance in language S, even if imperfect,
must nevertheless approximate the phonemics of S sufficiently to be intelligible
to its unilingual hearers. On the contrary, the use of a word borrowed from S in
a P-utterance is not inhibited by the need to conform to an extraneous phonemic
norm; the mechanisms of interference therefore affect individual loanwords with
particular force. If the speaker's intent is to integrate the loanword, the same
mechanisms dictate a sweeping substitution of phonemes. Thus, Spanish *yegua*
'mare' becomes, in Taos, /ˌjɑwoˈʔonɑ/;[37] Italians in the United States adopt
Brooklyn as /brokoˈlino/, *husband* as /ˈosbiru/, *box* as /ˈbokisɑ/;[38] Hawaiian
borrows *George* as /keoki/, *rice* as /lɑiki/, *brush* as /pɑlɑki/.[39] In addition to the
simple substitution of phonemes, various analogy patterns become operative:
Danes adopt German *Maschine* as *maskine* on the analogy of such cognates as
Schuh ~ *sko*. Some Yiddish speakers modify *painter* to /pejntner/ and *coat* to
/kojt/.[40] Longer words, undergoing folk etymology, are reinterpreted as meaningful compounds and their phonemic shape is adjusted accordingly (e.g. the famous
asparagus > *sparrowgrass*),[41] or, by metanalysis, parts of words are productivized
for compounding (e.g. *hamburg-er* > *ham-burger* > *burger, beef-burger*).

Since words can also be borrowed from a language in its written form, phonic
integration sometimes starts with the spelled form of a word. Because of the
transcription *tsar*, this Russian loanword is pronounced with /ts-/ in Amer.
English, while German *Zwieback* has been adopted as /ˈzwijbak/, even though in
the source languages both words have the same initial sound.[42] English loanwords
have been treated differently in Hawaiian spoken Japanese, which received many
of them by the "ear route," and in standard Japanese, which (until 1945, at
least) received its English material from the printed page. Thus standard Japanese borrowed *gasoline* in its spelled form and obtained *gasoriñ*; colloquial Japanese in Hawaii has /gʼɑsɯriṇ/, since the Japanese hear the initial English consonant as a palatal and the [ə] as most nearly [ɯ].[43]

The phonic integration of a corpus of loanwords has been satisfactorily described for many languages;[44] but a systematic survey of all possible processes
and mechanisms, in the light of both structural and cultural considerations,
remains to be made.

[37] Trager (576), 146.

[38] Menarini (353).

[39] Carr (96), 18.

[40] This adaptation must have originated with speakers of Yiddish dialects which have
no /oˑ/ or /ow/, but who feel—as a result of their contact with central ("Polish") Yiddish—
that /ow, oˑ/ corresponds to their own /oj/; therefore, /kojt/ is to /kowt/ as northeastern
("Lithuanian") Yiddish /hojz, bojx/ is to central Yiddish /hoˑz, boˑx/ 'house, belly'. On a
parallel dialect problem in Amer. Norwegian, see Haugen (203), 222f.

[41] Cf. Lommel (321).

[42] Cf. Bloomfield (55, 448) for this and other examples. See also Haugen (203, 223) on
Amer. Norwegian, and Møller (374, 10–2) on Danish.

[43] Carr (96).

[44] See, for example, Frey's study (153) of English loanwords in Pennsylvania German or
Lytkin's analysis (330) of Russian loanwords in Komi.

2.3 Grammatical Interference

2.31 Plan of Analysis

The problem of grammatical interference—currently among the most debated questions of general linguistics[1]—is one of considerable complexity. Many linguists of repute have questioned the possibility of grammatical, at least morphological, influence altogether. "The grammatical systems of two languages . . . are impenetrable to each other," said Meillet (**350**, I, 82), and he was echoed by Sapir: "Nowhere do we find any but superficial morphological interinfluencings" (**472**, 217). With equal vigor, the opposite view has been defended by Schuchardt (**497**, 195): "Even closely knit structures [*dichte Zusammenschlüsse*], like inflectional endings, are not secure against invasion by foreign material." According to a contemporary restatement, "there is no limit in principle to the influence which one morphological system may have upon another."[2]

That entirely contradictory views could be held by such responsible scholars is apparently due to the lack of agreement between them on fundamental terms and concepts. To this day, there is little uniformity in the drawing of lines between morphology and syntax, grammar and lexicon.[3] But this need not be an obstacle to a systematic analysis of grammatical interference. The main requirement is that in a given contact situation, both languages be described in the same terms. Beyond that, it is possible to steer clear of the fluid and controversial borders between words and non-words, syntax and morphology, and so forth, by treating these distinctions, for comparative purposes, as matters of degree. Thus, while morphemes that are words (free) and those that are not (bound) may be distinguished absolutely in some languages or language types, in a general synopsis the "degree of boundness" of morphemes is easily handled as a variable; correspondingly, a commitment as to the absolute limits between morphology, word-formation, syntax, and phraseology can be avoided.

The analysis attempted here skirts the treacherous classificatory problems of general grammar by recourse to one absolute and two relative distinctions:

a. MORPHEMES (segments of utterances, including prosodic features which differentiate simple morphemes) are distinguished from GRAMMATICAL RELATIONS, including: (1) order; (2) agreement, dependence, and similar relations between grammatical units; and (3) modulations of stress and pitch. This distinction is of significance here because grammatical functions which are performed in one language by morphemes may be identified by bilinguals with relations of another language. For example, a Russian-English bilingual may

---

[1] The question figured on the agenda of the International Congresses of Linguists in 1939 (Brussels), 1948 (Paris), and 1952 (London); see bibliography (**230–232**).

[2] Bazell (**32**), 303. Rosetti (**454**, 73) uses the interpenetration of two morphologies as the criterion for defining a *langue mixte*, which he contrasts with a *langue mélangée* containing but isolated borrowings.

[3] Cf. Vogt (**599**), 33.

identify the order relation between *loves* and *Mary* in *John loves Mary* with the morpheme *-u* in the Russian sentence *Ivan Mari-u ljubit*, where it expresses the accusative and thus makes *Maria* the direct object.

b. More or less OBLIGATORY categories. In a language, the expression of some categories is obviously more obligatory than that of others. Whenever an action is described by a finite verb in English, for example, its time in relation to the speech event must be expressed by a tense. This category is therefore more obligatory than, say, the sex of animate objects, whose specification is optional even with nouns capable of gender differentiation (*teacher—woman teacher, friend—boy friend, poet—poetess, wolf—she-wolf,* etc.). In the more obligatory distinctions, a zero morpheme can signify one member of the opposition. Thus the absence of *-s* in *(he) put* signifies past tense, while the absence of *she-* in *wolf* does not necessarily signify masculinity. Relations, too, can be more and less obligatory. For instance, word order patterns covering subject and verb are less obligatory in German than in English, and in Russian they are more optional than in either of the former.

c. Greater or lesser syntagmatic BOUNDNESS of morphemes used to express categories. For example, *-t* in Latin *amaui-t* is more bound (i.e. less separable) than *il* in French /il-emɛ/ *(il aimait)*. The English morpheme *he* in *he loved*, is, in turn, less bound than the French *il*, since it is even more separable and is used in other functions.

This scheme, it is hoped, will make possible an examination of the evidence without the bias reflected in strongly worded, and possibly premature, declarations like Meillet's (quoted on p. 29 above). But two additional premises underlying the analysis must be stated. First, morphemes and grammatical relations belonging to one language can occur in the speech of another language as "borrowings." Secondly, morphemes and grammatical relations, as well as morpheme classes, are subject to interlingual identifications in the sense defined in §2.11.

In these terms, given the contact of two languages, A and B, the following types of grammatical interference of A with B (or vice versa) are to be expected:

(1) The use of A-morphemes in speaking (or writing) language B. Example: Amer. Yiddish /nit er bʌt ix/ 'not he but I'. It is to be investigated whether forms belonging to some classes are more subject to transfer than others (§2.32); also, how the transferred morphemes are integrated with the recipient grammar (§2.37).

(2) The application of a grammatical relation of language A to B-morphemes in B-speech, or the neglect of a relation of B which has no prototype in A (§2.53). Example: *he comes tomorrow home*, with the German word order pattern (cf. *er kommt morgen nach Hause*) applied to English morphemes.

(3) Through the identification of a specific B-morpheme with a specific A-morpheme, a change (extension, reduction) in the functions of the B-morpheme on the model of the grammar of language A (§2.34). Example: The identification by bilinguals of Yiddish *ver* with English *who*, and the resulting use of *ver* in the capacity of a relative pronoun (*der menš ver iz do* instead of *der menš vos iz do* on the model of *the man who is here*). On the model of language A, a

set of existing categories of language *B* may come to be expressed by new morphemes, or entirely new obligatory categories may even be established; also, existing categories may be eliminated on the model of another language (§2.35).

For interference of type (1), where a transfer of morphemes is involved, it is convenient to speak of the source language and the recipient language. For types (2) and (3), where no morphemes are transferred, we may speak rather of the model language and the replica language.

2.32 Grammatical Function of Morphemes and Likelihood of Transfer

The outright transfer of morphemes from one language into speech in another, viewed as a means of correcting the inadequacies of a lexicon, is considered in §2.4. In this section, the transferability of morphemes is considered as a correlate of their grammatical function in the source language and the resistance of the recipient language.

The transfer of morphemes which are as strongly bound as inflectional endings in many European languages seems to be extremely rare. The study of the phenomenon is unfortunately encumbered by the often unsatisfactory description of its few known instances.

What appears at first blush to be a transfer of highly bound morphemes often turns out, upon a fuller analysis, to be something else.[4] It sometimes happens that free forms are transferred into a language in pairs, with and without an affix. The presence of the pair in the recipient language enables even its unilingual user to analyze the two-morpheme compound into a base and affix, and to extend the affix to other, indigenous bases. Thus the plural ending *-im* in Yiddish *pójerim* 'peasants,' *doktójrim* 'doctors' is only ultimately, but not directly, of Hebrew origin; it is rather an analogical extension of the *-im*-plural from such Yiddish couples as *min—mínim* 'sort,' *giber—gibójrim* 'strong man', etc., etc.— free morphemes borrowed in pairs from Hebrew. The English diminutive *-ette* in words like *kitchenette* represents a productive device introduced in such word pairs as *statue—statuette* or *cigar—cigarette*, rather than a direct transfer of a bound morpheme from French.[5]

After such items are discounted,[6] however, there remains a residue of cases

[4] This point was raised by Schuchardt (496), 9f.

[5] Cf. also the rare examples of the penetration of a Latvian prefix into Livonian and of a German prefix into Old Prussian, cited, alongside of the well known Slavic prefixes in Rumanian, by Kiparsky (272, 501-3). It is interesting that such affixes are frequently utilized for facetious purposes, e.g. *-ität, -ibus* in German (*Grobität, Gründibus*) or *-ition* in Rumanian (e.g. *furculition* for *furculiţă* 'fork'); see Graur (175). Cf. also the humorous phrase of Yiddish slang, /far'štande-vu/ 'do you understand?' after French *comprenez-vous*.

[6] Many alleged instances of bound-morpheme borrowing are not described in sufficient detail to permit a judgment as to whether analogical extension of the above type is involved or not; thus Schuchardt's reference to an Armenian *-kʰ* plural of Caucasian origin (497, 193) is all too curt; his view on the Latin origin of Basque plural *-eta* (*ibid.*) is doubted by Lafon (292, 507). In Zvegincev's assertion (658, 331) that modern Persian borrowed new plural suffixes, *-at* and *-džat*, not even the source of these loans is indicated. The Greek agentive suffix *-ci*, transferred into Turkish, according to Spitzer (537), is almost certainly

which can be explained in no other way than by the outright transfer of a highly bound morpheme. One such ascertained instance is the transfer of Bulgarian verb endings for the first and second persons singular into Meglenite Rumanian.[7] Thanks to the rigorous description by T. Capidan (**93**, 159 f.),[8] the facts and circumstances of the case are known. In that Rumanian dialect, the endings -*um* (-*ăm*) and -*iš*, of Bulgarian origin, occur in place of the older -*u*, -*i*: *aflum*, *afliš* 'I, you find' for *aflu*, *afli*. It is significant that in the surrounding Bulgarian dialect, the conjugation in -*am*, -*iš* is the most productive of several types. Some Bulgarian verbs formerly of the -*ă* conjugation have adopted the -*am* paradigm (*pletă* > *pletam* 'I twist, knit', *rastă* > *rastam* 'I grow,' etc.). It is as if the analogical expansion of the -*am* verb class overflowed the boundaries of the Bulgarian language into the Rumanian dialect. Of course, the category of first person singular, present indicative, already existed in Rumanian when the new morpheme to express it was introduced. A rather special condition is therefore involved here, namely the congruence in structure of the Rumanian and Bulgarian conjugations prior to the transfer. The case plainly resembles the spread of inflectional morphemes among closely related dialects of one language,[9] where two prerequisites are satisfied: congruent grammatical structures and *apriori* similar vocabularies.[10] Almost equally favorable conditions characterize the Romansh-Schwyzertütsch contact, where a case bordering on bound-morpheme transfer has occurred. Bilingual children have been replacing the Romansh feminine indefinite article *in*, an alternant of *ina* used before vowels, by *ina-n* (*ina-n-ura* 'an hour' for *in' ura*) on the model of Schwyzertütsch, where, just as in English, the article *a* has an extended alternant, *an*, before vowels (*a p'luag* 'a plough', *an ap'al* 'an apple'). In Welsh, where an English -*s* is sometimes used to reinforce the plurality of a collective noun (e.g. *sɛren* 'star', *sēr* 'stars, collectively', *sērs* 'stars, plurally'),[11] there was also a preëxisting plural category.

---

an analogical extension. Jaberg's curious case (**237**, 65) of the adoption of -*en* from (standard?) German into the Romance dialect of a Swiss Grison valley to differentiate the plural (*la vacchen*) from the formerly identical singular (*la vacca*) also possibly has to be discounted on the grounds of analogy; his data are inconclusive. Incomplete, too, is the assertion by Hardie (**194**, 122) that French -*amant* was transferred as an adverb-forming suffix into Breton. Schuchardt's example (**496**, 8, 10) of the transfer of English possessive -'*s* into insular Portuguese (*gobernadors casa*) has been used as a stock illustration by Meillet (**350**, I, 87), Vendryes (**594**, 343–4), and many others who were unaware that Schuchardt himself retracted it (**498**, 524, footnote 1), reanalyzing the phrase as *gobernador su casa* ('the governor his house'). On the other hand, Spanish-English bilingual children in Tampa, Florida, have been overheard saying *Juan's padre vive aquí* 'Juan's father lives here'; cf. Ortoz (**390**).

[7] A dialect spoken north of Salonica.

[8] Summarized by himself (**91**), 91.

[9] E.g. the spread in Schwyzertütsch of the first and second plural ending -*nt* (replacing zero, -*t*) from Uri into Urseren, described by Bangerter (**15**, 11). Even Meillet (**350**, I, 87) admitted the possibility of this type of morpheme transfer.

[10] The similarity of vocabulary, cognate and borrowed, in Bulgarian and Meglenite Rumanian may have been a facilitating factor even in the morpheme transfer discussed here.

[11] Sommerfelt (**534**), 8.

Indeed, it stands very much to reason that the transfer of morphemes is facilitated between highly congruent structures;[12] for a highly bound morpheme is so dependent on its grammatical function (as opposed to its designative value) that it is useless in an alien system unless there is a ready function for it.

One reason why bound-morpheme transfers have so rarely been detected[13] is that observers have sought them predominantly in fixed languages, rather than in the flowing speech of bilinguals.[14] There is little doubt that careful listening to speech, particularly in circumstances where interference is little inhibited (cf. §3.4), would reveal many interesting transfers of even the most strongly bound morphemes.[15]

That such transfers are ephemeral and are rarely established in the recipient language is a different matter and deserves separate study. Cultural reasons (cf. §42) may be at play, but structural factors, too, may be involved. Significantly, the transferred morphemes in several of the cited examples are introduced to replace zeros or phonemically less bulky forms: -en replacing zero for the plural in a Swiss Italian dialect, -o replacing zero for the vocative in Rumanian, ge- replacing zero for the passive participle and -ke for the feminine in Yiddish-affected English; -um, -iš taking the place of the shorter -u, -i in Meglenite Rumanian, or -nt replacing mere -t (or zero) in Urseren Schwyzertütsch. The bilingual speaker apparently feels a need to express some categories of one system no less strongly than in the other, and transfers morphemes accordingly for purposes of reinforcement. The unilingual speaker of the recipient language, on the other hand, uncontaminated by another system, may not share the need for reinforcement. Moreover, because of their frequent inconspicuousness, the transferred bound morphemes occurring in the foreigner's speech easily escape his notice. Unaware of their presence, ignorant as to their function, he is not likely to adopt them. Caribbean Creole, for example, reflects a state of one-time

---

[12] This has been asserted in much more general form by Bartoli (22a, 90) in 1927 and by the Prague Linguistic Circle (420, 305) in 1948. While Vogt's remark (599, 38) on the unsuitability of the Indo-European field for grammatical interference study is valid with reference to replica functions (see p. 37, footnote 30), the exact opposite would seem to be true as far as the transfer of bound morphemes is concerned, since the condition of apriori congruent structure is so fully developed in the Indo-European family.

[13] Some other instances of bound-morpheme borrowing are the Rumanian feminine vocative ending -o, of Slavic origin, reported by Rosetti (454, 73); the Georgian instrumental in -iw of Armenian origin, mentioned by Schuchardt (497, 193); and a few scattered others.

[14] On differentiating language and speech, see §2.14.

[15] Thus Schuchardt (496, 101) heard, in the German speech of Czechs, forms like sie geht-e 'she goes' (present tense!), with a transfer of Czech -e; he also heard Slovaks saying, in German, in Pressburg-u, with a Czech locative suffix (ibid., 85). Cf. Kober's phrases, allegedly reproducing the English speech of native Yiddish speakers (279, 36): now is gebusted the cup 'now the cup is "busted" ', or like a . . . can from sardines was gepacked the train 'the train was packed like a can of sardines' (280, 25), where the morpheme ge- is transferred into English; Miss Fortune-Tellerke (ibid.), where the Yiddish formant -ke is added to reinforce the feminity of Miss Fortune-Teller. Cf. also the Polish-German forms cited by Mak (334, 49), e.g. to mi przyszlo komisch vor (<das kam mir komisch vor) 'this seemed funny to me'.

bilingualism when the functions of the strongly bound and alternating morpheme which differentiates French masculine /plẽ/ from feminine /plɛn/ 'full' were overlooked. Instead, these compound forms were borrowed as simple, semantically different words: plẽ 'full', plen 'pregnant (of animals and women); full (of moon)'; similarly for fẽ 'fine (delicate)', fin 'thin', etc.[16]

As a mechanism for the reinforcement of expression, the transfer of morphemes naturally flourishes where affective categories are concerned. Schuchardt (496, 86f.), in his still indispensable early study, noted the transferability of diminutive and endearing affixes. Diminutives of Polish origin have been shown to abound in Silesian German,[17] while in modern Hebrew endearing forms in -le, derived from Yiddish, have been regularly established.[18] A favorite Yiddish morphological device for the expression of disparagement, consisting in the repetition of a word with substitution of /šm-/ for the initial consonant (e.g. libe-šmibe 'love—what's love?'), has been applied by Yiddish speakers to many other languages; in Amer. English, as Spitzer has shown (537), the money-shmoney pattern seems to be catching on among non-bilinguals, too.

According to the conception of the relative boundness of morphemes (p. 30), it is now possible to pass from the unequivocally bound forms to freer ones and inquire whether some parts of speech, or form classes, are more amenable to transfer than others. It would be interesting, for example, to test the proposition that the transferability of a class of morphemes is a function of both systems in contact, not just of one. In other words, it might be possible to show, perhaps, that a relatively unbound morpheme is most likely to replace its counterpart in another language if the latter is more bound and is involved in a greater variation of alternants in fulfilling corresponding functions. Thus, Ukrainian and Rumanian both have adjective comparisons, but while in Ukrainian the comparative is expressed by an unstressed bound suffix (involving frequent root modifications), the Rumanian system is quite clearcut: To form the comparative, the detachable form mai is placed before the adjective, which is itself unaffected. A bilingual in this contact situation is reported to have reinforced her comparatives in Ukrainian by introducing mai from Rumanian (obtaining something like the redundant more older).[19]

Would the same speaker have introduced mai into French, where plus is just as unbound and invariant? The answer must remain speculative because, unfortunately, evidence of this type is still extremely scarce.

Other things being equal, and cultural considerations apart, morphemes with complex grammatical functions seem to be less likely to be transferred by the bilingual than those with simpler functions. For example, a preposition which determines one of several cases is less likely to be transferred than a freely occurring noun;[20] an auxiliary verb, governed by conjunctions or governing moods

[16] Taylor (565), 43, footnote 2.
[17] Pritzwald (422).
[18] Rubin (457), 308.
[19] Racoviță (424).
[20] Schuchardt already noted (496, 9, 85) that "in regard to their independence, preposi-

of the main verb, is perhaps less transferable than a full-fledged verb. On the contrary, such unintegrated morphemes as sentence-words and interjections would appear to be transferable almost at will.[21] Of course, the structure of the recipient language is also involved. If it contains cases which the bilingual can identify with the case system of the other language in contact, the transfer of a preposition may be facilitated.

It may be possible to range the morpheme classes of a language in a continuous series from the most structurally and syntagmatically integrated inflectional ending, through such "grammatical words" as prepositions, articles, or auxiliary verbs, to full-fledged words like nouns, verbs, and adjectives, and on to independent adverbs and completely unintegrated interjections. Then this hypothesis might be set up: The fuller the integration of the morpheme, the less likelihood of its transfer.[22] A scale of this type was envisaged by Whitney in 1881 (637) and by many linguists since. Haugen (203, 224) discusses it as the "scale of adoptability," without, perhaps, sufficiently emphasizing its still hypothetical nature as far as bilinguals' speech is concerned. It should be clear how much painstaking observation and analysis is necessary before this hypothesis can be put to the test.[23]

While the flowing speech of bilinguals has been neglected, statistical analyses

---

tions differ little from suffixes." He quotes an Italian who said, in German, *er wohnt nella Heinrichstrasse* 'he lives on Heinrich Street'. Here the place name, which in this community was as much Italian as German, was transferred into German speech along with its invariant preposition, much as the French *statuette* was transferred into English with its formative suffix. The same speaker, Schuchardt writes, would not have used *nella* in a free construction like **er ist nella Küche*.

[21] Some bilinguals appear to transfer these unintegrated words in both directions, until they form a single, merged lexical subsystem used in speaking either language; in Roberts' terminology (450, 34), there takes place lexical "interfusion," i.e. reciprocal borrowing. The native-language speech of American immigrants swarms with English interjections. But while words like *sure, never mind, well,* and *O.K.* are freely used, say, in immigrant Yiddish, the uninhibited English speech of the same speakers, and even that of their children, is full of *táke* 'indeed', *kejnenhóre* 'not bad!', *nébex* 'poor thing', and similar grammatically unintegrated adverbs of which Yiddish has so many. As Sjœstedt points out (521, 100), "such little words . . . are the forerunners of the invasion of a vocabulary by a foreign one"; but after the language shift has taken place, such words of the receding language "are often the last ones to survive and to attest the existence of the extinct language."

[22] The confirmation of this hypothesis would be fully in keeping with the decisive role assigned to grammatical criteria, as the most conservative, in establishing genetic relationships among languages; cf. Meillet (350), I, 84.

[23] Students of acculturation face a similar problem—almost equally unexplored—of rating culture elements according to their transferability. "It seems," says Linton in a tentative remark (312, 485), "that, other things [e.g. prestige associations] being equal, certain sorts of culture elements are more easily transferable than others. Tangible objects such as tools, utensils, or ornaments are taken over with great ease, in fact they are usually the first things transferred in contact situations. . . . The transfer of elements which lack the concreteness and ready observability of objects is the most difficult of all. . . . In general, the more abstract the element, the more difficult the transfer."

In the future it may be feasible to formulate a theory of transferability as a function of structure comprehensive enough to cover both linguistic items and extralinguistic elements of culture.

have been made of the form classes contained in lists of loanwords. In a count of this type, Haugen (**203**, 224) computed the proportion of each part of speech in several lists of English loanwords in Amer. Norwegian and Amer. Swedish. The result was in conflict even with Haugen's own concept of transferability; in one list, there were 75% nouns but only 1.4% interjections (though the latter would be expected to be at least as transferable as nouns in view of their structural independence). Perhaps the statistical procedure could be refined a bit. In the first place, the text frequency of the classes of loanwords would have to be determined. Interjections, for instance, might be only one in a hundred different loanwords, but might be twenty or thirty of every hundred loanwords as they occur in speech. In the second place, the ratio of form classes among the loanwords should be compared with the ratio of these classes in the total vocabulary of the recipient and source languages (in terms of both text occurence and dictionary listings). It might turn out then that, say, only one out of thirty occurring nouns is a loanword, but as many as one out of every three interjections is transferred.

If one could somehow measure the frequency of particular words in the speech of various members of a language community, it might be possible to show the diminishing frequency of certain transferred forms as one moves from the highly bilingual speakers—the agents of the transfer—to the more unilingual bulk of the group.[24] It might be feasible to prove or disprove then what so far has had to be asserted only hypothetically—that the reception of transferred forms, especially by unilinguals, is subject to a selective resistance inherent in the recipient grammar.

It has been suggested, for example, that the inflected[25] verb systems of the Indo-European and Semitic languages are recalcitrant at the introduction of new stems, while their noun classes are more open. Indeed, a language like Hebrew cannot use a verb of more than four stem consonants;[26] but other languages, whose stems are also inflected but not limited in length, have means to handle new additions. When it comes to mobilizing verbs, -*ieren* can be suffixed to a new stem in German, -*irovat'* in Russian, -*adzi* in modern Greek,[27] -*i* or -*ari* in Amer. Sicilian;[28] Yiddish has a special periphrastic conjugation for the use of

---

[24] In Switzerland, it has been proposed to study this aspect of language contact in a spatial projection. Jaberg (**238**, 55ff.), commenting on Tappolet's collection of Schwyzertütsch loanwords in Swiss French patois (**563**), showed that if the occurrence of loanwords were indicated by dots on a map, the contact areas on the language border would be darkest. Cf. also Steiner (**546**, 31) on the "density of borrowing" of French words in Schwyzertütsch. Unfortunately this line of research was never pursued, and no information on form classes has been produced.

[25] I.e. those utilizing highly bound morphemes with many alternants in their paradigms, and not excluding inflectional changes in stems.

[26] Even so, *t-l-g-r-f* 'to telegraph' does function as a five-consonant verb; cf. Weiman (**615**), 66.

[27] Graur (**174**).

[28] Menarini (**353**), 156f. Unless otherwise indicated, examples of interference cited from Amer. Italian, Amer. German, Amer. Norwegian, Amer. Yiddish, and other immigrant languages belong to substandard usage and are not admitted to the cultivated forms of these languages even in the United States.

most verbs of Hebrew origin (e.g. *mekane zajn, ix bin mekane* 'to envy, I envy' <
mᵉqanê? < *q-n-?*); Amer. Portuguese can not only inflect English verb stems
directly, but also resorts to periphrasis: *fazer o boda* 'to bother', and even *fazer
o find-out*.[29] Similar devices can be named for other morpheme classes in these inflected languages.

Why is it, then, that in the usual lists of loanwords, nouns figure so predominantly? The reason is probably of a lexical-semantic, rather than a grammatical and structural nature. In the languages in which borrowing has been
studied, and under the type of language and culture contact that has existed,
the items for which new designations were needed (cf. §2.44) have been, to an
overwhelming degree, such as are indicated by nouns. Under different structural
or cultural contact conditions, the ratio might be different.[30] For example, in the
contact of a European language, where many concrete "things" are generally
indicated by nouns, with a language in which verbs fulfill some of the same
functions (e.g. Nootka), the ratio of nouns among the loanwords would probably
be lower than usual. Further, in a cultural setting where the emphasis in borrowing is on things spiritual and abstract, loanwords other than nouns may again
occupy a larger place, even in a European language. In this way one may account,
for example, for the relatively large proportion of such classes as verbs, adverbs,
conjunctions, and prepositions among the loanwords from Hebrew into Yiddish
(although here, too, nouns predominate).

In themselves, the existence of an inflection or the restrictions on the phonemic
make-up of stems (e.g. their length) are hardly an obstacle to borrowing. Where
there are inflections, there are usually also base-extending affixes to adapt new
stems; where the stem must have a prescribed phonemic form, it can be forced
into that form (see §2.37). Some morpheme classes of a language (like inflectional endings or pronouns) do indeed seem less hospitable to newcomers than
others, but only insofar as those classes are more self-sufficient in the face of
cultural innovation, at least of a concrete, material kind.

2.33 Interference in Grammatical Relations

The sentence *he comes tomorrow home* was cited on p. 30 as an example of
the application of a grammatical relation of word order from one language
(German) to morphemes of another (English). Such interference in the domain
of grammatical relations is extremely common in the speech of bilinguals.

Interference of relations can be of several types. (1) The replica of the relation
of another language explicitly conveys an unintended meaning. Example: A
German speaker says in English *this woman loves the man* on the model of German
diese Frau liebt der Mann, intending to communicate the message 'the man
loves this woman', but producing the opposite effect. (2) The replica of the
relation of another language violates an existing relation pattern, producing

[29] Pap (395), 100, 105. In Amer. Lithuanian, according to Senn (514, 47ff.), English
adjectives are most difficult to accept; verbs are easiest. Nevertheless, adjectives, too, are
transferred: *dòrtinas* < *dirty, fòniškas* < *funny*.

[30] Here, Vogt's recommendation that other than Indo-European languages be examined
(599, 38) is fully to the point (cf. p. 33, footnote 12).

nonsense or a statement which is understandable by implication. Example: A German speaker says in English *yesterday came he* on the model of German *gestern kam er*, meaning 'he came yesterday'. A third type, which constitutes interference only theoretically, consists in the unnecessary imposition of a relation to a language where no obligatory relations exist in the equivalent domain. For example, if a native English speaker were to maintain the English-type word order of SUBJECT + VERB + OBJECT in his Russian speech, this would be superfluously monotonous, but would not violate Russian grammar.[31]

All types of interference can affect every type of relation: order, modulation, agreement and dependence.

a. ORDER. Examples of interference in word order are plentiful. Swiss bilingual children have been recorded saying, in Romansh, /ˈɪɲa ˈkotʃna tʃaˈpetʃa/, instead of /ˈɪɲa tʃaˈpetʃa ˈkotʃna/ 'a red hat', on the model of the Schwyzertütsch order pattern ARTICLE + ADJECTIVE + NOUN; also, /ɛl a la tʃaˈpetʃa aɲ/ for /ɛl a aɲ la tʃaˈpetʃa/ 'he has his hat on', on the Schwyzertütsch pattern in which adverbal complements come last in the main clause. In idiomatic Yaqui, words like *betčiʔibo* 'for' generally follow the noun: *ʔin-áčai betčiʔibo* 'my-father for', i.e. 'for my father'; but on the pattern of Spanish PREpositions, the word order is being shifted to make the relational word precede the noun: *bétčiʔibo ʔin-áčai*.[32] In Amer. Portuguese, nouns are compounded in an Anglicized order: *Português Recreativo Club* for *Club Recreativo Português*.[33]

b. MODULATIONS. The systematic description of modulation patterns available in a language is still in its infancy; it is too early, therefore, to expect exact statements of the impact of one language on another in this domain.[34] Let two examples suffice.

(1) Yiddish has an intonation pattern which designates a yes-or-no question with an expected negative reply. It consists in a rise, as if for a normal yes-or-no question, which turns into a fall after the high pitch level is reached.[35] Thus, *du vilst smétene* (with final contour ‾−_) 'you want sour cream' is distinguished from the same sentence with final contour _−‾ ('do you want sour cream?') and from the same sentence with the final contour −‾\ ('you don't want sour cream, do you?'). Some native speakers of Yiddish may be heard to apply this special contour to sentences in other languages, e.g. *you're going home* (−‾\), intended to mean: 'you aren't going home, are you?'.

(2) The rules of Yiddish noun compounding require a distinctly stronger stress on the first element: /ˈkix-meser/ 'kitchen knife', /ˈbixer-ˌojsʃtelung/

[31] While comparisons between phonemic and grammatical processes have their dangers, it may be safe to point out the parallelism of the first type of interference of grammatical relations with phonemic under-differentiation, the second type with phone subsitution, and the third type with phonemic over-differentiation.

[32] Johnson (252).

[33] Pap (395), 85.

[34] Dreher's study (129) deals with a related problem but does not fit into the framework of the present discussion.

[35] In the notation of Trager and Smith (577), this would correspond approximately to [. . .²⁺⁻] or /. . .² ‖ ⫽/.

'book exhibition'. Under English influence, this relation is sometimes neglected in Amer. Yiddish; one hears forms like /₁arbeter-ˈring/ 'Workmen's Circle' (properly /ˈarbeter-₁ring/), /ˈperets-ˈmitlšul/ 'Peretz High School' (properly /ˈperets-₁mitlšul/), and the like.

c. AGREEMENT AND DEPENDENCE. Interference among relations of this type is easily observed. Bilingual children in Switzerland say, in Romansh, /la tʃa-ˈpetʃa ε ˈkotʃan/ 'the hat is red', failing to select for the predicate adjective the same gender (feminine) as for the subject (i.e. /... ε ˈkotʃna/), on the model of neighboring Schwyzertütsch, where the pattern of agreement does not exist. The Italian model leads Slovenian bilinguals to neglect the selection of the accusative in the direct object in Slovene.[36] Chuvash speakers fail to make the past-tense verb in Russian agree in gender with the subject, on the Chuvash model: *syn ne pila čaj* for ... *ne pil* ... 'the son did not drink tea'.[37] On the other hand, a possessive relationship is sometimes superfluously distinguished in Amer. Yiddish on the English model: *er šnajtst zajn noz* 'he blows his nose' for the more idiomatic *er šnajtst di noz* ʻ... the nose'.

Examples of all kinds could be cited without limit, for the misapplication and neglect of grammatical relations is well attested. This type of interference is so very common probably because grammatical relations, not being segments of utterances, are least noticed by naïve speakers.[38] If the available evidence contains mostly cases of the type where the intended meaning is understandable at least by implication (cf. p. 37), it is clearly because the pressure against relational interference resulting in unintended meanings is considerably stronger.

Interference may also affect functions performed in one language by morphemes but rendered in another by grammatical relations. For example, the function of the German morpheme *dieser*, as distinct from *die*, is often performed in Yiddish by stress: *af der ˈgas = auf der Strasse* 'in the street'; *af ˈder ₁gas = auf dieser Strasse* 'in this street'. This difference leads German-Yiddish bilinguals either to transfer the German morpheme or to utilize—often superfluously— Yiddish patterns of emphasis by morphemes: *af ot der gas, af der dóziker gas,* etc.

2.34 Replica Functions for Equivalent Morphemes

If the bilingual identifies a morpheme or grammatical category of language *A* with one in language *B*, he may apply the *B* form in grammatical functions which he derives from the system of *A*.

What leads the bilingual to establish the interlingual equivalence of the morphemes or categories is either their FORMAL SIMILARITY or a SIMILARITY IN PREËXISTING FUNCTIONS. Formal similarity enables Amer. Yiddish speakers to

---

[36] Vendryes (594), 341. Actually, a pattern of order is substituted for the requirement of the accusative in the direct object.

[37] Seliščev (509). Many similar instances of interference of Estonian and Chuvash with Russian are cited by Raun (427), 9f.

[38] Language teachers instructing relatively young children feel it necessary to make their pupils aware of the subtle relations of their native grammar before exposing them to the new system; cf. Nikol'skij's experiences (386) in teaching Russian to Tatar children.

identify *op* 'off, down' with English *up*, leading to such innovations as *op-rufn* (after *to call up*). The Hungarian deverbal adjectives in *-andó/-endö* have been given gerundival functions by identification, on formal grounds, with Latin *-andus/-endus*.[39]

Similarity in function, on the other hand, causes Uzbeks to equate the Russian construction *iz* + genitive with their native partitive and to use it even where idiomatic Russian requires other prepositions (*ot, u*, etc.).[40] On the same basis— through a process identical with loan translation in the lexical domain (cf. §2.41) —the Balkan languages have each developed a set of two specialized conjunctions to introduce complementary clauses, one (e.g. Rumanian *ca*) after 'to say, to think, to believe', the other (e.g. Rumanian *să*) after 'to want, to demand', etc., all corresponding to the Middle Greek distinction between ὅτι and νά.[41] In Hungarian, the conjunction *akár* 'or' has been identified with Slavic equivalents (e.g. Serbocroatian *volja*), yielding, on that model, an extended construction *akár ... akár* 'either ... or' (Serbocroatian *volja ... volja*).[42] The Finnish form *epä*, originally the present participle of the verb of negation, has been mobilized in compounds as a prefix meaning 'non-', after the fashion of Swedish *om-, on-*.[43] In many European languages, a full system of adverbal complements has been reproduced from another language: Romansh after German,[44] Welsh after English,[45] Hungarian (to some extent) after German,[46] Yiddish after Slavic.[47] In Yiddish, for example, the adverbal complements of Germanic origin *far-, tse-, on, der-* have aspective functions closely resembling Polish *za-, roz-, na-, do-*, respectively.[48] Sometimes entire grammatical categories of two languages are identified because of a partial similarity in function. For example, Amer. German speakers, identifying the English with the German present tense, may say *how long are you here?* for *how long have you been here?*. In Silesia, the identification of the third person plural of the local Polish dialect ("Wasserpolnisch") with the equivalent category in German has led to the unexpected use, completely unknown in Polish, of the third person plural for polite address (e.g. *dokąd idą?* = *wohin gehen Sie?*).[49]

Taking its cue from the speech of bilinguals, a language community can, by systematically extending the functions of morphemes in its language, not only change the use of individual forms, but also develop a full new paradigm of ob-

[39] Sauvageot (**474**). On identification by form in lexical interference, see below, pp. 48, 50f:
[40] Xajrulla (**654**).
[41] Sandfeld (**468**).
[42] Simonyi (**519**).
[43] Sauvageot (**474**), 498.
[44] Jaberg (**236; 238**, 287f.).
[45] E.g. Vendryes (**594**), 343.
[46] Sauvageot (**474**), 498.
[47] Landau (**294**).
[48] Cf. Yiddish *šrajbn* with Polish *pisać* 'to write (*imperfective*)' and *on-šrajbn* with *na-pisać* 'to write (*perfective*)'.
[49] Müller (**380**). The same phenomenon occurs in Italian speech influenced by Slovene; cf. Schuchardt (**496**), 99.

ligatory categories on the model of another language. Such is the origin of grammatical calques like the new Breton perfect with *am euz* based on the French indefinite past with *avoir*;[50] the postposited definite article in Rumanian, Bulgarian, Albanian, and Modern Greek;[51] the disappearance of the infinitive and the differentiation between two conjunctions in the Balkan languages under Middle Greek influence;[52] the differentiation between the purely grammatical copula and the verb 'to be' in Tigre and Tigrinya on the pattern of Cushitic languages in Ethiopia;[53] the future tense in Romansh and Schwyzertütsch formed with /vɛɲ/ and /kʰun/ ('come'), respectively, as auxiliaries;[54] the passive voice in Estonian, Sorbian,[55] and Slovene[56] based on German; the partial aspective system of Yiddish based on Slavic;[57] the partial aspective system in Irish based on English.[58] In Silesia, the German verbal construction *haben* + past participle has been reproduced in Polish to function as a past tense: *ja to mam sprzedane* 'I have sold it', after *ich habe es verkauft*[59]—much like the new preterite in late Latin, *habēo scriptum*, which is said to be a replica of the Greek γεγραμμένον ἔχω,[60] or like the new Hungarian pluperfect formed with *volt* 'to have' following the past form of the verb, on the pattern of the German pluperfect;[61] and so on and on.

Significantly, in the interference of two grammatical patterns it is ordinarily the one which uses relatively free and invariant morphemes in its paradigm—one might say, the more explicit pattern—which serves as the model for imitation.[62] This seems to be true not only in the creation of new categories, as in the above examples, but also in those changes due to language contact where a new set of formants is developed to fulfill a preëxisting grammatical function. Estonian, for example, has developed a system for denoting possession by the genitive of the personal pronoun (a free form), in the German fashion, to replace the personal suffix (bound form), a pattern which still survives in Finnish. It thus has *minu kodu, sinu kodu* 'my house, your house' where Finnish (and

---

[50] Hardie (**194**), 103.

[51] Sandfeld (**467**), 165–73; despite overall similarities, the functions of the article do differ in the four languages; cf. Michov (**360**). Caution against simplifications is also urged by Iorga (**233**).

[52] Sandfeld (**468**); cf. p. 40 above.

[53] Leslau (**306**), 72.

[54] Szadrowsky (**561**), 9.

[55] Sandfeld (**466**), 60. While Estonian uses an equivalent auxiliary, Sorbian has transferred the German *werden* bodily.

[56] Vendryes (**594**), 343.

[57] On the aspective system of Yiddish, see Schächter (**481, 482**) and Weinreich (**625**).

[58] Sjœstedt (**521**), 112ff.

[59] Vendryes (**594**), 343.

[60] Bonfante (**68**), 304.

[61] Sauvageot (**474**), 498.

[62] A case in which the expression of a category was made more explicit by the TRANSFER of a morpheme was described on p. 34. Incidentally, the psychological reasons for which the more explicit, the more consciously experienced pattern is easier to imitate should not be difficult to formulate. Note that the transfer of morphemes also seems to be favored by relatively greater (i.e. more explicit) phonemic bulk; cf. p. 33.

presumably older Estonian) has *koti-ni*, *koti-si*.[63] Similarly, in Amharic there has developed, beside the possessive-suffix pattern *bet-kä* 'your house', a more explicit pronoun construction (*yaantä bet* < *yä-antä bet* 'of-you house') after the Cushitic pattern.[64] In much the same way, the possessive suffixes are falling into disuse in colloquial Israeli Hebrew (*bet-xa* 'house-your' is much less common than *ha-bait šel-xa* 'the-house of-you') under the pressure of the more explicit pattern of Yiddish and other European mother-tongues of so many Israelis.[65] Language contact can result in such far reaching changes that the affected language assumes a different structural type.[66]

The reverse type of influence—the change of a grammatical system toward a less explicit form—is generally recognized to be quite rare,[67] but some instances have nevertheless been attested. Thus, in the dialect of Tadzhik spoken in the north of the Tadzhik S.S.R. (around Khodzhent and Samarkand), where the contact with Uzbek is particularly strong, the Tadzhik conjugation has been evolving from an isolating toward a more agglutinative form, with the auxiliary verbs becoming affixes, i.e. growing more bound, on the Uzbek model. In standard Tadzhik, for example, there is a present progressive form of the type *man xurda istoda-am* 'I eating am-I', i.e. 'I am eating'. In the Uzbek-influenced dialect, a new pattern has been developing: *man xur(d)-sod-am*, where the auxiliary *istoda-* has been reduced to a suffix of the main verb (> *-sod-*), the personal ending now being added to the main verb. The Uzbek prototype is *kel-vat-man* 'coming-am-I', where the suffix *-vat-*, indicating the progressive aspect, has, incidentally, also evolved from a free auxiliary verb. Many other Tadzhik verbal forms have developed likewise.[68] In Serbocroatian, a productive pattern of forming absolute superlatives by means of bound morphemes has developed as a replica of the Turkish model (*beli* 'truly'—*bezbeli* 'quite truly'); for example, *go* 'nude'—*gozgo* 'quite naked'; *ravno* 'even'—*ravravno* 'entirely horizontal', etc.[69] But despite the unusual trend toward more strongly bound forms demonstrated in the above cases, the model patterns have nevertheless been explicit enough. The formant morphemes in the model were easily recognizable, the occurrence of alternants was regular.

2.35 Abandonment of Obligatory Distinctions

Finally the type of grammatical interference resulting in the disappearance of grammatical categories should be referred to. One need only think of a foreign-language classroom where English-speaking students fail to distinguish cases, genders, or aspects in a foreign language. In situations of natural language contact, the same process occurs. In Gurage (Southern Ethiopia), for example, the

---

[63] Sauvageot (474), 498.

[64] Leslau (306), 71.

[65] Weiman (615), 7.

[66] Belić (38), 304. The partial "Indo-Europeanization" of modern Hebrew, a secondary language for many European bilinguals, could probably be demonstrated; cf. Weiman (615), *passim*; Larish (295); Rubin (457).

[67] E.g. by Vogt (599), 39

[68] Stavrulli (543), 40f

[69] Skok (522).

gender of adjectives, under the influence of Sidamo, is no longer expressed consistently;[70] that is, as a result of language contact the expression of the category has become less obligatory in the sense defined on p. 30. Similarly, German speakers in Texas, under the influence of English, neglect the distinction between dative and accusative in certain constructions.[71] In Yaqui verbs, the obligatory indication of incorporated direct object, transitiveness (with regard to an indirect object), and person is being eliminated under the impact of Spanish; the pattern ʔínepo ʔenči-ʔa-mák-ria-ne 'I you-it-give-trans.-I' is replaced by the rudimentary ʔínepo ʔen-máka 'I you-give', i.e. 'I give (it to) you'.[72] In Udi, a North Caucasian language, the ergative construction has given way to a nominative under Armenian and Tatar influence.[73] But while the violation of such highly obligatory categories is quite conspicuous, astute observation reveals the desuetude of more optional types as well. In Ireland, for example, "there is no doubt that a speaker who knows some English often tends to prefer the Irish construction which least shocks the English language habits [i.e. the grammatical system serving as a model], unless he is reacting consciously, in which case the reverse effect will be produced. . . . Even where the details of the process escape observation, the total result is considerable, as shown by the growing banalization of Irish in areas where it is spoken concurrently with English."[74]

In the highly hybridized makeshift trade languages, most obligatory categories expressed by bound morphemes are well known to be abandoned.[75] These tongues have by and large been formed from structurally very different languages; the failure to perceive non-explicit grammatical categories has therefore been widespread on both sides. Also, considering that trade tongues begin with a very sketchy learning of both second languages, and that only the bare essentials of existence are given expression in the hybrid form, the necessity for observing grammatical distinctions is so reduced that free and non-obligatory forms suffice as means of expressing them.

2.36 Role of Extra-Structural Factors

It follows from the preceding discussion that a simple statement of the form "Morphologies can(not) be mixed" is premature at the present state of our knowledge. The transfer of a full grammatical paradigm, with its formant mor-

[70] Leslau (306), 69.

[71] Eikel (133), 279.

[72] Johnson (252).

[73] Dirr (122), 306.

[74] Sjœstedt (521), 121. Cf. also Heberle (207), 31.

[75] Cf. Broch's description of Russenorsk (81). On the other hand, the more stable Creole languages have developed articulate grammatical systems, including obligatory categories, based on free forms; cf. Taylor's analysis of the Caribbean Creole conjugation (565, 84), in which mwɛ tan 'I hear', mwɛ te tan 'I heard', mwɛ ke tan 'I will hear', etc., represent a perfect tense paradigm. Silesian bilingual Poles who, according to Hoffman (223, 276), say in German ich bekommen täglich 3 Mark Lohn 'I receive 3 marks a day in wages', seem to depend on the free and explicit pronoun ich to denote the first person, not troubling with the proper inflection of the verb itself (which should, of course, be bekomme). Hjelmslev has shown (221) that Creole languages have a theoretical optimum, rather than a minimum, of grammar.

phemes, from one language into another has apparently never been recorded. But the transfer of individual morphemes of all types is definitely possible under certain favorable structural conditions, such as a preëxisting similarity in patterns or the relatively unbound and invariant form of the morpheme. Furthermore, obligatory categories have become optional or abandoned and replica patterns established on the model of another language, again favored by such factors as relative explicitness of the model categories.

And yet, not every conjuncture of favorable structural conditions results in permanent grammatical interference of the type one might predict. Clearly, fewer phenomena of interference are incorporated in the language as a code than occur in the speech of bilinguals. There is a selection of phenomena, and a complex resistance to interference. The conventional evidence does not enable us to analyze the components of such resistance—purely structural considerations (incompatibility of new forms with existing ones), psychological reasons (e.g. unwillingness to adopt for ordinary usage material transferred in affective speech), and socio-cultural factors (favorable or unfavorable prestige associations of the transferred or reproduced forms, etc.).

For an analysis that can do justice to the complexity of linguistic facts, the data must be obtained, first and foremost, from the flowing speech of bilinguals in the natural setting of language contact; the usual sort of evidence, taken from relatively well established languages, cannot be a substitute.[76]

2.37 Grammatical Integration of Transferred Words

A word which has been transferred from one language into another is itself subject to the interference of the grammatical, as well as the phonic, system of the recipient language, especially at the hands of its unilingual speakers. As in the case of phonic treatment (cf. §2.25), a scale of effects ranging from complete non-adaptation to full grammatical integration of a word can be formulated.

By far the most usual procedure is the grammatical adaptation of loanwords.[77] Amer. Polish, receiving *bootlegger* from English, declines it: *jeden z butlegerów*, 'one of the bootleggers', and forms new words on native derivation patterns: *rokińczer-ować* 'to rock in a rocking chair'.[78] Amer. Greek adds inflectional endings: *bossis* 'boss', *bommis* 'bum', *grihonnis* 'greenhorn', and also forms new derivatives: *sain-atiko* '(shoe) shine parlor'.[79] Amer. Lithuanian classifies nouns: *týčeris* 'teacher', *drèsė* 'dress', *grýnorius* 'greenhorn'.[80] Amer. Yiddish conjugates: *badern* 'to bother', *er hot gebadert* 'he bothered', and derives: *holdópnik* 'gangster who performs a holdup', *olrájtnik* (*<allright*) 'self-satisfied parvenu'. Some of these American innovations have even found their way into the corresponding languages of the Old World.

---

[76] Little has been done in grammar that would correspond, for example, to studies of foreign "accents" in the phonic domain.

[77] Bloomfield (55), 453ff.; see also Migliorini's study (361) of the problem.

[78] Doroszewski (125).

[79] Lontos (323).

[80] Senn (514), 50.

Particularly interesting is the grammatical integration of loanwords where several classes are potentially open for them in the recipient language. Thus, English verbs borrowed into Amer. Portuguese are, if they are conjugated at all, generally placed in the first conjugation (*chinjar* 'to change', *jampar* 'to jump', etc.); only rarely do they join the *-ear* class (*faitear* 'to fight').[81]

In the assignment of borrowed nouns to grammatical genders, various criteria are at play. Generally, it appears, nouns denoting animate beings receive genders according to their sex; thus, *a norsa* (<*nurse*) in Amer. Portuguese, *di noj(r)s* in Amer. Yiddish are feminine, *o boquipa* (<*bookkeeper*) and *der bukkiper* are masculine in each language.[82] With inanimate nouns, the form of the word may be paramount: *cracker*, becoming *craca* in Amer. Portuguese, is feminine by virtue of its *-a* and *krėkė* in Amer. Lithuanian is feminine for its *-ė*;[83] in Amer. Yiddish, the ending of *kreker* classifies it as masculine. Some nouns seem to bequeath their gender to the loanwords by which they are replaced: in Pennsylvania German, *bailer* 'boiler' is masculine because it replaced *kesel* (*m.*), while *pigder* 'picture' is neuter because it replaced *bild* (*n.*). The word *sing* has split: it is *der sing* in the sense of 'kitchen sink' (substituting for *der waseršang*), but *di· sing* in the sense of 'laundry sink' (for *di· wešbang*).[84] In Amer. Norwegian, *inč* is masculine because it replaces *tomme*, while *jågg* 'yoke' is explained to be feminine because of *krukka*.[85] In other cases, however, the basis of classification must be assumed to be the greater productiveness of one of the genders in the recipient language: masculine in Amer. Norwegian,[86] Amer. Lithuanian,[87] and Amer. Portuguese;[88] feminine in Amer. German[89] and, to a lesser extent, in Amer. Yiddish[90] (e.g. *train* > Amer. Port. *o treno*, Amer. Yiddish *di trejn*). In still others, the classification is unexplained; why, for example, does Amer. Italian have *lo storo*<*store*, but *la yarda*<*yard*?[91] It would be most desirable to have a comparative study of the reactions of all American immigrant languages to English loanwords in the way of gender and other categories;[92] the fact that the source of the loanwords is the same—a common denominator in the comparison—would bring to the fore the structural criteria which are at play in the grammatical integration of loanwords.

[81] Pap (**395**), 100. Why some verbs do join the *-ear* conjugation is not made clear.

[82] In Amer. Yiddish, a 'lady bookkeeper' would be *bukkiperke*. The source for the Portuguese examples is Pap (**395**), 100–4.

[83] Senn (**514**), 50.

[84] Reed (**436**).

[85] Flom (**152**).

[86] *Ibid.*, 28, 31.

[87] Senn (**514**), 48ff.

[88] Pap (**395**), 102.

[89] Aron (**5**).

[90] Neumann (**383**), 418.

[91] Vaughan (**591**). As Pap (**395, 104**) and Neumann (**383, 417**) point out, the borrowed vocabulary is still in a "transitional" stage and there is a considerable amount of fluctuation in the assignment of genders. The problem is also discussed by Møller (**374**), 45ff.

[92] Pennsylvania German, for example, uses not only the plural in *-e*, but also vowel alternation: *di· gaund* 'ladies' dress' (< *gown*), plural: *di· gaind*; cf. Reed (**435**). Similarly, in Amer. Yiddish: *der šap* 'workshop', plural: *di šeper*.

In all the cited examples, the transferred word was, for better or for worse, integrated with the recipient grammar. Under certain circumstances, bilingual speakers display an indifference as to the grammatical treatment of transferred material. Entire sentences may even be transferred in unanalyzed form, as in Amer. Italian *azzoraiti* 'that's all right', *variuvanni* 'what do you want', *goraelli* 'go to hell'.[93] The special speech situation necessary for such grammatical indifference is discussed in §3.43.

In still other circumstances, a conscious effort is made to retain the morphology of the source language for transferred words, as in the use of the Latin-type plurals *minim-a, foc-i, formula-e* instead of the English-type *minimums, focuses, formulas*; the use of the Russian-type plural in *Bolsheviki* in a variety of English; the declension of Latin loanwords in an antiquated, learned type of German (*unter den Verbis* 'among the verbs'), etc.[94] In all these instances, a desire to display the learning associated with the knowledge of the source language, or the prestige of the source language itself, underlies the practice. An important cultural factor is manifested here.

Thus, a choice is often made by the speaker between integrating and not integrating the transferred words—a choice which seems even more clearcut in the matter of grammar than in sounds (cf. §2.25). The choice itself would appear to depend not on the structures of the languages in contact, but rather on individual psychological and socio-cultural factors prevailing in the contact situation. These must be analyzed independently (see chaps. 3, 4).

[93] Menarini (**353**).

[94] Even the indeclinability of loanwords like those in *-o, -um* in standard Polish (e.g.: *radio: bez radio* 'without a radio', but *okno: bez okna* 'without a window') reflect an unwillingness to tamper with a foreign morpheme.

2.4 Lexical Interference

2.41 Mechanisms of Lexical Interference

The ways in which one vocabulary can interfere with another are various. Given two languages, A and B, morphemes may be transferred from A into B, or B morphemes may be used in new designative functions on the model of A-morphemes with whose content they are identified;[1] finally, in the case of compound lexical elements, both processes may be combined.

a. SIMPLE WORDS.

(1) In the case of simple (non-compound) lexical elements, the most common type of interference is the outright transfer of the phonemic sequence from one language to another. Examples of such loanwords are available from practically every language described.

"Simple" in this connection must be defined from the point of view of the bilinguals who perform the transfer, rather than that of the descriptive linguist. Accordingly, the category of "simple" words also includes compounds that are transferred in unanalyzed form. Many interjections belong in this class, e.g. Penna. German *holišmok* < *holy smoke(s)!*,[2] as well as whole interjectional sentences of the type of American Italian *azzoraiti* 'that's all right', *vazzumara* 'what's the matter?'.[3] There are also the nominalized interjections, like Acadian French *faire la didouce à* 'to say hello to' (<*how do you do*)[4] or *le donquia* 'care-free person' (<*don't care*),[5] and words of other classes: Amer. Italian *siriollo* 'city hall', *sanemagogna* 'son of a gun',[6] Amer. Norwegian *blakkvalnot* 'black walnut',[7] Amer. Portuguese *o fòdejulai(a)* 'Fourth of July',[8] Volga German *saditsen* 'to sit down' (<Russian *sadít'-sja*),[9] and so on and on. Italian *pizza* 'large, hot, open cheese pie (with various salty fillings)', which has been adopted in Amer. English and "reinforced" into *pizza pie*, has even been retransferred as an unanalyzed compound into Amer. Italian: *la pizza-paia*.[10]

---

[1] The parallelism with the formulation of grammatical interference (cf. §2.31, p. 30) is evident. Equivalence of designative function here corresponds to identity of grammatical function in the previous chapter. The separation of the grammatical and lexical aspects of interference presupposes, of course, that many morphemes do have a designative function distinct from their purely grammatical function. The author regrets that to those formalistically inclined readers who cannot conceive of linguistic meaning other than distribution and of linguistic semantics beyond context analysis, the material in this chapter will appear either repetitious or linguistically irrelevant.

[2] Werner (**634**).

[3] Menarini (**353**), 159.

[4] Poirier (**411**), 281.

[5] Smith and Phillips (**527**).

[6] Menarini (**353**), 159, 175ff.

[7] Haugen (**203**), 219.

[8] Pap (**395**), 98.

[9] Braun (**77**).

[10] Menarini (**353**), 163.

The transferred word is occasionally of such form as to resemble phonemically a potential or actual word in the recipient language. In New Mexican Spanish, *bate* 'baseball bat', *troca* 'truck', *torque* 'turkey', *escore* 'baseball score',[11] in Colorado Spanish *percolador* 'coffee percolator',[12] in Louisiana French *guimbleur* 'gambler'[13] or Canadian French *baquer* 'to back' (*c'est son père qui le baque*), *guésser* 'to guess',[14] there is little or nothing to betray the fact that the word was borrowed but recently. The words *asesamiento* 'assessment' of New Mexico Spanish,[15] *alimonio* 'alimony' of Florida Spanish,[16] *o alvacote* 'overcoat' and *os alvarozes* 'overalls' of Amer. Portuguese[17] also seem completely assimilated.

(2) The other major type of interference involves the extension of the use of an indigenous word of the influenced language in conformity with a foreign model. If two languages have semantemes, or units of content, which are partly similar, the interference consists in the identification and adjustment of the semantemes to fuller congruence.[18] In Russian, for example, the semanteme represented by the expression *úroven'* comprises the concept of 'level', concrete and abstract. In Yakut, the semanteme represented by *tahym* was originally restricted to 'water level'. Through the interference of Russian, *tahym* has been extended to represent all 'levels', whether of water or of development, skill, etc.[19]

Often two existing semantemes, X and Y, of one language are merged on the model of another language, where the combined content of X and Y is represented by a single sign, Z. In the process, the expression of either X or Y is utilized for the merged pair and the other is discarded. For example, in dialectal Yiddish, the semantemes 'bridge' and 'floor' have been merged on the model of Belorussian *most*,[20] with *brik* (originally 'bridge') expressing the combined content, and the earlier word discarded.

Since lexical interference has been particularly well studied among genetically or culturally related languages, a great many cases could be discovered where the expressions in the two languages in contact were already similar before the units of content were brought into alignment. In Colorado Spanish, for example, *ministro* 'cabinet official' acquired the new meaning of 'Protestant ecclesiastic' on the model of English *minister*,[21] extending the previous similarity of expression to the content as well. Polish-Russian bilinguals are reported to broaden the use of Polish *tylko* to cover all meanings of the similar Russian *tól'ko*, even in such

[11] Kercheville (265).

[12] Trager and Valdez (578).

[13] Smith and Phillips (527).

[14] Barbeau (16), 105.

[15] Kercheville (265).

[16] Ortoz (390).

[17] Pap (395), 101. On the integration of loanwords, see §2.25 (phonic) and §2.37 (grammatical).

[18] The result is called a semantic loan, or an extension, by Haugen (203, 219), and is classed with loan-shifts. In Betz's scheme (42), it is a case of "loan meaning" (*Lehnbedeutung*).

[19] Mordinov and Sanžejev (375), 41.

[20] Shklyar (515), 66.

[21] Trager and Valdez (578).

phrases as *tylko wczoraj* 'only yesterday' (for *dopiero wczoraj*) on the model of Russian *tól'ko včerá*.[22] No Romance language in America seems to have escaped the interference of English *introduce* in the sense of 'to acquaint, to present formally': Portuguese *introduzir*,[23] Italian *introdurre*,[24] Louisiana and Canadian French *introduire*,[25] which originally meant merely 'to bring in', have all been so affected. But the change in the content of signs on the basis of homophonous signs in another language may go beyond a mere extension; the old content may even be discarded entirely. Amer. Italian *fattoria* has acquired the meaning 'factory', and no longer expresses its original content of 'farm'.[26] In many examples cited in the literature, it is unfortunately not indicated whether the old content is still covered by the expression; it is difficult to ascertain, for example, whether Amer. Portuguese *livraria*[27] and Amer. Italian *libreria*,[28] which are used to express 'library' on the model of the homophonous English word, continue also to denote 'bookstore' or not; or if Amer. Greek *karro*, used to express 'automobile' on the model of *car*,[29] still means 'cart, wagon' as well.

As a theoretical point, it may be noted that an adjustment in the content of signs with a considerable degree of homophony is a borderline case between the alternatives of (1) word transfer and (2) semantic extension due to contact. When Amer. Yiddish *korn* (originally 'rye') or Amer. Norwegian *korn* (originally 'grain')[30] are used in the sense of 'maize', it is impossible to say whether the Amer. English *corn* has been transferred, or the content of the indigenous words extended: In either case, the result is a broadening in the semantic function of the word in the recipient language.[31] Occasionally it is feasible to distinguish two types of interference involving homophony according to the nature of this semantic broadening.[32] If there is a "leap" in meaning, a HOMONYM is established in the recipient language; for example, the addition of the unrelated content of 'pinching' to 'jumping' in Amer. Portuguese *pinchar*,[33] or of the content 'to care' to the

[22] Jakubowski (**248**).

[23] Pap (**395**), 88.

[24] Menarini (**353**), 161.

[25] Read (**429**); Barbeau (**16**), 105. In a contact situation with as much homophony as between Italian and Spanish in Latin America, influence of this type is particularly common; cf. Riegler (**447**).

[26] Menarini (**353**). 'Farm' is now expressed by *farma*.

[27] Pap (**395**), 88.

[28] Vaughan (**591**), 433.

[29] Lontos (**323**).

[30] Haugen (**203**), 228.

[31] An equivalent phenomenon in culture contact is represented by the so-called syncretisms, or unified entities of bi-cultural derivation. Greenberg has shown (**179**) that North African Negroes easily accept the belief in the Mohammedan *jinn* because they identify it with their aboriginal *ʔiskoki* spirits, just as Catholic saints have been identified by Latin American Negroes with African deities. As Herskovits puts it (**218**, 5f.), "the fact that the receiving group can find in the traditions of the donors something understandable in terms of their own patterns makes for a lack of resistance and accelerates acceptance."

[32] Cf. Pap (**395**), 89f.; Haugen (**203**), 220.

[33] Pap (**395**), 88.

originally unconnected content 'to sweep' in Amer. Yiddish *kern*. If there is no such leap, but a "logical," gradual extension of meaning, the result is rather PO-LYSEMY, as in the above named cases of Amer. Norwegian *korn* 'grain' + 'maize' and Amer. Yiddish *korn* 'rye' + 'maize'.[34]

(3) Finally, a mild type of lexical interference occurs when the expression of a sign is changed on the model of a cognate in a language in contact, without effect on the content, e.g. when Spanish *Europa* becomes *Uropa* in Tampa, Florida,[35] or when *vakátsje* 'vacation' becomes *vekejšn* in Amer. Yiddish.

b. COMPOUND WORDS AND PHRASES.

Three types of interference are possible for multiple lexical units consisting of more than one morpheme. All the elements may be transferred, in analyzed form; all elements may be reproduced by semantic extensions; or some elements may be transferred, while others are reproduced.

(1) Transfer of analyzed compounds occurs when the elements of a compound or phrase are adapted to word-formative or syntactic patterns of the recipient language (if the elements are transferred unanalyzed, the word is to be considered simple). An example of a compound analyzed in the process of transfer is *conscientious objectors*, which Florida Spanish has borrowed as *objetores concientes*,[36] recompounding the elements in Spanish fashion. In Amer. Yiddish, the phrase *he changed his mind* is analyzed and resynthesized as *er hot gečéjndžt zajn majnd*, according to the demands of Yiddish grammar.[37]

(2) Reproduction in terms of equivalent native words can be carried out with compounds, phrases, and even larger units such as proverbs.[38] Thus, English *skyscraper* has served as a more or less exact model for German *Wolkenkratzer*, French *gratte-ciel*, Spanish *rascacielos*, Russian *neboskrjób*, Polish *drapacz chmur*, etc.; Penna. German *es gebbt rejje*[39] is reproduced in English as *it gives rain* 'it is going to rain', word for word. In the Balkans, all languages render 'may God punish you' by their equivalents of the phrase 'may you find it from God':[40]

      Aromunian: *S-ţĭ-o-afli dila Dumniđắŭ!*
      Albanian: *E đetš nga Perɛndìa!*
      Greek: *Apò tò theò tóbrɛs!*
      Bulgarian: *Ot Boga da mu se naměri!*
      Serbocroatian: *Da ot Boga nadješ!*

[34] The terms HOMONYMY and POLYSEMY, common in semantics—cf. Ullman (585), 48—seem more convenient than "loan homonyms" and "loan synonyms," or homophonous and homologous extensions, proposed by Haugen (203, 219; 203a, 94).

[35] Hayes (206). It is not entirely clear whether this form is /uˈropa/ or /juˈropa/.

[36] Ortoz (390). Neither component exists in standard Spanish.

[37] It might be possible to distinguish two separate loanwords here: *change* and *mind*; but *mind* is not used in Amer. Yiddish in any context but this and *making up one's mind*.

[38] Sandfeld's classic paper on calques (469) is full of examples. Cf. Unbegaun (586) on calques in Slavic. Replica proverbs in German are described by Seiler (507), vol. 5–8. A high number of lexical replicas has been interpreted as a symptom of "translated culture": see the discussion by Bauer (28).

[39] Wilson (644).

[40] Papahagi (396), 128.

The Yiddish proverb, *a šlext vajb is erger vi der tojt*, is a verbatim reproduction of the Hebrew *ʔiša raʕa mar mimavet* 'a bad wife is worse than death'.

This form of interference, generally called loan translation,[41] has been subdivided as follows:[42]

(a) LOAN TRANSLATIONS proper, in which the model is reproduced exactly, element by element: Louisiana French *marchandises sèches* 'dry goods' (i.e. textile fabrics for sale);[43] Huguenot French *avoir droit* after German *recht haben*,[44] Amer. Portuguese *estar direito* 'to be right', after English.[45]

(b) LOAN RENDITIONS (*Lehnübertragungen*), in which the model compound only furnishes a general hint for the reproduction, e.g. German *Vater-land* after Latin *patr-ia*, *Halb-insel* 'half-island' after *paen-insula* 'almost-island'; *Wolken-kratzer* 'cloud scraper' after *sky-scraper*.

(c) LOAN CREATIONS (*Lehnschöpfungen*), a term applied to new coinages which are stimulated not by cultural innovations, but by the need to match designations available in a language in contact: e.g. Yiddish *mitkind* 'sibling' (literally 'fellow child')[46] created on the stimulus of English *sibling*, German *Geschwister*, and equivalent terms much in vogue in present-day social science.

Among loan translations, one can also distinguish those in which the components appear with their familiar semantemes (only the particular combination of them being due to another language) from those where one or more of the components is involved in a semantic extension.[47] An example of the first type is Florida Spanish *poner a dormir* 'to put to sleep' (standard Spanish *hacer dormir*, *adormecer*), where *poner* and *dormir* appear with ordinary meanings, only the combination being unusual; the second kind is exemplified by such forms as Canadian French *escalier de feu* 'fire staircase, fire escape', where *feu* appears in place of standard *incendie* (the whole compound corresponds to standard French *escalier de sauvetage*); the substandard English *yes well* modeled after Penna. German *jawell* 'to be sure';[48] or the Wisconsin German *Pferds-Rettich* 'horse radish'.[49]

(3) The third type of interference in compound lexical units involves the transfer of some elements and the reproduction of others.[50] An excellent study

[41] Haugen (**203a**, 80) is proposing the term "novation" as opposed to mere "extension."
[42] Betz (**42; 41**, 9–31).
[43] Read (**429**).
[44] Erbe (**139**).
[45] Pap (**395**), 88.
[46] It is possible, on the other hand, to consider the CONCEPT of 'sibling' an innovation in the culture of Yiddish speakers much as it was in the English-language world, where the word *sibling* is said to be a coinage (or perhaps a revival) dating back to 1897. Betz himself (**41, 42**) applies the term "loan creation" (*Lehnschöpfung*) to such forms as *Kraftwagen* for *Automobil*, where the reference to the model form in another language is quite vague.
[47] "Evolving" (*entwickelnde*) and "enriching" (*bereichernde*) loan translations, according to Betz (**41, 42**).
[48] Wilson (**644**).
[49] Seifert (**506**).
[50] Loanblends, in Haugen's terminology (**203**, 218f.). Cf. also Møller (**374**, 55).

has been made of such hybrid compounds in Penna. German,[51] where forms like *fleˑš-pai* 'meat pie' or *esix-jug* 'vinegar jug' abound, and where even the suffix *-cvor* has been utilized in such hybrids as *waˑ(r)-ewe(r)* 'whoever', *was-ewe(r)* 'whatever'. In Tampa (Fla.) Spanish, many hybrid compounds are found in baseball vocabulary, such as *home plato* 'home plate', *pelota de fly* 'fly ball', and the like.[52]

The reproduced element of a hybrid compound, like a simple word or the elements of a loan translation semantically extended (type *a*(2) above, pp. 48f.), can be affected by homophony. For example, in the Wisconsin German hybrid compound *Grund-floor* 'ground floor',[53] the second element is transferred, while the first, *ground*, is reproduced by a homophonous indigenous sign whose seman-teme is perhaps slightly extended.[54]

Among the hybrid compounds one may also distinguish those in which the stem is transferred and a derivative affix reproduced, e.g. Amer. Yiddish *far-pójzenen* 'to poison', Swiss French patois *de-štopfe* 'to unplug' (using Schwyzer-tütsch *štopfe*),[55] or Penna. German *fils-ig* (after *filth-y*), *šip-ig* (after *sheep-ish*);[56] and those in which the stem is indigenous and an affix transferred, e.g. Amer. Norwegian *kårrna* 'corner', apparently a blend of English *corn-er* and Norwegian *hyrrn-a*,[57] or German *Futter-age* 'forage', a nonce-word formed, by popular ety-mology, after French *four-age*.[58] This last type might be called interlingual port-manteaus.

Finally, a special type of hybrid compound is represented by forms like Amer. Italian *canabuldogga* 'bulldog',[59] where one element of a compound (*dog*) is both transferred and reproduced (*cana-*).

All that has been said about forms of lexical interference applies not only to common words but to proper names as well.[60] Proper-name interference is par-ticularly common; that the same place or person should be called by unrelated names in a language-contact situation is in fact the rarer case.[61] Pairs of place-

---

[51] Schach (**478**).

[52] Ortoz (**390**).

[53] Seifert (**506**). For an analysis of interesting English and standard German hybrid compounds, see Rothenberg (**455**).

[54] On the contrary, in the Canadian French *grand plancher* for 'ground floor', reported by Barbeau (**16**), both elements seem to have been reproduced; the homophonous French *grand* had its content polysemantically extended.

[55] Zimmerli (**657**), I, 32.

[56] See Schach's special paper on blended derivatives in Pennsylvania German (**480**), 120. Sadlo (**459**, 112) cites interesting Polish blended derivatives coined by children of Polish miners in France, e.g. *glisadka* 'skating rink' after *glissade* × *ślizgaw-ka*.

[57] Haugen (**203**), 218.

[58] Mackensen (**332**).

[59] Livingston (**314**); Menarini (**353**), 163. Occasionally, even simple words undergo a similar process of repetition in translation: Willems (**640**, 299, 306) cites Brazilian German *presus-holen* 'to fetch', *cavalho-Pferd* 'horse'. Cf. also the compound forms in the Schwy-zertütsch of Biel: *fini-fertig*, *grad-žüst*, analyzed by Baumgartner (**29**).

[60] The best survey of research on bilingual place names appears to be that by Draye (**127**). No equivalent study for personal names seems to have been made.

[61] Kranzmayer (**286**) calls them "free pairs."

names like Italian *Monfalcone*—Slovene *Tržič* in Italy, Romansh *Mustér*—German *Disentis* in Switzerland, German *Wittingau*—Czech *Třeboň* in the Sudeten,[62] Polish *Tarnobrzeg*—Yiddish *Džikev* in Poland, are not common. In the most usual case a name is transferred from one language to another, e.g. Italian *Trieste*—Slovene *Trst*; Ukrainian *Vladimir*—Yiddish *Lúdmir*; German *Pfauen*—French *Faoug*. Sometimes analyzable place names are "translated," i.e. their components are reproduced from indigenous vocabulary, e.g. Czech *Vrch-labí*—German *Hohen-elbe*;[63] Afrikaans *Kap-stad*—English *Cape-town*; Italian *Abbazia*—Slovene *Opatija*.[64] In the case of compounds, hybrids may result from the transfer of only one element: In the German name of the Sudeten village of *Darkendorf*, for example, the first part of the Czech name *Darkovice*, was adopted, but a German final element substituted.[65]

Similar choices are open for rendering personal names in another language: direct transfer (with phonemic adaptation, as in Norwegian *Hæve* > English *Harvey*, or without it); translations (e.g. Norwegian *Langhoug* > English *Long-hill*);[66] and hybrids (e.g. Yiddish *Finkl-štejn* > English *Finkle-stone*). In the case of unanalyzable and untranslatable names—both first and last names—a "pseudo-translation" of sorts is sometimes made, consisting of the replacement of the old name by a new one whose first consonant, at least, is the same; cf. the equivalences of Yiddish *Mójše* with English *Morris, Morton*; Yiddish *Herš* with *Herbert, Harry*; Yiddish *Rabinóvitš* with *Robbins*, and so on. A comprehensive study of the patterns of personal name changing has not yet been made, not even for a single socio-geographic area like immigrant America.

2.42 Lexical Integration of Loanwords

While the phonic and grammatical integration of loanwords has engaged the attention of many scholars (cf. §§2.25, 2.37), their purely lexical integration has hardly been touched upon.[67] And yet the consequences of a word transfer or a word reproduction on the miniature semantic system (or "field") of which the new word becomes a member are as much a part of the interference as the transfer or reproduction themselves.

Only the most concrete loanwords, such as designations for newly invented or imported objects, can be thought of as mere additions to the vocabulary. For example, the word /televiʒn/, introduced into Amer. German from English, cannot have had much of an effect on existing German vocabulary. Sometimes loanwords which are more abstract are also asserted to be mere additions; it is

---

[62] Schwarz (502), 214.

[63] *Ibid.*, p. 210.

[64] Kranzmayer (286).

[65] Schwarz (502), 207.

[66] Kimmerle (267), 28. Cf. also Portuguese *Caranguejo* > Engl. *Crabtree*, etc., cited by Pap (395), 135.

[67] Vočadlo (596) proposed this problem as the subject matter of "comparative lexicology." In the field of culture contact also, according to Linton (312, 478f.), "what happens to preëxisting culture elements when new ones are introduced . . . has unfortunately received little attention."

claimed, for example, that Amer. Italian *giobba* 'job' corresponds to neither *arte, mestiere, professione, impiego,* nor *occupazione,* since it designates a new concept, viz. 'work that is found, and for which one has no attachment and no spiritual interest'.[68] But although there is no full correspondence between *giobba* and any preëxisting word, there is a partial overlapping of content, at least with *impiego* 'employment' and *lavoro* 'work'. If *giobba* is now used exclusively to express this overlapping content, *impiego* and *lavoro* can be said to have undergone a corresponding semantic restriction due to the interference of English. In the immigrant English expression *give me the knife once* (after German *gib mir mal das Messer*),[69] the unusual function of *once* might appear to be an addition, pure and simple, to the familiar content of this sign; in ordinary English usage, the content of German *mal* would not be expressed at all: *give me the knife*. But since the English language does contain signs for rendering this content (e.g. *come* as in *come, give me the knife!*), these unused signs can be said to undergo a restriction in function at the same time as the content of *once* is broadened. The transfer of *giobba* and the extension of *once* are thus not without effect on the existing vocabulary.

Except for loanwords with entirely new content, the transfer or reproduction of foreign words must affect the existing vocabulary in one of three ways: (1) confusion between the content of the new and old word; (2) disappearance of the old word; (3) survival of both the new and old word, with a specialization in content.

(1) CONFUSION IN USAGE, or full identity of content, between the old and the new word is probably restricted to the early stages of language contact.[70] One can imagine the initial stage in the development of Amer. Yiddish, for example, when the old *féntster* 'window' and the newly transferred *vínde* were used at random to express the same content. Even without transfer, a set of specialized signs in one language may become confused due to interference of another language where the same content is not similarly subdivided. For example, in Amer. Yiddish *gejn* (originally 'to go on foot') has almost displaced *forn* 'to go by vehicle' on the model of English *go*. In the Russian speech of Bessarabians, *postávit'* 'to put (an upright object)' and *položít'* 'to put (a predominantly horizontal or soft object)' are confused on the model of a single Moldavian verb;[71] similarly in Amer. Yiddish, some speakers confuse *šteln* 'to put (upright)' and *lejgn* 'to put (horizontally or without regard to position)'—even *zetsn* 'to put (a person at a table)'—on the model of the single English *put*. In each of these cases of semantic confusion, one of the terms may eventually become fixed as an expression of the combined content, and the other abandoned.

(2) Old words may be DISCARDED as their content becomes fully covered by

[68] Prezzolini (**421**).

[69] Harris (**196**).

[70] An anthropological parallel discussed by Linton (**312,** 481): "Cultures seem to be almost infinitely tolerant of duplications in function. In fact at least temporary duplication is an inseparable accompaniment of culture change."

[71] Racoviță (**424**).

the loanword.[72] This obtains both when foreign words are transferred and when they are reproduced. When English *paper* 'newspaper', for example, was transferred into Amer. Yiddish (*péjper*), the old words, *blat* or *tsajtung*, were discarded. In Amer. Portuguese, the semantic extension of *papel* (on the model of English *paper*)[73] also led to the discarding of the old *gazeta*. In the Amer. Yiddish of some speakers, the loanwords *dólar* and *sent* have even driven out terms like *rubl* 'ruble' and *kópike* 'kopeck'; such speakers refer to old-country prices in terms of 'dollars' and 'cents'. It may not always be easy to test whether the old word has been discarded or merely restricted in usage; but anyone who has seen an American immigrant break into a smile at the mention of an old-country word, with the comment, "I hadn't heard that one for thirty years," will know how effective the discarding of lexical elements can be.

One type of interference in which words are discarded although no equivalents are transferred has been described by M. Haas (187). She found Thai-English bilinguals avoiding the use of certain innocuous Thai words because of their phonic resemblance to obscene words in English.

(3) Finally, the content of the clashing old and borrowed words may become SPECIALIZED.[74] Strictly speaking, the specialization in content, usually affects both the old word and the loanword if both survive. In literary Amer. Yiddish, for example, *lójer* is accepted as a term for 'a lawyer in the U. S.'; it is thus more specialized than the English *lawyer*. The content of the old word, *advokát*, has in turn become specialized accordingly to denote 'a lawyer elsewhere but in the U. S.', or just 'lawyer', without regard to country. Karelian *künži* 'nail' has been borrowed in dialectal Russian (Archangel) as *kinža*, not to replace the established word for 'nail', but to designate 'nail or wedge which fastens an axe to its handle'.[75] As Gurage (Ethiopia) borrowed the Qabena word *mata* 'younger brother', the established *waği* 'brother' was specialized to mean 'older brother'.[76] Specialization can develop even if the transferred word is genetically related to the established form. The terms are then designated as "doublets." Thus, the French *cause*, borrowed from Latin, has a meaning different from that of *chose*;[77] in the patois of the Vosges, French *metier* was borrowed for 'profession', while the indigenous /mtei/ was retained for 'loom'.[78] Yiddish *kort* denotes 'playing card' while the doublet *karte* (a transfer of the German *Karte*) means only 'map'; the well-established word *kíbuts* (from medieval Hebrew) denotes 'community',

---

[72] Lee (298). As pointed out on p. 49, there is often insufficient information in loanword studies to decide whether the old word has become specialized or discarded.

[73] Pap (395), 88.

[74] Similarly in culture contact. "The substitution of a new culture element," Linton writes (312, 481), "by no means always results in the complete elimination of the old one. There are many cases of partial . . . replacement. . . . Stone knives may continue to be used for ritual purposes long after the metal ones have superseded them elsewhere."

[75] Jakubinskij (247), 9–11.

[76] Leslau (306), 80.

[77] Cf. Meillet (350), II, 36ff. for this and additional examples.

[78] Bloch (50), 110ff.

while the loanword *kibúts*, transferred from modern Hebrew, has the specialized meaning 'collective settlement in Israel'.

One way in which loanwords may be specialized is according to style. For example, in the Vosges patois, where French *vomir* was borrowed for 'to vomit', the indigenous word acquired a crude connotation as it became obsolete.[79] In some contact situations, the borrowed elements all enter the "learned" stylistic stratum of the recipient language, e.g. most Greek loanwords in English. Frequently, on the other hand, the transferred elements occupy a familiar or slangy stylistic stratum, acquiring pejorative connotations which they lacked in the mother-tongue; curiously, this is reported both for German loanwords in Czech[80] (e.g. *ksiht* 'mug' < *Gesicht* 'face') and for Czech loanwords in Sudeten German (e.g. *Nusch* 'bad pocket knife' < *nůž* 'knife').[81] Yiddish offers many interesting illustrations of stylistic specialization. A series of Slavic adjectives in -*ne*, for example, have acquired an ironical meaning lacking in the source language: *glávne* 'principal', *gromádne* 'enormous'; Hebrew elements have entered both the elegant style (*ben-ódom* 'human being') and slang (*bónim* 'sons').

2.43 Reasons for Lexical Borrowing

There is no doubt that lexical borrowing is less restricted to the bilingual portion of a language community than phonic or grammatical interference.

The vocabulary of a language, considerably more loosely structured than its phonemics and its grammar, is beyond question the domain of borrowing *par excellence*.[82] In exploring the causes of lexical borrowing, it may therefore be well to inquire first as to the reasons which motivate ANY speaker—unilinguals included—to accept new loanwords in his vocabulary, i.e. to be an agent in their diffusion; and then to consider bilinguals as but a special type of speaker. Also, since loanwords are in many cases not recognizable as such to the unilingual,[83] one must look first for the reasons of lexical innovation in general. While this field of general lexicology is little developed, a number of tentative statements can be made.

The need to designate new things, persons, places, and concepts is, obviously, a universal cause of lexical innovation. By determining which innovations of this type are loanwords, the linguist may help to show what one language community has learned from another.[84] Polish and Ukrainian, for example, have imported Rumanian designations mostly in the sphere of mountain habitat and cattle

---

[79] *Ibid.*, 110. Cf. also §4.31, p. 95.

[80] Vočadlo (596), 171.

[81] Pritzwald (422).

[82] Meillet (350), I, 84; Pisani (409), 332.

[83] Haugen (203), 229; Fries and Pike (154), 31.

[84] Bloomfield (55), 458ff. Incidentally, Bloomfield defines "cultural borrowing" merely as borrowing from another language, which he opposes to "dialect borrowing" from the same "speech-area" (*ibid.*, 444). He further divides cultural borrowing into "ordinary" and "intimate," the latter involving bilingualism (461). Since cultural and intimate borrowing are not contrasted, Dillon's (121) and Pap's (395, 189, footnote 260) criticisms are not quite well taken.

grazing;[85] the peoples of the Volga have, according to linguistic evidence, learned architecture from the Russians;[86] the Raetoromans have acquired almost all the products of industrial civilization from the German-speaking North,[87] while the Schwyzertütsch speakers learned some domestic and agricultural techniques, as well as mountain customs, from the Raetoromans and acquired the Romansh terms with them.[88] A considerable body of common culture in Europe is reflected in the large corpus of common vocabulary in all European languages.[89] The wide acceptance of indigenous place names by a migrating group may also be mentioned here; in Amer. English, the numerous names of Indian origin are almost the only loanwords from that source. Lexical borrowing of this type can be described as a result of the fact that using ready-made designations is more economical than describing things afresh. Few users of language are poets.

But the designative inadequacy of a vocabulary in naming new things is not the only cause of lexical innovation. Internal linguistic factors also contribute to the innovating process.

One such internal factor is the LOW FREQUENCY of words. It has been shown that, other things being equal, the frequent words come easily to mind and are therefore more stable; relatively infrequent words of the vocabulary are, accordingly, less stable, more subject to oblivion and replacement.[90] In dialectal Russian, for example, the infrequent and unstable designations for parts of tools, which vary greatly from one locality to the next, are, in the Finnish contact area, represented by Finnish loanwords, although there has been no corresponding cultural borrowing. In other words, the reason which has led to the fluctuation of indigenous words for 'the place on a scythe where the blade is attached to the handle' has, in the bilingual zone, caused a Finnish loanword to be adopted.[91] The instability reflected in the diversity of expressions for 'pine cone' in the patois of the Vosges may have invited the penetration of the dialectal French *pomme (de sapin)*.[92] In Yaqui, the greater number of ramified associations has prevented the word for 'mother', *ʔáe*, from being replaced by a Spanish loanword like the other kinship terms.[93]

Another internal factor conducive to lexical innovation is pernicious HOMONYMY. The celebrated cases of lexical pathology and therapy discovered by Gilliéron need not be cited here. Suffice it to say that sometimes a word seems to have been borrowed from another language in order to resolve the clash of homonyms. For example, it is alleged that because of the clash between the words

---

[85] Łukasik (327); Scheludko (483).

[86] Räsänen (425).

[87] Cf. the lists by Brandstetter (76) and Genelin (164).

[88] Szadrowsky (561), 17ff.

[89] Much of this vocabulary based on cultural innovation was of course formed by loan translation. Cf. Betz's interesting proposal (41, 31ff.) for a dictionary of European loan translations.

[90] Jakubinskij (247), 7; Mulch (378), 8, 57ff.; Schuchardt (497), 157.

[91] Jakubinskij (247), 7f.

[92] Bloch (50), 80.

[93] Spicer (536), 426.

for 'cart' (<CARRUM) and 'meat' (<CARNEM), the Vosges patois borrowed *voiture* and *viande* from French.[94] Granting the validity of Gilliéron's theory in the unilingual situations which he described, the explanation by homonymy must nevertheless be applied to the behavior of bilinguals only with great care, for in many cases the existence of homonyms has definitely not prevented borrowing. The case of Amer. Portuguese *pinchar* 'jump' + 'pinch' was cited on p. 49. An Amer. Polish speaker has been heard to say *ci na kornerze muwią* 'those on the corner are moving', despite the existence of the homophonous *mówią* 'speak'. Even the presence of a homophonous obscene term for 'female genitals' has not barred Amer. Portuguese from borrowing Eng. *corner* > *cona*.[95] In Penna. German, the existence of the form *ufle·se* 'pick up' has not precluded the loan translation of English *to read up on* as *uf-le·se* (in this case *le·se* = 'read'), nor even the formation of the hybrid derivative *uf-le·se* 'to lace up' (designating also, through the homonymy of *uf-*, the antonymous 'to unlace'!);[96] here, lexical interference has produced at least a triple homonym.[97]

A third reason for lexical innovation is related to the well-known tendency of affective words to lose their expressive force.[98] As Jakubinskij has vividly put it (247, 13ff.), certain notions seem to attract a multitude of designations, just as some individuals tend to evoke nicknames while others do not. In such semantic fields as 'talking', 'beating', 'sleeping', 'tallness', or 'ugliness', there is in many languages a constant NEED FOR SYNONYMS, an onomastic low-pressure area, as it were. Where synonyms are available from another language, they are gladly accepted; the cause of the lexical aggrandizement can be said to be inherent in the recipient language.[99] Such is the reason for the borrowing of many words from Finnish into dialectal Russian, for example, which cannot be explained as designations of cultural innovations. A language can also satisfy its ever-present need for euphemisms and slangy "cacophemisms" by borrowing. In the Olonets dialect of Russian, for instance, the Finnish *repaki* became a welcome euphemism for 'menstruation'.[100] The patois of the Vosges at one time satisfied their euphemistic needs by borrowing, for 'vomit', the French word

[94] Bloch (50), 95. A special case of dangerous homonymy is the insufficient phonemic bulk of a word. This has been cited by Bloch (93f.) as the cause of the replacement, for example, of Vosges patois *v(e)hi* 'neighbor' by French *voisin* > /wɛzī/.

[95] Pap (395), 92 and footnote 66. Cf. the radically different reaction of bilingual Thais noted by Haas (187).

[96] Schach (479), 266.

[97] Capidan's attempt (91, 78) to explain the borrowing of Slavic *scump* 'expensive' in Rumanian by the fact that the indigenous CARUM had converged phonemically, in the seventh century, with CARRUM 'cart', must be regarded skeptically, since the homonymy of 'cart' and 'dear' is even less clashing than the above-named instances from American immigrant languages.

[98] Vendryes (594), 252-4.

[99] The fact that in Wintu· "words concerned with the formal aspect of an activity are losing to those concerned with the essential or kinaesthetic aspects," according to Lee (298), may be related to this hunger for synonyms.

[100] Jakubinskij (247), 11f.

vomir (see p. 56); in French itself, the same requirement has since led to replacement of *vomir* by more elegant synonyms (*rejeter, rendre*).[101]

Whereas the unilingual depends, in replenishing his vocabulary, on indigenous lexical material and whatever loanwords may happen to be transmitted to him, the BILINGUAL has the other language as a constantly available source of lexical innovations. The bilingual's vocabulary, of course, needs replenishment for the same reasons, internal (low frequency of words, pernicious homonymy, need for synonyms) as well as cultural. With regard to the latter, a bilingual is perhaps even more apt than the unilingual to accept loanword designations of new things because, through his familiarity with another culture, he is more strongly aware of their novel nature. Unilingual Portuguese speakers might perhaps have retained their native *sobretudo* for what to them would have been merely a new style of overcoat; but the bilingual Portuguese immigrants in America borrowed the English term (>*alvacote*), apparently seeing in this form of clothing a different type of object.[102] Norwegians at home might have applied native terms to isolated agricultural innovations; as immigrants to America, they borrowed a large farming vocabulary from English because they were particularly sensitive to the newness of the techniques and tools.[103]

Three additional factors may prompt lexical borrowing on the part of bilinguals. First, a comparison with the other language to which he is exposed may lead him to feel that some of his semantic fields are INSUFFICIENTLY DIFFERENTIATED. Thus, Italian dialect speakers in Switzerland seem to have gotten along with a single word, *corona*, to denote 'wreath' and 'crown'; but as a result of contact with German they are reported to have felt the need to differentiate and borrowed *Kranz* for 'wreath', retaining *corona* as a designation for 'crown'.[104] The Slavic settlers of the Russian North felt their one designation for 'stallion' inadequate when Finnish had at least two; accordingly, they borrowed *varža* from Finnish to designate 'a bad or very young stallion'.[105] In the Vosges patois, *sõže* became too crude in the face of the French differentiation between *songer* and *rêver*; accordingly, *rêver* was borrowed and a specialization of terms effected.[106] In Yiddish, *xólemen* 'to dream' was also insufficiently differentiated in contrast to such Slavic distinctions as Polish *śnić* 'to dream in one's sleep'—*marzyć* 'to fancy'; hence the German loanword *trójmen* (<*träumen*) was introduced, and the meaning was apportioned between *xólemen* and *trójmen* on the Slavic model.

A second consideration affecting bilinguals in particular is the symbolic association of the source language in a contact situation with SOCIAL VALUES, either positive or negative. If one language is endowed with prestige, the bilingual is

[101] Vendryes (**594**), 257.

[102] Pap (**395**), 109.

[103] Haugen (**199**), 32f.

[104] Jaberg (**237**).

[105] Jakubinskij (**247**), 7. A similar point is made, and illustrated by West European examples, by Møller (**374**), 18.

[106] Bloch (**50**), 95.

likely to use what are identifiable loanwords from it as a means of displaying the social status which its knowledge symbolizes (cf. §3.35.) This can be observed both in learned borrowings, e.g. of Latin phrases in English, and in the intimate, "unnecessary" borrowing of everyday designations for things which have excellent names in the language which is being spoken. "Why use the word *belt* when the [Irish] word *crios* exists? Surely here the feeling that English is a superior language, and that an English word confers distinction upon an Irish sentence, plays an important part."[107] Those American immigrants who borrow as "heavily" as possible to show their advanced state of acculturation, act upon a similar motive. It would be enlightening to study whether Indian languages, which are even more forced to borrow from English for cultural reasons, in the sense defined above, than the immigrant tongues, are equally avid borrowers from English for reasons of social prestige.

In some contact situations, on the contrary, lexical borrowing is utilized for cacophemistic purposes, in slangy speech, because of the unfavorable associations of the other tongue. The pejorative connotations of German and Czech loanwords in the respective languages has been mentioned (p. 56). The patois of French Switzerland have no morally favorable terms of German origin, but "they swarm with German words for disreputable or badly dressed women, . . . rudeness, coarseness, indolence, sloth, avarice," corresponding to the stereotyped "ridicule with which the French Swiss regards the German Swiss, his culture, and above all his language, of whose inferiority the former is deeply convinced."[108] The desire for comic effects may also motivate lexical mixture.[109] This is alleged to be the reason why German speakers borrowed from Yiddish, Parisian argot speakers from German, etc.[110] A study of Yiddish speakers in the United States would show that among those who, for cultural reasons, are most on their guard against the unchecked influx of borrowings from English the intentional use of "Anglicisms" is a frequent comic device.

Finally, a bilingual's speech may suffer from the interference of another vocabulary through mere OVERSIGHT; that is, the limitations on the distribution of certain words to utterances belonging to one language are violated. In affective speech, when the speaker's attention is almost completely diverted from the form of the message to its topic, the transfer of words is particularly common. (Cf. also §3.43.)[111]

[107] Sjœstedt (**521**), 97. See also Møller (**374**), 20ff.

[108] Jaberg (**238**), 60f.

[109] Cf. Skwarczyńska (**524**) on the esthetics of macaronic texts and Weinreich (**620**) on macaronic folksongs.

[110] Öhmann (**388**).

[111] One way in which bilinguals differ from unilinguals, as Petrovici (**402**) and Møller (**374**, 9) have pointed out, is that the former, because of their knowledge of the source language, recognize many of the oldest and best assimilated loanwords as "foreign." If the resistance to borrowing is great enough (cf. §4.4), the bilingual, according to Petrovici, "who is trying to speak a pure language may replace the loanword by a word which he believes to be [more genuinely] a part of his mother-tongue." Racoviţă (**424**) cites the typical case of a bilingual Bessarabian who said in Russian *institucja*; then, at the thought that

This section may be concluded on a word of caution. The borrowing of any one word can be explained by one or several of the various enumerated causes of lexical interference. Yet, remarkably, some words seem never to be transferred. In Amer. Yiddish, for example, *vínde* has replaced *féntster* 'window', *flor* is common for *pódloge* 'floor', but English *door* is never borrowed; *točn* has practically replaced *rirn, on-rirn, tsu-rirn zix tsu* 'to touch'; but *buy* or *sell* are not used even in the most careless Yiddish speech. *Walk* is borrowed; *talk* is not. From a study of the general causes of interference, the transfer of many of these words might have been predicted, but it has not taken place. This resistance to transfer on the part of some words has so far not received any explanation. It is one of the unsolved problems of language contact.

2.44 Selection of Interference Mechanism

In lexical interference the bilingual is faced with a choice of mechanisms. As shown in §2.41, a simple word to be borrowed can be transferred or reproduced by a semantic extension; a compound may be transferred in analyzed form or reproduced as a loan translation or hybrid compound. For example, in forming a single word to express both 'paper material' and 'newspaper', Amer. Yiddish resorted to the transfer of English *paper*, while Amer. Portuguese extended the content of the indigenous word, *papel*. Do structural reasons ever determine the choice of mechanism?

In a specific instance, an existing word in the recipient language might be supposed to repel a homophonous transfer; to avoid homonymy, loan translation (or semantic extension) might be preferred. And yet §2.41 contains ample evidence of homonymy created by word transfer (cf. especially p. 58). Potential homonymy as a source of resistance to transfer—at least as far as bilinguals are concerned—must therefore be regarded with skepticism.

Theoretically, too, a language with many restrictions on the form of words may be proportionately more resistant to outright transfer and favor semantic extension and loan translation instead.[112] Such resistance would, of course, be a function not of the structure of the recipient language, but of the difference in the structures of the recipient and source languages. If Tibetan resisted transfers from Sanskrit and restricted its borrowing to loan translations,[113] it was only because the structure of Sanskrit words was so different from its own·structure; the resistance to transfers from a language with more congenial word structure, like Chinese, has not been so great.[114] And it must always be borne in mind that transferred words can be phonemically adapted to the recipient language (§2.25).

---

this might be an illegitimate Rumanian loanword, he replaced it by a "purer" *učreždenije*. Similar considerations seem to underlie the fact that there is a more hospitable attitude to Slavic loanwords in American standard Yiddish than there was in the old-world literary language; see M. Weinreich's preface to Stutchkoff (553), xivf.

[112] Vočadlo (596, 170) divides languages into homogeneous, amalgamate, and heterogeneous ones, with receptivity to transferred words greatest in the latter group.

[113] Sapir (472), 209f.

[114] Laufer (297).

To be sure, in a language with homogeneous word structure, unadapted forms transferred from a language with very different word structure are easily recognizable.[115] But that there exists structural resistance other than the recognizability of transferred forms has not been proved. Many European languages have even lost their homogeneity of word structure precisely as a result of the acceptance of large numbers of transferred words without disintegrating. German, Polish, and other languages alleged to be structurally resistant to transfers have in the United States absorbed an enormous corpus of English words—adapting them phonically and grammatically as necessary—and yet continue to function, for better or for worse.[116] The difference between American Spanish speakers who say /eu'ropa/ and those who say /ju'ropa/ on the model of English *Europe*, between Yiddish speakers who say *dženosajd* 'genocide' and those who insist on *genotsíd* (the Yiddishized version of the neo-Latin word) or *félkermord* (a loan translation), cannot stem from the structure of the language they speak, for they all use the same language. Similarly, the fact that 'library' in standard Belorussian was called *kniharnja* (a loan rendition) in the 1920's and *biblioteka* (a transfer from Russian) in the 1940's[117] was not due to an intervening change in the structure of the language. The unequal degrees of resistance to transfers and the preference for loan translation over transfers are a result of complex socio-cultural factors which are not describable in linguistic terms alone.[118] Some ways of approaching these factors are discussed in chaps. 3 and 4.

[115] Even Fries and Pike (**154**), who deny this on principle, speak of (diachronically) unassimilated phonemic sequences in loanwords (p. 39).

[116] Cf. Kaufmann (**263**) on Amer. German. In Brazil, cases of German loan translation from Portuguese have been found to be extremely rare; see Willems (**640**), 279.

[117] Lomtev (**322**), 135.

[118] Cf. Kiparsky (**271**), Kaufmann (**263**), Bloomfield (**55**), 468. In Modern Hebrew, structural factors make transferred words recognizable, but, as Weiman writes (**615**, 5), "the cultural and religious prestige of the Hebrew pattern . . . [has] contributed to keeping the two patterns—native and foreign—distinct."

2.5 Total Amount of Interference

At this point, it may be useful to recapitulate the extent to which interference in the several domains of language is structurally determined. A number of general questions, not related to any one domain, also remain to be clarified.

2.51 Quantification of Interference

No easy way of measuring or characterizing the total impact of one language on another in the speech of bilinguals has been, or probably can be, devised. The only possible procedure is to describe the various forms of interference and to tabulate their frequency. This has been done for small samples of bilinguals' speech. Smith (**531**), for example, computed the frequency of certain types of deviation from the norm in the English of Hawaiian children with different native languages, comparing it with their sex, age, and parents' occupation. While her description of the "errors" and their classification is inadequate from the linguistic point of view, the study does illustrate the feasibility of quantifying data on interference.

For the very special type of speech situation in which a speaker consciously tries to suppress interference as fully as he can, the customary language-proficiency test is a practical summary measure of interference. Its validity is limited by the unusualness of the testing situation, by the ordinarily crude classification of "errors," and by the fact that poverty of expression in the second language (i.e. exaggerated concentration on high-frequency forms and a propensity for circumlocution of difficult forms) is as a rule not recorded as a lack of proficiency, even though it is a result of interference. Moreover, not every gap in proficiency can be attributed to interference; after all, unilingual persons would also achieve unequal scores for proficiency in their own language.[1] Nevertheless, the foreign-language proficiency test can be employed as a crude instrument, especially if response time and similar factors are taken into account. Paralleling written tests which provide for limited time periods, the Bikčentajs (**44**), the Galis (**156,** 4ff.; **156a**), and Saer (**73, 462**) measured response times in oral tests with considerable precision. Taute (**564**) even correlated speech hesitancy and general shyness with gaps in proficiency, since a retarded rate of speech can also be interpreted as an effect of interference.

2.52 Structure As a Determinant of Interference

The following table summarizes the various factors governing interference which were referred to in §§2.2–4. The phenomena of interference are considered

---

[1] To correct this, it is customary, in studies of bilingualism, to use RELATIVE proficiency scores for the second language. Thus, the South African Survey of Bilingualism in 1938, according to Malherbe (**335,** 18ff.), employed a BILINGUAL QUOTIENT computed as the quotient of the proficiency scores in the second and first languages. Taute (**564**) calculated his bilingual INDEX as the square root of the product of the two scores. For the formulas used by H. Saer, see Bovet (**73**), 4ff.

| FORM OF INTERFERENCE | EXAMPLE | STR... |
		STIMULI
All interference		Any points of difference betwee[n] two systems
Phonic		
Under-differentiation of pho-nemes (p. 18)	/d/ and /t/ not differentiated	Absence of corresponding dis-tinctions in primary language
Over-differentiation of pho-nemes (p. 18)	[k] and [kʰ] treated as separate phonemes	Presence of distinction (only) in primary language
Reinterpretation of relevant features (p. 18)	Voiceless /p/ treated as pho-nemically tense and only con-comitantly voiceless	Different phonemic systems
Phone substitution (p. 19)	[r] for [ʀ] where there is only one trill phoneme	Different pronunciations of equivalent phonemes
Integration of loanwords (pp. 26–8)	English /rajs/ into Hawaiian /lɑiki/	Difference in phonemic systems; homogeneous but different type of word structure in re-cipient language
Grammatical		
Transfer of morphemes (pp. 31–7)	Slovak-German *in Pressburg-u*; Yiddish-English *job-shmob*	Congruent systems, much com-mon vocabulary, relatively unbound morphemes, greater phonemic bulk
Transfer of grammatical rela-tions (pp. 37–9)	German-English *I come soon home*	Different relation patterns
Change in function of "indig-enous" morpheme or cate-gory (pp. 39–42)	German-English *how long are you here?*	Greater explicitness of model (usually)
Abandonment of obligatory categories (pp. 42ff.)	Loss of old French tense sys-tem in Creole	Very different grammatical sys-tems
Integration of loanwords (pp. 44–6)	English *change* into Amer. Portuguese *chinjar*	Homogeneous word structure in recipient language
Lexical		
Lexical interference as such (§2.4)	—	Structural weak points in recipi-ent vocabulary, need to match differentiations in source lan-guage
Outright transfer of words (rather than semantic exten-sion) (pp. 47f., 50)	German *Telephon* rather than *Fernsprecher*	Congenial form of word; pos-sibility of polysemy (?)
Phonic adjustment of cognates (p. 50)	Spanish /euˈropa/ into /juˈro-pa/ on English model	Economy of a single form
Specialized retention of an "indigenous" word after borrowing of an equivalent (pp. 55f.)	French *chose*, retained and dis-tinguished from *cause*	No confusion in semantemes

STRUCTURAL	NON-STRUCTURAL	
RESISTANCE FACTORS	STIMULI	RESISTANCE FACTORS
Stability of systems; requirements of intelligibility	Social value of source (model, primary) language; bilingual interlocutors; affective speech; individual propensity for speech mixture; etc.	Social value of recipient language; intolerance of interference; puristic attitudes toward recipient (secondary) language; loyalty to mother-tongue; unilingual interlocutors; etc.
Functional yield of the distinction	—	Loyalty to secondary language
—	—	—
Existence of appropriate holes in the pattern	—	—
Danger of confusion with another pheneme	Social value of primary language	Loyalty to secondary language
Potential homonymy (?)	Intolerance of recognizable loanwords; unilingualism of speaker	Social value of source language
Non-congruent systems; complicated functions of morphemes	Affectiveness of categories	Loyalty to recipient language
Conflict with existing relations	Affectiveness of categories	Loyalty to recipient language
—	—	Loyalty to recipient language
—	Makeshift language	Loyalty to recipient language
—	Intolerance of recognizable loanwords; unilingualism of speaker	Social value of source language
Existence of adequate vocabulary	Lexical inadequacy in face of innovations; oblivion of infrequent words, need for synnyms, prestige of source language, stylistic effect of mixture	Loyalty to recipient language
Potential homonymy (?); uncongenial word form	Bilingualism of interlocutors	Loyalty to recipient language
—	—	Loyalty to recipient language
Elimination of superfluous terms	—	—

as resultants of two opposing forces: STIMULI of interference and RESISTANCE to interference. Both stimuli and resistance factors can be structural or non-structural in the linguistic sense. Economy and intelligibility have been classified as structural criteria because they are the functional bases on which linguistic systems are constructed. Language "loyalty" is used here in the sense defined in §4.4.

The forms of interference which appear in the first column and the causes of interference inherent in the structure of the languages in contact, as well as the resistance offered by the structures, are those that emerged from the discussion in §§2.2–4. As was shown there in some detail, certain forms of interference are called forth, facilitated, or inhibited by the concrete structural differences of the languages. But it was shown, too, that the total impact of the languages on each other—the extent to which interference of each structurally determined type is manifested—can hardly be accounted for by strictly linguistic data. Two examples, one lexical and one phonic, may be cited here. In a study of word borrowing in Amer. Yiddish, it was found that on the editorial and magazine page of an average Yiddish newspaper, 2.1% of the vocabulary was transferred from English; on the news page, 5.3% were loanwords; while the Anglicisms in the advertising material reached 20%.[2] Obviously, the structure of the two languages in contact was the same on all pages, while the difference in subject matter alone could not account for so great a discrepancy; a resistance of a cultural sort kept English words out of the news and especially of the editorial page. The other example is that of a native Yiddish speaker who reported:[3] "I have two accents for Russian. . . . In the society of Russians my pronunciation becomes pure, but when I find myself in Jewish company, my former [Yiddish] accent appears. The same thing happens when I am tired or excited." The nature of the potential foreign accent was, as always, determined by the structural relation of the primary and secondary sound systems; but the manifestation of the accent was here controlled by powerful social and psychological, i.e. nonstructural, factors.

For practically every form of interference, there is an interplay of factors external to the structures of the languages which favor or inhibit the development of interference of that type.[4] As the right half of the summary table (pp.

    [2] Neumann (**383**).

    [3] Epstein (**138**), 82.

    [4] Distinctions parallel to those between stimuli and resistance, structural and nonstructural factors, occur implicitly in studies of acculturation, too. Thus, Redfield, Linton, and Herskovits (**432**) distinguish culture traits "presented" (=stimuli) from those "selected" in acculturation situations, and stress the "significance of understanding the resistance to traits as well as the acceptance of them." They also name "congruity of existing culture-patterns" as a reason for a selection of traits; this corresponds to structural stimuli in language contact. When Linton observes (**312**, 488) that "new things are borrowed on the basis of their utility, compatibility with preëxisting culture patterns, and prestige associations," his three factors are equivalent, roughly, to structural stimuli of interference, structural resistance, and nonstructural stimuli, respectively. Kroeber (**287**, 415-8) devotes a special discussion to resistance against diffusion. Resistance to cultural borrowing is also the subject of a separate article by Devereux and Loeb (**119**), who dis-

64f.) shows, the external factors include individual traits of bilingual speakers, circumstances in the speech situation (the bilinguality of the interlocutors, emotional involvement of the speaker, etc.), and the socio-cultural context of the language contact, in which social value, purism, and similar considerations are operative. The element of time, or length of contact, may also be at play. These factors are examined in the remaining chapters—first from the point of view of the individual, who is the ultimate locus of contact (chap. 3), then from the point of view of the group which makes him the kind of bilingual he is and determines the prevalent speech situation (chap. 4).

It may be noted that, from the structural point of view, interference is to be expected in BOTH languages that are in contact. If, in practice, the interference occurs only in one direction, it is again such non-structural factors as speakers' linguistic life-histories and the cultural setting which are decisive.

2.53 Comparison of Interference in the Several Domains

A great many writers on language mixture have expressed opinions as to the relative amounts of borrowing in the various domains: sounds, grammar, vocabulary. Whitney (637) ranged words (nouns first), then suffixes, then inflections, then sounds according to the freedom with which they are borrowed. Pritzwald (422) lists the various domains in the order in which they are subject to foreign-language interference thus: vocabulary, sound system, word-formation and compounding, syntax, proper names. Dauzat (113, 49–55) asserts that vocabulary is most exposed to influence; then come the sounds, then syntax; while "morphology, . . . the fortress of a language, surrenders last."

The objection has been raised that "amounts of influence" in the various domains are incommensurable and that therefore no comparison is possible. Indeed, it seems necessary first to devise ways of formulating the degree of integratedness of a system, and to measure the affected proportion of the domain, before meaningful comparisons can be made. All the cited opinions on relative amounts of borrowing are rather superficial and premature, if they are meaningful at all.

What can be stated without resort to quantification is the direction of interference. One can say on a descriptive basis that in a contact situation which we may designate AB, for instance, A has had no influence on B-phonemics, but has influenced B-vocabulary; on the contrary, B has also influenced A-vocabulary and some of the A-grammar. The existence of an "algebra" for statements of this sort, however, does not mean that panchronic laws on the directions of interference are ready to be formulated. Tesnière (570, 85), following Meillet,

---

tinguish between "resistance to the cultural item"—corresponding roughly to structural resistance in language contact—and "resistance to the lender." These authors also discuss resistance ON THE PART OF the "lender," e.g. the attempts of the Dutch to prevent Malayans, by law, from learning the Dutch language. No equivalent lender's resistance seems to operate in language contact, unless the inconspicuousness of a strongly varying, phonemically slight morpheme with complicated grammatical functions be considered as a point of resistance to transfer within the source language (cf. p. 33); see also §4.31 (p. 96) on esoteric languages.

presumed to know that "mixture is impossible between corresponding systems of different languages; two morphologies do not mix; they can only exclude each other. . . . Wherever one observes mixture, it is always between dissimilar systems: a grammatical system of one language with the lexical system of another; a phonetic system of one language with the morphological system of another, etc." Such constructions are not only premature; they are plainly false. Both phonetic and morphological interference, even in the same language, had been documented long before Tesnière's statement was made.

2.54 Interference and Language Shift

A language shift may be defined as the change from the habitual use of one language to that of another. One may ask whether interference ever goes so far as to result in a language shift. In other words, can a bilingual's speech in language *A* become BY DEGREES so strongly influenced by language *B* as to be indistinguishable from *B*?

The language shift (cf. also §4.7) can be analyzed by reference to either the descriptive linguist's criteria or the subjective experience of the speaker himself. Descriptive linguists, in analyzing strongly mixed utterances of bilinguals, have been accustomed to grant priority to the grammar and to assign the utterance to the language whose grammar is utilized in it.[5] The following lines, for example, occurring in a humorous macaronic Yiddish song, would usually be considered Yiddish, and not Russian, by virtue of their grammar:

> *Mir veln* guljájen*en mit a* médlen*er* paxódkel*e*
> *Un firn a* néžnem razgavór.[6]

An equivalent sentence could be constructed using Yiddish vocabulary in a Russian grammatical frame; it would then be assigned to Russian. "No amount of lexical penetration can dislodge the grammatical barriers."[7] A methodological problem arises, however, when the grammar itself is mixed. A Yiddish-speaking immigrant who has been in the United States for thirty years or so, for example, has been heard to say: /aj hejt ðə dʌst vos æˈkjumjulejt zix/[8] 'I hate the dust which accumulates'. The main clause is English; in the relative clause, *accumulate*, though of English origin, is conjugated as a Yiddish reflexive verb (note the zero ending after a verbal base in *-t*), and the clause may therefore be designated as Yiddish. There is thus a switch of language within a single sentence. In the Slovak-German phrase *in Pressburg-u*, cited by Schuchardt (cf. p. 33, footnote 15), the grammar is both German (preposition) and Slovak (ending). There is some reason to believe that a facility in switching languages even within

---

[5] On the justness of assigning priority to grammar, cf. p. 35, esp. footnote 22.

[6] 'We shall walk (Russian *gulját'*) at a slow (R. *médlennyj*) gait (R. *poxódka*) and carry on a tender (R. *néžnyj*) conversation (R. *razgovór*)'. None of the Russian words belong to the regular Yiddish vocabulary; if they did, no comic effect would be achieved.

[7] Roberts (450), 37.

[8] Phonic interference (e.g. /dʌst/ $\geq$ /dost/) is disregarded.

a single sentence or phrase is characteristic of some bilinguals (cf. §3.22). It remains to be determined empirically whether habitual switching of this type represents a transitional stage in the shift from the regular use of one language to the regular use of the other. Of course, it is obvious that a shift does not necessarily have to pass through such a transitional stage.

The other approach is by way of the speaker's subjective experience. As was noted in §2.12, an utterance of a bilingual is USUALLY characterized by its overall Englishness, Frenchness, Russianness, etc. But such is not always the case. When Meillet (**350**, I, 82) asserts: "A speaker always knows that he is using the one system or the other," he obviously is not considering those bilinguals, who, under certain conditions, CANNOT say which language they meant to use in a sentence just uttered. They may even admit that their distinction between languages undergoes, as it were, a temporary collapse.[9] Whether such subjectively experienced, frequent collapses (which may correspond to the descriptively defined grammatical mixture) are a possible manner of transition to a regular shift has not yet been determined.

2.55 Crystallization of New Languages from Contact

New hybrid languages, such as the creoles and pidgins, have been formed as a result of the modifications in languages that have been in contact. Their status as new languages may be said to be due to the fact that they have attained some or all of the following: (1) a form palpably different from either stock language; (2) a certain stability of form after initial fluctuations; (3) functions other than those of a workaday vernacular (e.g. use in the family, in formalized communication, etc.); (4) a rating among the speakers themselves as a separate language.[10] In some contact situations, no new languages, in the above sense, have developed.

Can the descriptive linguist in an actual contact situation derive any indications from the speech of bilinguals as to whether a new language is in the making? Since criteria (3) and (4) are outside the province of linguistics proper, he can only deal with the specificness of the new type of speech and its stability of form. In regard to the latter, some deviant forms, or innovations, occur with distinctly greater constancy than others. Thus, a given Amer. Yiddish speaker may occasionally confuse *gejn* 'to go (on foot)' and *forn* 'to go (in a vehicle)' as a result of English interference (cf. p. 54), but he may use the transferred English *metš* (*<match*) in place of the indigenous *švébele* exclusively. On the whole, a preponderance of constantly occurring deviations from a previously valid

---

[9] For a "collapsed" French-Basque text, see Bouda (**72**). Slovak-German examples are cited by Schuchardt (**496**), 81–5. Sjœstedt (**521**) also discusses "precipitate" borrowing of this type.

[10] The importance of the last criterion has been repeatedly demonstrated, e.g. by Terracher (**567**). Kloss (**275**) operates with only two criteria, one linguistic and one sociolinguistic: *Abstandsprachen* are defined by criterion (1), while *Ausbausprachen* depend on criterion (3).

norm in speech exposed to contact suggests that a new language may be on its way.[11] As for the matter of difference from the stock languages, because of the prime importance of grammar (cf. p. 35, n. 22), it is major deviations of a grammatical type, above all, that are interpreted as signs of a split between the affected sector and the rest of the language. Also, structurally unpredictable adaptations of transferred elements indicate that the bilingual fringe is handling interference with a certain degree of independence from the language community as a whole. For example, the consistent adoption of the English verb *vote* as Amer. Yiddish *vutn* deviates not only from the older (and standard) Yiddish expression of this semanteme (*štimen*), but also from the predictable integration pattern of English /ow/ > Yiddish /o, o·/ (e.g. *wholesale* > /holsejl/).[12]

But beyond such general hints, the descriptive linguist can say little, because the other two criteria of what constitutes a separate language lie in the domain of sociolinguistics, not in linguistics proper. To answer the question as to a new language in a way which would correspond to reality, the attitudes of the speakers must be taken account of. After all, the fact that the language of the United States is still (American) "English," while Czech and Slovak are two languages, not one, is not deducible from linguistic analysis.[13]

Sociolinguistic factors in the crystallization of a new language are discussed in §4.6.

[11] On the contrary, the improvised, *ad-hoc* nature of some hybrid jargons can be inferred from the relative inconstancy of their forms. Contrast the improvised French-Turkish school jargon described by Rottenberg (**456**) with the medieval Anglo-French hybrid jargon which, according to Albert (**2**), had stable forms and underwent independent internal developments.

[12] There are only a few other cases of /ow/> /u/, e.g. *Coney Island* > Amer. Yiddish /kuni ajlend/, *to smoke* >/smukn/, *slow* > /slu/; cf. Jaffe (**239**), 133. If these adaptations were made by speakers of the so-called Yiddish *u*-dialects, on the analogy *vutn* : *votn as *vugn* : *vogn* 'cart', we then have here an interdialectal relationship which is the reverse of that represented by *coat* >/kojt/ (cf. p. 28, footnote 34). It is nonetheless, of course, an internal development of the type under discussion.

[13] As a curiosity, it may be noted that in the so-called "debate" which rocked Soviet linguistics in 1950, one of the views for which Marr, the dethroned prophet of the "new doctrine," was reproached was that language interference "results in the formation of a new language by means of an explosion, a [dialectical] leap from an old quality to a new quality." According to Stalin, "this is quite wrong" (**535**, 75). When caught at the contradiction between this verdict and earlier pronouncements of his to the contrary, Stalin extricated himself by declaring that only "after the victory of socialism on a world-wide scale" will language contact result in the emergence of new languages (*ibid.*, 98).

3 The Bilingual Individual

A series of non-structural stimuli and resistance factors which help to determine linguistic interference emerged in §2.52. They might be divided, offhand, into individual and socio-cultural. When one considers, however, that the bilingual speaker is the ultimate locus of language contact, it is clear that even socio-cultural factors regulate interference through the mediation of individual speakers. The problem of the bilingual individual as a determinant of interference is therefore of central importance and must be examined first. The psychological effects of bilingualism on non-verbal behavior, which are of only subsidiary importance to the present treatment, are summarized in the Appendix, pp. 116ff.

3.1 Psychological Theories of Bilingualism

Psychological conceptions of bilingualism and interference are contingent on theories of speech behavior in general; hence they vary from one school of psychology to another, and one is again confronted with the much discussed difficulty of finding a common denominator to which they might be reduced.

From the point of view of the individual, the two languages are two types of activity in which the same organs are employed. A comprehensive psychological theory of bilingualism ought therefore to account for both the effectively separated use of the two languages and for interference of the languages with one another. It is the latter aspect which has received most attention.

An early coherent theory of interference was constructed by a student of associational psychology, I. Epstein (**138**). A man with a multilingual background of his own, Epstein turned to observation and introspection for answers to questions prompted by his own experience. Thinking, as Epstein sees it, is the association between ideas and words. A direct association between an idea and a foreign word, he finds, is possible. But the knowledge of one language intervenes in the learning of subsequent ones; for, according to earlier studies on memory, when an association ab has been established, the formation of a second association, ac, is inhibited, and once ac is also formed, the reproduction of either b or c in association with a is inhibited. For each idea, therefore, the bilingual's multiple concurrent word associations interfere with each other, especially in the "expressive" uses of language (i.e. speaking and writing). It follows that bilingualism is an obstacle to ideation. Particular embarrassment is caused by the use of the uncustomary language in a given domain or in talking to a person with whom another language was used previously.

Although Epstein's work was widely praised, it ran into immediate criticism on theoretical grounds. W. Stern, the noted student of child language, pointed out (**550**, 107) that Epstein's conclusions applied only to adults, and that his associational psychology had been superseded by a more modern "psychology of thought." As Stern saw it, "the difference in languages . . . not only leads to the associative phenomenon of interference, but is a powerful stimulus to individual acts of thought, to comparisons and differentiations, to the realization of the scopes and limitations of concepts, to the understanding of nice shadings of meaning."

The importance of associational interference has subsequently been questioned even by those who do not deny its theoretical premises.[1] The issue has been taken up repeatedly in the debate on the "direct" vs. "indirect" methods of foreign-language teaching. A further elaboration of the theory of interference has come from scholars who have suggested that the greater the differentiation in the topical and environmental domains in which two languages are used, the less interference in association; only a functionally undifferentiated use of two languages induces "inorganic" bilingualism that is subject to interferences of associations.[2]

American psychologists so far have apparently refrained from formulating theories on bilingualism, as no experiments in this field seem to have been undertaken.[3] It is encouraging, however, that recent research trends in psycholinguistics are at last taking cognizance of developments in linguistic and communication theory by distinguishing between code and message (language and speech).[4] On the basis of this distinction, it is to be hoped, the psycholinguists will succeed in throwing light on the psychological mechanisms of switching code.[5]

The study of aphasia in bilinguals has, by and large, been carried on without a commitment to any psychological or neurological explanation of bilingualism, in terms either of function or of localization of the languages in the brain.[6] Recently, however, at least a partial neurological theory of bilingualism was formulated, according to which there exists at the posterior edge of the Sylvian fossa and in the adjoining parietal regions of the brain a special language-switching mechanism. "Complete rigidity [*Erstarrung*] in one language or the ability to switch at will from one language to the other are the only ways in which this switching center can function or be disturbed."[7] This hypothesis of an anatomically localized control center in bilinguals, if confirmed, may some day help to account for individual differences among bilinguals with respect to the amount of speech mixture (cf. §3.22 below).

3.2 Characteristics of the Bilingual Speaker

There are at least two characteristics of a bilingual person which predispose him to specific modes of behavior as an agent of language contact even before

---

[1] A brief survey of the criticism is to be found in Braunshausen (**79**), 35ff.

[2] Cf. Ittenbach (**235**), Volkmer (**601**), Geissler (**163**), 100.

[3] Esper (**140**) and Wolfle (**649**) do not specify the relevance for language-contact studies of their experiments on associative interference within a single artificial structure.

[4] Cf. Miller (**363**), 7; Osgood (**391**), 45.

[5] On the problem as seen from the communication point of view, see Fano (**144**), 696.

[6] E.g. Goldstein (**172**), 138–46; Kainz (**256**), II, 300–3.

[7] Leischner (**301**), 773. Goldstein, without benefit of the latest evidence, doubted the possibility of localizing the switching function (**172, 140f.**).

the actual speech situation arises. While they are easy to identify, they have yet to be correlated with the total amount of interference, or with specific types of interference, occurring in bilinguals' speech under otherwise equal conditions. This is a field in which experimentation and group testing promise important new insights. At this time, the research problems can only be suggested in broad outline.

3.21 Aptitude

The individual's aptitude for learning a foreign language is almost by definition a factor in his performance in the second language. Tests for language-learning aptitude are available[8] and have been used, but the testable aptitude remains to be compared with amounts and types of interference. To be sure, a rough correlation between second-language aptitude and attained proficiency underlies the tests themselves; still, in practice, the proficiency scores turn out to be insufficiently differentiated to serve as substitutes for a description of interference. Specialized procedures must be devised to investigate the problem.

According to one school of thought, very early bilingualism affects adversely an individual's aptitude for language learning. Tireman (573), however, found that the child bilingual's handicap in acquiring a second vocabulary is not as great as is sometimes supposed. Spoerl (540), comparing the mental performance of 69 bilingual college freshmen with that of a control group, discovered that the bilinguals surpassed the unilinguals slightly in English ability.[9] On the other hand, Toussaint (575) found the performance of Flemish-French bilinguals in dictation to be far inferior to that of unilinguals. Obviously, only additional research can establish a basis for explaining such discrepancies.

A special claim made in favor of bilingualism is that it helps in the acquisition of a third language[10]—not because of the similarity of the third language to one of the first two, but simply because of the greater experience of the bilingual in language learning. This point, too, awaits clarification by research.

3.22 Switching Facility

The ideal bilingual switches from one language to the other according to appropriate changes in the speech situation (interlocutors, topics, etc.), but not in an unchanged speech situation, and certainly not within a single sentence. If he does include expressions from another language, he may mark them off explicitly as "quotations" by quotation marks in writing and by special voice modifications (slight pause, change in tempo, and the like) in speech. There is reason to suspect that considerable individual differences exist between those who have control of their switching, holding it close to this ideal pattern, and those who have difficulty in maintaining or switching codes as required. The-oretically, one could visualize two types of deviation from the norm: one in the

[8] Buros (87), 265f.

[9] Speakers of Romance languages, of course, have a special advantage in learning English because of the peculiar role of Romance vocabulary in "advanced" English.

[10] Cf. Stecker (545). Gali (156) proposed an appropriate line of experimental investigation.

direction of excessively rigid adherence to a language, the other in the direction
of insufficient adherence to one language in a constant speech situation.[11] An
explanation of the former type of deviation has tentatively been advanced by
neurological research (see p. 72). On the other hand, the opposite tendency
(abnormal proneness to switching) has been attributed to persons who, in early
childhood, were addressed by the same familiar interlocutors indiscriminately
in both languages. Such was the conclusion, for example, of M. E. Smith (530)
in an experiment on eight children in 1935. Maurice Grammont, the French
phonetician, had the same idea when he counseled Ronjat, in bringing up a bilingual child, to use only French, while the mother was to keep to her native
language, viz. German, exclusively (451, 3). Even Stern (551) expressed the opinion that "the imbedding [*Einbettung*] of a language in a definite and constant
situation facilitates its learning" in unmixed form—a rather premature conclusion in view of the limited number of cases examined. The whole problem has
hardly been explored. On the basis of future tests, it may be possible to determine whether one or two (or more) deviant behavior patterns exist, and whether
bilingual individuals can be classified according to them.

3.3 Relative Status of Languages

Throughout the analysis of the forms of linguistic interference (chap. 2),
conventional terms like "mother-tongue," "first," "second," or "native language"
were avoided; for, from the structural point of view, the genetic question of
which of the two systems in contact was learned first by a given speaker or group
of speakers is irrelevant. All that matters is to know, for every instance of interference, which language is the source or model and which the recipient or replica,
and also whether in a given contact situation, a language can be both a source
and a recipient of interference (as noted in §2.53, it can). Accordingly, the terms
"source" and "recipient" were employed, with the equivalents of "primary"
and "secondary" in the section on phonemics (§2.2).

And yet, in a given case of contact, the prevalent type, direction, and extent
of interference may change with time. Since the languages themselves remain
the same, it must be their relative status with the agents of the contact and of
interference—the bilingual individuals—that is undergoing the modification.
From this point of view, it is legitimate to ask what the bilingual's position with

---

[11] Rosetti (454, 76f.), for example, cites the case of a woman "who, in her native Tran-
sylvanian village, had learned Rumanian and Hungarian in childhood, but who was unable
to translate a sentence from one language to the other. In her mind the two languages
formed systems separated by a staunch wall." Christophersen, too (101, 6), speaks of "bilinguals [who] cannot always translate well." These cases contrast with the bilingual Sorbians described by Ščerba (477), who seem to have had but a single language
with two "modes of expression," German and Sorbian. (On merged systems as a problem
in language theory, see §2.12.) Graur (176) suggests a connection between switching facility
and changes in proficiency. As his fluency in French decreased with lack of practice, so
did his switching facility; he found himself continuing in French whenever he had occasion
to introduce a single French name into a Rumanian utterance. On individual differences in
language learning and switching, see also Weightman (612), 41–5.

regard to the two languages is, since two bilinguals knowing the same languages and having identical aptitudes and switching facility may differ, nevertheless, in the status which they accord to each language.

Suppose that it is determined which of a bilingual's two languages, if any, is "dominant" by given psychological criteria.[12] It then becomes the task of inter-disciplinary, psycholinguistic research to investigate to what extent (other things being equal) the individual's "dominant" language serves as the source of interference in his speech. There is a formidable difficulty, however, to be resolved first. It inheres in the fact that the criteria by which a language might be characterized as dominant are numerous: proficiency, order of learning, atti-tudes might all be considered. Since these criteria are not mutually exclusive, it would seem necessary to correlate each one of them with typical forms of interference—a vast research program in itself. Only then could CONFIGURATIONS OF DOMINANCE CRITERIA be compared with bilinguals' speech behavior (see the discussion in §3.38).

Some of the possible criteria are enumerated below.

3.31 Relative Proficiency

A bilingual's relative proficiency in two languages is easily measured (cf. p. 63, footnote 1); one of the languages can hence be designated as dominant by virtue of the speaker's greater proficiency in it. However, in the interests of interference studies, proficiency tests must satisfy certain special requirements. First, care must be taken to test proficiency against a realistic scale which is impartially determined from a description of the "normal" form of the language, not imposed by prescription. Secondly, proficiency should be measured separately on various levels: understanding, expression, and inner speech[13] (the ordinary tests cover all three levels at once). Thirdly, relative proficiency should be meas-ured for a given moment in the bilingual's life, since the ratio can change in the course of time.[14]

3.32 Mode of Use

The visual reinforcement in the use of a language that a bilingual gets by read-ing and writing it may put that language in a dominant position over a purely oral one. The generally accepted notion that visual aids reinforce language learn-

[12] The complex term "dominant" covers what is often indiscriminately lumped together under "mother-tongue," a concept judiciously criticized by Christophersen (101, 2–4). All criteria of dominance, of course, may be socio-culturally determined; those mentioned under §3.36 below almost always are. The socio-cultural determination of dominance is discussed in chap. 4.

[13] For example, many bilinguals who are equally proficient in speaking both languages can nevertheless do their arithmetic ("inner speech") in one language better than in the other; this is particularly true of using the multiplication table, which is memorized as a verbal text in one language; see Epstein (138), 52ff; Lagarde-Quost (293), 2nd part, 14. Cf. also Michel's three "powers" of bilingualism (359).

[14] Christophersen (101, 8) vividly describes bilinguals with changing relative proficiency in their two languages. Incidentally, tests of the type used by Saer (see p. 10) may be utilized with good results for proficiency studies.

ing finds support in two cases reported by Minkowski (365) in which Swiss bilinguals recovering from aphasia regained the use of standard German and French, respectively, before their native Schwyzertütsch—presumably because they had used the standard languages in their written forms.[15]

3.33 Order of Learning and Age

The distinction of having been learned first is so great that the first-learned language, the "mother-tongue," is generally considered dominant by definition. In the initial stage of bilingualism, the mother-tongue is, indeed, at the same time the language of greatest proficiency; but later on, many bilinguals exceed their mother-tongue proficiency in the second language under certain circumstances. Many immigrants in the United States, for example, have a greater facility in English than in their native languages. On the other hand, a speaker's emotional involvement with his mother-tongue (§3.35) is rarely transferred to another language in full. In those cases of bilingual aphasia in which the mother-tongue was recovered first, it is the subject's greater emotional involvement with it that has been called upon as an explanation.[16]

The effects of exposing children to a second language at various ages have never been properly tested. The concentration of foreign-language teaching upon the high-school and college level, on the one hand, and the fact that in bilingual areas instruction in the second language is usually kept out of at least the early grades of primary school,[17] reflects the general view as to the optimum age for language learning:[18] ten to eleven years. An educational experiment, with the cooperation of qualified linguists, on the performance effects of earlier and later exposure to a second language would doubtless be a worthwhile undertaking.[19]

[15] Cf. also Goldstein (172), 144-6.

[16] This explanation seems today to be preferred to the so-called Rule of Ribot, according to which material memorized earlier is damaged less extensively. Of course, there are many cases where the mother-tongue is recovered second. This is attributed, among others, to the greater automatization of mother-tongue speech; cf. Goldstein (172), 138ff., especially 144; Kainz (256), II, 301.

[17] Cebollero (98), 72. It is interesting that where the desire or pressure to teach children the second language is particularly great, the age of first exposure is lowered. In Switzerland, for example, many Romansh schools voluntarily depart from the cantonal curriculum by introducing German as early as in the first grade. In the Soviet Union since 1938, children in four-year national-minority schools have been compelled to study Russian from the second grade on (cf. 67, 1221). Hardy (195) discusses the deplorable results of the too early, or exclusive, use of the second language in schools of colonial countries. Cf. also Appendix, pp. 121f.

[18] As Swadesh puts it (556, 60), we consider "an empiric fact the observation that the more fully adult a person is at the time he comes in contact with a new language, the less likely he is to obtain full control of it." Symonds (560) has shown that attendance of Chinese elementary school does not affect the second-language (English) performance of young Hawaiian children.

[19] Arsenian urged such research in 1937 (6, 143). Geissler's descriptive and speculative material (163), though suggestive, is based on only 17 actual cases, and is therefore hardly conclusive. In a larger sample of Romansh children in Switzerland, this author (624, 283)

Some children learn two languages from the start; they may be said to have two mother-tongues. These infant bilinguals face many problems of a special kind.[20] It has been asked, for example, at what age children become aware that they are learning two languages. One writer claims that not until the age of three does a child take note of its bilingualism.[21] Another observer recorded the first consciousness of bilingualism at 1;6 and full awareness of it at the age of 3;0.[22] A third child was reported to know the names of the two languages at the age of 2;12.[23] Whether the early or late cognizance of his or her bilingualism correlates with the individual's subsequent behavior in regard to interference remains to be investigated.

3.34 Usefulness in Communication

The greater utility of a language, or the extent to which it is actually used, is an easily measurable factor which serves to establish the dominance of one of two languages. In many cases of aphasia, the language most used in the period immediately preceding the trauma is recovered first.[24] "Schedules" of the general type devised by Hoffman (224) show up the extent to which each language is used by a given subject.[25] Bilinguals also can be questioned as to their own opinions of the usefulness of each language. In tests made in an English school of a bilingual area in Wales, for example, 91% of the pupils asserted the usefulness of studying and knowing Welsh.[26] In an inquiry made by this author in Switzerland, a group of Romansh-speaking students convincingly testified to the usefulness of German to them. Not only is the usefulness of a language the foremost reason for learning it (i.e. a cause of language contact), but the greater extent to which one language is used may make it a source of interference for that very reason.

3.35 Emotional Involvement

Many persons, if not most, develop an emotional, pre-rational attachment to the language in which they receive their fundamental training in semiotic be-

---

found early German learners (age 4–5) to be concentrated in certain parts of the canton of Grisons. If early learning of the second language can be shown to be a cause of interference in the first, this fact is an important omen of change in the Romansh dialects of those areas where German is learned most early.

[20] See Leopold (305).

[21] Geissler (163), 23.

[22] Ronjat (451), 81.

[23] Leopold (304), IV, 14.

[24] This was discovered by Pitres (410). Kainz (256, II, 300f.) cites more recent cases and additional literature.

[25] Hoffman's "schedule" was used in expanded or modified form by Arsenian (6) and Fishman (148, 149). It must, of course, be adapted to every concrete contact situation; as Lehrer showed (300, 320), Hoffman's form would prove inadequate outside the United States, where the role of the common language cannot be assumed to be as uniform as that of English in this country.

[26] Jones (253).

havior. Because unanalyzed "total situations,"[27] in which such behavior is learned, are more frequent in childhood, it is usually the childhood language, or mother-tongue, which enjoys the resulting strong attachments.[28] The total situations usually also provide the basis for mastery of the language which is not to be equaled later for any other tongue; as he rationalizes a person may conclude that his native language is richer, more subtle, more expressive than others. However, emotional involvements of later life (e.g. love affairs,[29] friendships,[30] patriotic attachment to a new country,[31] etc.) are apt to produce conflicting or superior bonds. Bilingual aphasics sometimes recover a language other than the mother-tongue because of greater subsequent emotional involvement.[32] Thus not every bilingual can unequivocally rank one of his languages as dominant on the grounds of emotional attachment.

3.36 Function in Social Advance

Under certain social conditions, the mastery of a language becomes important for an individual not merely as a medium of communication, but as a means to social advance. In Switzerland, for example, French in former patois territory was learned for its value in securing social status. Sometimes the conditions of social advance may even require the ostensible ignorance of another language —which may be a person's mother-tongue.[33] The usefulness of a language in social advance usually has a highly significant corollary: the importance of knowing that language well. In a situation of this type, there may even be a premium set on the concealment of the fact that a language was secondarily acquired. The effort exerted to overcome all traces of interference is therefore particularly strong; Bossard (71), for example, found "meticulous English" to be one of the "protective devices" of American bilinguals. The dominance of a language on these grounds can be expected to have a high negative correlation with all types of interference; but such a correlation remains to be documented by actual studies.

[27] The term is borrowed from Segerstedt (503) to designate a situation in which the meaning of forms is established by direct association of signifier and reference, without the mediation of other signs.

[28] Récatas (431) has demonstrated on the basis of field studies in Macedonia how the prestige of the mother-tongue outweighs all considerations against it. On the other hand, Weightman (612, 41–5) aptly characterizes a type of "unstabilized" bilingual whose attachment to one language is never strong.

[29] Cf. the case described by Minkowski (367).

[30] Minkowski (365); Goldstein (172), 145.

[31] See Schneerson's description (494) of changing language attitudes among immigrant children in Palestine.

[32] Minkowski (365, 367); Pötzl (415, 416); Kainz (256), II, 302f.

[33] Barker (20, 196) tells of bilinguals in Tucson, Arizona, who, in order to improve their relations with the "Anglos" (English unilinguals) will even deny that they know Spanish. For an illustration from the field of aphasia, see Pîtres (410), 877f. An interesting instance, on the contrary, of a foreign accent becoming a social advantage in an American environment has been described by Bossard (71, 704f.).

The value of a language in social advance might be designated PRESTIGE.[34] More than any other criterion of dominance, it is socially determined.

3.37 Literary-Cultural Value

A further point on which one language may be designated as dominant is the bilingual's intellectual or esthetic appreciation of the literary culture which is expressed in that language. In many countries the learning of the great languages of civilization occupies a prominent place in the higher educational system and "culture" is practically synonymous with bilingualism.[35] To German Swiss bilinguals, for example, standard German, which ranks lower in proficiency, emotional involvment, and usefulness than Schwyzertütsch, is nevertheless unequivocally the dominant language as far as literary-cultural appreciation is concerned.

3.38 The Dominance Configuration

The preceding discussion brought out a multiplicity of factors—and others may have to be added—by each of which one of a bilingual's two languages may be termed "dominant." These factors appear to be incommensurable.[36] The dominance of a language for a bilingual individual can only be interpreted as a specific configuration or syndrome of characteristics on which the language is rated. Using a + to indicate the positive rating of a language on a certain point, we may visualize bilinguals with typical dominance configurations such as shown in the table on page 80.

A great many additional variations, needless to say, are possible.

Logically, it would seem as if each one of the factors in the dominance configuration should first be correlated with typical forms of linguistic interference in the speech of bilinguals in each language, while the other factors are held constant. It should be determined, for example, whether it is true that greater emotional involvement in one language produces the transfer of affective grammatical categories into the other; that learning one language first secures some of its parts against all subsequent interference; that early unilingualism is necessary to make one of the two phonemic systems primary (as defined in §2.21),[37] and so

[34] The term "prestige" is often used indiscriminately to cover also (or rather) the usefulness of a language as a means of communication, its literary-cultural worth (see §3.37), possibly even its emotional significance, or the total dominance configuration (see §3.38). As a technical term, however, "prestige" had better be restricted to a language's value in social advance, or dispensed with altogether as too imprecise.

[35] Cf. Meillet and Sauvageot (351), 8f.

[36] The problem of multiple prestige rating is, of course, not confined to languages in contact; it arises often in social psychology, since the value that a thing possesses which allows it to be ranked in a hierarchical order is so often derived from several mutually irreducible sources.

[37] As Fries and Pike put it (154, 40), "it is also theoretically possible that for bilinguals the effect of their second language may be the phonemic breakup of conditioned variants of phonemes in their native language," i.e. that the first-learned language may become phonemically secondary; under precisely what conditions this may occur is still unknown.

forth. However, the number of individuals whose speech and life histories would have to be examined in order to correlate each factor separately may be prohibitive; it may not even be possible to find enough different individuals in a single contact situation to isolate all the factors. In practice there can therefore be no objection to correlating types of interference with groups of dominance factors, or even with entire dominance configurations, as long as the complexity of the configurations is borne in mind at all times, and only individuals with similar configurations are considered together.[38]

	ADULT U. S. IMMIGRANT, SEMI-LITERATE		ADULT U. S. IMMIGRANT, CULTURED		CHILD IMMIGRANT (U. S.)		GERMAN SWISS		FRENCH SWISS	
	Native	*English*	*Native*	*English*	*Native*	*English*	*Schwyzertütsch*	*Std. German*	*Patois*	*Std. French*
Relative Proficiency...	+		+			+	+		+	
Mode of Use (Visual)..		+	+	+		+		+		+
First Learning........	+		+		+		+		+	
Emotional Involvement..............	+		+		+	+	+		+	+
Usefulness in Communication.........		+		+		+	+			+
Function in Social Advance...........		+		+		+		+		+
Literary-Cultural Value..............			+	+		+		+		+

When the connection between types of interference and certain dominance configurations is successfully established, many linguistic changes which will until then have appeared accidental or even paradoxical will be able to be explained. Appropriate extensive study of bilinguals will not only elucidate the psychological factors in interference; it is also a prerequisite to an understanding of how socio-cultural determinants affect the bilingual. It may, in addition, clarify a number of basic questions in the psychology of language use in general.

3.4 The Speech Situation and Interference

The same bilingual may display varying amounts of interference in his speech according to circumstances in the immediate speech situation. Three such circumstances are discussed here.

[38] A parallel from social psychology: Osgood and Stagner (393) studied the prestige of various occupations. They obtained prestige ratings of 15 occupations on ten different traits, and found that each judgment of an occupation represented an irreducible configuration; yet, in a second test, the subjects were able to rank the same occupations according to "overall" prestige on a single continuous gradient. These more abstract judgments are of some significance, too, because attitudes based on them tend to become polarized—especially, as Osgood writes (392), when emotional thinking places them on an all-or-none basis. Presumably, the several traits making up the dominance configuration of a language could be similarly overlooked and an abstract judgment of "overall" dominance obtained; but the usefulness of the resulting general characterization of a language for interference studies must itself be proven.

3.41 Bilinguality of Interlocutors

In speaking to a unilingual, the bilingual often tends to limit interference and to eliminate even habitualized borrowings from his speech.[39] He is subject to what has been called interlocutory constraint,[40] which requires that he somehow make himself understood in his unilingual interlocutor's tongue. In those specific situations where a mere trace of another language is regarded as a social stigma, the speaker is, of course, constrained to much more than mere intelligibility (cf. §3.35). But when the other interlocutor is also bilingual, the requirements of intelligibility and status assertion are drastically reduced. Under such circumstances, there is hardly any limit to interference (cf. §2.53); forms can be transferred freely from one language to the other and often used in unadapted shape. No wonder that American immigrant languages, for example—spoken mostly BY AND TO bilinguals—have been subject to such extensive interference.

3.42 Departure from Specialized Uses of a Language

Many bilinguals are accustomed to discuss some topics in only one of their languages or to use only one language on given occasions; a sudden transition to the other language opens the door to interference.[41] A child learning both languages in its familial and play environment, for example, may be equipped to deal with everyday things in both tongues; but if it studies certain subjects in a unilingual school, it will have difficulty in discussing these "learned" topics in the other language, and in an attempt to do so, it will be prone to mix the languages. This is an everyday problem in German Switzerland, for example, where both Schwyzertütsch and Standard German are used. The functions of familiar dialogue, as contrasted with formal monologue (public addresses, lectures, sermons, etc.), are served by Schwyzertütsch.[42] Also, ordinary subject matter, as contrasted with technical matter, is dealt with in this language. Occasionally, however, the topic conflicts with the occasion. When technicians converse informally about machinery for which there is no adequate Schwyzertütsch terminology, or when a formal speech (requiring Standard German) is made about a homely topic which is more easily discussed in Schwyzertütsch, interference of the languages is quite marked.[43]

Some bilinguals, too, are accustomed to use only one language with a given person, and find the transition to another language extremely difficult. Here, too, a violation of the specialized use of the languages is involved, and increased interference is likely to result.

A number of writers have suggested that a person's bilingualism can be characterized on the basis of specialized or unspecialized use. The differentiation between "organic" and "inorganic" bilingualism was mentioned above (p. 10).[44]

---

[39] Cf. p. 60, footnote 111.

[40] *Partnerzwang*; cf. Braun (**77**).

[41] Cf. Epstein (**138**), 58–61; Lagarde-Quost (**293**), 2nd part, 17.

[42] On the basic differences between dialogic and monologic discourse, see Jakubinskij (**246**). For details on the Swiss problem, see Weinreich (**624**), 122–31.

[43] Cf. Racoviţă (**424**).

[44] Weiss (**628**) criticizes this dual typology as an oversimplification.

Geissler (**163,** 24ff.) distinguishes between orderly (*geordnet*) bilingualism, in which each language is assigned to its sphere of persons, and disorderly (*ungeordnet*) bilingualism, in which specialization is blurred. This, in turn, can pass into contrary (*entgegengesetzt*) bilingualism, in which the domains are not separated.[45] Michel (**359**) designates the two kinds of bilingualism as *in sensu distincto* and *in sensu composito*. Barker (**20,** 201) speaks of the "systematic patterning" of some bilinguals' language usage; the converse would be "unpatterned" usage.

These generalizations may prove of value in correlating "inorganic," "disorderly," "unpatterned" bilingualism with greater and lesser, or different types of, interference; the problem, however, stands.

3.43 Emotional Stress

The relation of the amount or type of interference with varying degrees of emotional stress under which the speaker acts is a psycholinguistic problem of some complexity and can only be mentioned here. The existence of the relation is suggested by the relatively frequent transfer of so-called "affective" grammatical categories and words;[46] even though satisfactory frequency tabulations are not yet available, it is significant that in many lists of loanwords, after the transfer of all possible items has been accounted for by reasons of structure, cultural innovation, and the like, a residue of words remains which is termed "affective borrowing."[47] Here, too, is an important task for interdisciplinary investigation.

[45] Cf. p. 35, footnote 21.

[46] Cf. p. 34.

[47] Out of many possible examples, Łukasik's analysis of Polish-Rumanian borrowing (**327**) and Scheludko's study of Rumanian loanwords in Ukrainian (**483**) may be cited. Both reveal, besides the alpine-pastoral "culture" designations, practically only "affective" words.

4 The Socio-Cultural Setting of Language Contact

4.1 The Role of the Socio-Cultural Setting

The bilinguality of some individuals is, no doubt, a socially isolated phenomenon. A lone missionary with an African tribe or an accidental Basque immigrant in an American town form practically unique points of language contact. Any of their language-usage habits which are of interest to students of interference must be described separately for each case. But when a group of some size brings two languages into contact, idiosyncrasies in linguistic behavior tend to cancel each other, while socially determined speech habits and processes characteristic of the group as a whole become significant. To delineate such patterns of language usage as characterize large groups—not to erect a futile dichotomy between individual and group—is the purpose of the present chapter.

It is clear that of the factors which make a language dominant for a bilingual (see §3.3), the usefulness of a language, its role in social advance, and its literary-cultural value are given to the individual by his surroundings; the relative status of the languages is therefore likely to be the same for most bilinguals in an undifferentiated environment. But even the order in which, and the age at which, the languages are learned, the extent of written usage, the relative proficiency, and the emotional involvement with the languages are frequently laid down for the language users by their society. Furthermore, the environment may make certain types of speech situation more prevalent than others. Thus, American immigrants, in their specific conditions of life, have occasion to speak a great deal with bilingual interlocutors; this cannot be without consequences for interference in their speech (cf. §3.41). One may go a step further and say that a person's predisposition to submit to or resist interference also has an environmental determinant, even if proneness to excessive "switching" is an individual personality trait. "A culture, as a preference for certain modes of behavior, involves a preference for certain personality structures rather than others; the kind of person favored in one group may be condemned in another."[1] Switching and speech mixture thus may come to be condemned by a society like any other undesirable trait.[2]

When a language-contact situation is examined in detail, the interrelation of socio-cultural conditions and linguistic phenomena is apparent. As an illustration, the case of Romansh-German bilingualism in Switzerland can be cited.[3]

---

[1] Morris (377), 209. Cf. the preference of certain types of speech behavior in Mohave culture described by Devereux (118), 268.

[2] Thus, the Mohaves, according to Devereux (118, 270), "show a singular reluctance to speak English unless they speak English well." If excessive switching should be demonstrated to be the result of too early and unspecialized use of two languages (§3.21), the possibility of social causation is all the more far-reaching.

[3] Studied by this author in 1949/50 (624, 268–436).

The Raetoroman language community is rapidly approaching a state of total bilinguality. In the present territory of Romansh, which is the remnant of a much larger Romance area subjected to continuous Germanization from two directions for over a millennium, the practical need to know German extends to almost all speakers. Familiarity with the Schwyzertütsch vernacular, in addition to the traditionally taught Standard German, is also on the increase. In one section of this area, the so-called Sutselva (Central Grisons), consisting of the Domleschg and Schams valleys (Romansh: Tumleastga, Schons), the exposure of the Romansh-language population to contact with German is particularly intense. Even within the family—as a result both of intermarriage and of the progressing language shift—the functions of German and Romansh often overlap. Children of Romansh mother-tongue consequently become bilingual very early. If it is true that children learn languages more easily and correctly than adults (cf. §3.33), a degree of purity of speech may be expected among the Raetoromans which cannot be sought, say, in an adult immigrant group coming to a new country and picking up the new language rapidly but poorly.

There are no clearcut language borders or mutually exclusive language territories in this contact situation. The Raetoromans in particular realize that they have no solidly unilingual hinterland and no city to serve as a cultural center.

As a result of the functional overlapping of the languages in everyday usage, many children learn both languages from the same persons, namely, their parents. It has been alleged that this fact in itself inhibits satisfactory language learning (cf. §3.22). What is certain is that if the parents are their children's teachers of both languages, then their own errors in both languages are transmitted to the next generation. This is in marked contrast, for example, to certain situations of French-German contact in western Switzerland, where bilingualism is also widespread but children as a rule learn each language from native, if not unilingual, speakers.

The overlapping of functions of the languages in the Romansh Sutselva leads to the use of both languages between the same interlocutors. This, added to the fact that both languages are learned so early, virtually blurs the distinction between mother-tongue and second language.

Furthermore, it is reasonable to suppose that in a bilingual community the general level of language cultivation (*Sprachkultur*), which is independent of the extent of bilingualism, accounts for the predominant types of speakers in the population. Since this is largely a peasant population with little schooling and a loose social hierarchy, one is led to expect that the type of bilingual who mixes both languages indiscriminately will be relatively frequent.

The population of the Sutselva is undergoing a language shift in favor of German. This fact of prime importance is deducible not only from the comparison of the data of the decennial censuses, but also from a synchronic analysis of figures regarding knowledge of each language among various age groups. It is a corollary of the shift that most bilingual speakers are of Romansh mother-tongue, for it is not often, in the Sutselva at least, that native German speakers learn Romansh subsequently, in opposition to the "trend of the times." There is thus a core of German unilinguals but practically no Romansh unilinguals in the population. The significance of this would in itself perhaps be ambiguous. On the one hand, the unilingual speakers of German form a nucleus of resistance against interference in German; on the other hand, German rather than Romansh is the second language to many speakers, and since the most natural direction of influence is generally thought to be from the mother-tongue upon the other tongue, the greatest potential influence might be expected from Romansh upon German.

However, the likelihood of this influence is counteracted by the fact that the social control of speech mixture affects the two languages quite unequally. While German elements in Romansh speech are tolerated practically without any limit, the reverse trend—Romansh influence in German speech—is kept within bounds. The knowledge of German is treated as an essential of acculturation, and is a prerequisite to social advance (urbanization); hence, the premium on good German is extremely high. When speaking German, the bilingual must guard himself against Romansh borrowings not only for fear of being misunderstood by the unilingual German speaker, but also because, in the area under discussion, slips may give away his Romansh origin at an inopportune moment or be taken as indices of his incomplete acculturation. In Romansh speech, on the contrary, there are no such regulative socio-cultural factors. Generally, no value is locally attached to purity in Romansh. Moreover, the Romansh listener is bilingual as a matter of certainty and will understand a borrowed German form. Nor is any loss of status possible through admixture of German forms or Romansh replica forms on German models. Thus, while potentially the major amount of influence could occur in German speech, actually, considering the effects of social control, most of the interference must be expected to take place in Romansh speech.

Until the Romansh revival movement of the past decade or two, there was practically no control opposing the habitualization of the results of German interference. The Sutselvan Romansh community is, to a degree, isolated linguistically as well as geographically from the speakers of other Romansh dialects; the cohesive forces within the community are few; no unilingual hinterland supports it or demands from it a "correct," uninfluenced language. If isolated cries for purity are voiced occasionally, they cannot be backed up by tangible cultural or social sanctions. Furthermore, institutional means for perpetuating a conservative language are almost lacking for Romansh. There has been little or no Romansh instruction in the schools of most villages of the area in over a century. The use of Romansh in such prestige-endowing functions as sermons has also been declining, especially in Protestant churches (for various complicated reasons). All instances of interference in speech are therefore candidates for becoming elements of Sutselvan Romansh—provided this dialect continues to be spoken, and unless the endeavors of the Romansh League to establish Romansh schools are successful.

Quite the contrary, of course, is true of German. There is a tendency for borrowings to become habitual, insofar as Romansh bilingual parents are also the German teachers of their children; but this is corrected by the rising volume of contact with non-Romansh, unilingual German speakers. To be sure, in the spoken form of German, i.e. the Chur dialect of Schwyzertütsch (to define it simply), there is no standardizing tendency and there is room for new borrowings from Romansh. But the unilingual bulk of the speakers of this dialect, bolstered by the urban center of Chur, is an important countervailing factor.

This socio-cultural setting of language contact and its linguistic-effects are radically different from French-German contact in western Switzerland. There it is widely felt that French is a standardized language with zealously guarded norms propagated by the schools. If there is any habitualized interference, it is therefore in the direction of French on Schwyzertütsch.

The likelihood of errors checked by the tolerance of interference in speech among native speakers of Romansh in the area discussed might be summarized as giving the following possibilities of linguistic influence:

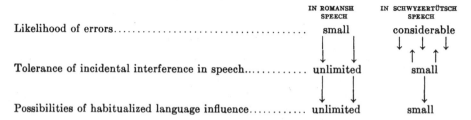

	IN ROMANSH SPEECH	IN SCHWYZERTÜTSCH SPEECH
Likelihood of errors.....................................	small	considerable
Tolerance of incidental interference in speech............	unlimited	small
Possibilities of habitualized language influence............	unlimited	small

The fullest freedom of integration of such borrowing as does occur can be expected in Romansh. In Schwyzertütsch a conflict exists between the inclination to borrow and regulative control of borrowing.

It should be evident even from an informal analysis like the preceding one that socio-cultural factors which can determine personality traits, preferred language habits, and typical speech situations are relevant to the control of interference. To ascertain how the various factors may best be grouped and studied is a formidable sociolinguistic research problem in itself. Programmatic works by German scholars like Kuhn (**290**) or Pritzwald (**422**), although prepared with somewhat different applications in mind, contain many useful ideas on this point. The following treatment is necessarily tentative and is designed primarily to stress the variety of factors that need to be considered. First, the functions of languages in a bilingual group are discussed (§4.2); then other group divisions paralleling the language division (§4.3) and the development and operation of language loyalty (§4.4) are taken up. Finally, some problems of the crystallization of new languages in contact situations and of language shifts are dealt with (§§4.6, 4.7).

One important limitation has to be pointed out. To predict typical forms of interference from the sociolinguistic description of a bilingual community and a structural description of its languages is the ultimate goal of interference studies. Unfortunately this aim cannot be attained till the missing link—the correlations between characteristics of individual bilinguals and interference in their speech—is supplied. In the ideal case of the future, the argument may run something like this. We are told that in a certain contact situation there is much intermarriage between the groups in contact. We infer from this that many children grow up in bilingual families, learning both languages simultaneously. Consequently (and this is the link which so far is only hypothetical) the children can be expected to have difficulties, say, with the grammar of both languages. A direct connection between intermarriage and proneness to grammatical interference—other things being equal—could then be postulated. To supply the missing middle of the argument, the psychological factors in interference, which were outlined in chap. 3, must be explored. But one can anticipate some of the aspects of the socio-cultural setting of language contact which are likely to be pinned down eventually as the ultimate extra-linguistic stimuli and resistance factors of interference.

4.2 Language Functions in Bilingual Groups

4.21 Classifying and Weighting the Functions

The functions of the languages in a bilingual community can be analyzed and classified in more than one way. Schmidt-Rohr, for example (**488**, 183), distinguishes nine "domains of language use," to wit, the family, the playground, the school (with subdivisions), the church, literature, the press, the army, the courts, the administration. This scheme may be adequate for some situations, but a domain like "The Family" is hardly differentiated enough. As one critic puts it, "often the parents are of different stocks and insist on initiating their children from the beginning in the native tongue of the father as well as of the mother. Sometimes parents entrust children from a very early age to governesses or tutors who speak different languages with a view to inculcating in them several tongues simultaneously or successively. Finally, families which have immigrated to foreign countries often speak their native language at home while the children use the language of the adopted country in their relations with domestic servants and the native population."[4] Mak (**334**) has used a more detailed schedule of functions, while Barker (**20**, 195), on the contrary, divides the social functions of language simply into familial, or intimate; informal; formal; and inter-group. This scheme, too, seems insufficiently articulated for many bilingual communities. A general survey of language functions in the bilingual communities of the world is not yet available.

From the special point of view of interference, the various functions of languages can be significantly graded according to the conservatory effect which they produce on speech behavior. In some functions, obviously, language usage is more subject than in others to corrective forces that counteract the habitualization of interference phenomena. In the kind of everyday discourse which aims at intelligibility only, careful diction is overlooked; there, interference may be rife. On other levels, however, conservative, "standardizing" forces may be operative at the same time. The school, for instance, in most literate societies checks people's freedom of speech behavior and acts as a deterrent to the "free"

[4] Braunshausen (**78**).

development of the language. In the unilingual situation it helps maintain a conservative, standardized language; in the bilingual situation it supports, in addition, the norms of the language against unchecked foreign borrowings. For the purpose of understanding and predicting language influences, the fact that one of the languages is used in the educational system (if any) is therefore of great importance. What the school achieves as a conservatory agency in language development is, however, not accidental, but part of a broader cultural setting with its specific prevailing attitudes on language purity. For example, if there is a strong and living literary culture transmitted through the schools, an attitude of caution against borrowing may be effectively communicated to the younger generations. The use of a language for literary functions is thus a hint that the conservative language forces symbolized by literature may be at work.

The realization that one's mother-tongue is not a standardized language applicable in all types of formalized communication (governmental activities, literature, radio, schools, etc.) often makes people indifferent to interference in it. In Switzerland, the functional "inferiority" of Schwyzertütsch (predominantly a spoken language) as against French—a language of unrestricted functions—is so deeply felt by many bilinguals of both mother-tongues that the flow of borrowings from French to Schwyzertütsch in border areas is considered as natural as the inhospitality of French to loanwords from Schwyzertütsch. Dialectal diversity, too, is often seized on as a token of the "unstandardized" state of a language and its functional inferiority, with a resulting indifference to interference in it. The Swiss Raetoromans of the Sutselva area, for example, are distinctly aware of the dialectal variations in local Romansh. Can it be a real language, many local inhabitants ask, if bread is called [paŋ] in one village, [pawŋ] in another, and [pœwŋ] in a third? This variation contributes to the contempt in which the language is held, a contempt so great that the mere suggestion of purism appears ridiculous to most of its speakers. Thus the loanwords from Schwyzertütsch stream in *en masse*. That Schwyzertütsch, which is here the "superior" language, is itself dialectally diverse elsewhere, is immaterial, since practically every Romansh community is in contact with only one variety of it.

From a sociolinguistic evaluation of the conservatory effect which standardized uniformity and a variety of functions produces, a scale could be derived for weighting the several functions in which one or the other language predominates in a contact situation.

4.22 Functions of a Language According to Mother-Tongue Groups

It is a conclusion of common experience, if not yet a finding of psycholinguistic research, that the language which has been learned first, or the mother-tongue,[5] is in a privileged position to resist interference. The importance of priority in learning is likely to be so great in comparison with other psychological factors governing interference that the description of functions in bilingual situations ought to be refined to take the factor of mother-tongue into account from the start.

---

[5] Notwithstanding the reservations about the term "mother-tongue" when applied vaguely (§3.32), the expression can be utilized in the present technical sense as 'the language learned first.'

To do this, one might define as a MOTHER-TONGUE GROUP the class of all those people involved in a language-contact situation who learned one of the languages first. In a bilingual group, one would accordingly expect to find two mother-tongue groups, and perhaps an intermediate set of persons who actually learned both languages simultaneously.

The characteristic use of languages in various functions should preferably be described separately for each mother-tongue group, not merely for the bilingual community as a whole. This additional breakdown might show, for example, that the burden of bilingualism is borne entirely by one of the mother-tongue groups, while the other group expects to be addressed in its own language in all cases of intergroup communication. Thus in a French-Schwyzertütsch bilingual village like Meyriez (near Murten, Switzerland), the bilinguals belong predominantly to the Schwyzertütsch mother-tongue group; few native French speakers learn Schwyzertütsch at all. It may furthermore appear from this additional analysis that though a community is bilingual, it contains only one mother-tongue group; the other language may not be spoken natively by anyone. The functional division between the languages is then uniform for the entire bilingual community.[6] Such is the case in German Switzerland, where the population is generally bilingual (Schwyzertütsch and Standard German), but the mother-tongue is exclusively Schwyzertütsch. Standard German is functionally restricted to written usage, to formal (monologic) discourse, and to subject matter technical in nature (cf. p. 81). The absence of a significant Standard German mother-tongue group deprives the language of that resistance to interference with which a group of native speakers would endow it. Ashkenazic Hebrew, which in its millenarian contact with Yiddish was largely limited in function to liturgical use and rabbinical literature and correspondence, was not represented by a mother-tongue group, either, and experienced profound interference as a consequence, splitting up dialectally in its phonology as Yiddish did: Just as the word for 'year' appears in some Yiddish dialects as *jor* and as *jur* in others, Hebrew 'blessed art Thou' corresponds to *borux ato* or *burɔx atu*, according to the area.

The psychological importance of priority of learning thus has a concomitant on the sociolinguistic plane. It is the importance to a language of being represented by a sizable mother-tongue group in a contact situation.

4.3 Congruence of Linguistic and Socio-Cultural Divisions

In any concrete contact situation, the division between mother-tongue groups is usually congruent with one or more other divisions of a non-linguistic nature. Some of these are outlined in the present section, with the stress on such factors as may be relevant to the stimulation or inhibition of interference.

4.31 Types of Congruence

(1) GEOGRAPHIC AREAS. Among the most common parallels to the division between mother-tongue groups is a geographic line. Unless it coincides with high

[6] Grootaers (182) terms this "stylistic bilingualism," as distinct from "social bilingualism," where two mother-tongue groups are involved.

mountains, seas, or other physical obstacles, there is likely to be contact between the mother-tongue groups across the line, and hence bilingualism.[7] Language contact along many European language borders has been described in great detail, and data are available on the extent of bilingualism for every community in those areas.[8] It appears that if the geographic division is clearcut, especially in rural surroundings, the language contact tends to be rather restricted. The purpose of intergroup communication in such cases is mainly trade,[9] whether the geographic line is a county boundary or an ocean. For example, the German-language part of the Sarine valley, canton of Fribourg (Switzerland), "is oriented predominantly westward [because] economic and social intercourse with the [French-language] Pays d'Enhaut, . . . the Ormont Valley, and its market center, Aigle, is more important than that with the [German-language] Simmental."[10] Consequently, the relations between mother-tongue groups are fluid and limited in scope. There is a great turnover of interlocutors; the means used to communicate are frequently improvised. Although interference in speech is likely to be quite heavy, it is not apt to be habitualized. On the other hand, since language contact congruent with area contact involves travel into a strange environment, new things are likely to be encountered and their names adopted. Sporadic lexical borrowing is therefore to be expected.

In one type of congruent language-and-area division, the intergroup contact is more developed: in isolated enclaves, such as the so-called language "islands" (*Sprachinseln*) of pre-war Europe or the rural immigrant settlements of the Americas. There the population is dependent on the surrounding area in proportion to its isolation from its own hinterland or homeland, and interference can accordingly be expected to be more profound. In the study of German-language enclaves in Eastern Europe, the precise nature of the relations with the new environment as a determinant or interference has been carefully considered.[11]

The congruence of language and area may be disturbed even in rural communities, especially if located precisely on a language border;[12] in city surround-

---

[7] The role of physical obstacles in the cultural and linguistic isolation of German ethnic enclaves in Slovakia has been graphically portrayed by Kuhn (291).

[8] Cf. Draye (127), Dhondt (120), and Valkhoff (588) on the French-Flemish border in Belgium, Lévy (310) on Alsace-Lorraine, Zimmerli (657) on the German-French border in Switzerland, Waltershausen (606) on the German-Romansh line, Bock (58) on German and Danish in Central Schleswig, Kloss (276) on a section of the German-Dutch language border.

[9] In Switzerland, the population of a village sometimes also crosses the language border to a neighboring community to attend church services, e.g. the German-speaking Catholics of the village of La Scheulte; cf. Wartburg (607), 158.

[10] Steiner (546), 31, footnote 13.

[11] See Kuhn (290); also Pritzwald (422), Mackensen (331).

[12] For example, Wallenried near Murten, Switzerland, described by Weinreich (624), 233–5. Concerning the cartographic problems created by blurred language borders, cf. Pfaundler (403), Sieger (518), and Sidaritsch (517), as well as the Styrian map by Schmidt and Neumann (487), where the new principles are utilized; cf. also Weinreich (624), 52f., 100, 103.

ings, an unblurred language border is quite unusual. In the bilingual (French and German) Swiss city of Biel, for example, no topographical language border appears to exist.[13] But of course there are exceptions. A city like Fribourg (Switzerland) is divided: In the lowest quarter (German *Au*, French *Auge*), inhabited mostly by German speakers, the signs are in German, the police officials and the salespeople are all conversant with German. While the entire upper portion of the city is French, the lower city enjoys a certain amount of linguistic (German) autarky. It is hardly surprising, then, that such widespread interference of French and German as is reported from Biel[14] is not typical of Fribourg.

There remains a need for precise sociolinguistic studies of bilingual urban communities,[15] since it is evident that linguistically unnucleated cities are foci of the most extensive and intimate interlingual contacts, both in the Old World and the New.

(2) INDIGENOUSNESS. The geographic separation of two mother-tongue groups may be canceled by migration, but a movement of one of the two groups seems frequently to result in a new characteristic socio-cultural division not without typical linguistic effects of its own. The immigrant language, rather than the indigenous one, appears to be the more exposed to interference for at least the following reasons: (a) The novelty of the habitat creates a need among the immigrants for adequate new vocabulary (cf. §2.43, p. 59); (b) The social and cultural disorientation of the immigrants undermines their inertial resistance to excessive borrowing into their language;[16] (c) Since many immigrant groups have a significantly low proportion of women among them, the necessity for intermarriage leads to a discontinuity of linguistic tradition. Bilingual Arizona, where there are both fresh Spanish-speaking immigrants and indigenous Spanish-speaking "Old Families," represents a curious test case for these hypotheses. And indeed, while the "Old Families" maintain their Spanish—with a preference for Standard Spanish—in the face of the ascendancy of English, the immigrants and their children, anxious to speak English, are generally negligent about their native Spanish.[17] Spanish as an immigrant language thus suffers considerably greater interference from English than Spanish as a coterritorial, indigenous tongue.

(3) CULTURAL OR ETHNIC GROUPS. In a great majority of contacts between groups speaking different mother-tongues, the groups constitute, at the same time, distinct ethnic or cultural communities.[18] Such contact entails biculturalism (participation in two cultures) as well as bilingualism, diffusion of cultural traits as well as of linguistic elements.[19]

---

[13] Detailed house-to-house inquiries might, however, reveal varying concentrations of mother-tongue groups.

[14] Kuenzi (289).

[15] Cf. the correlated studies of urban social structure and acculturation outlined by Caplow (95).

[16] See Willems (642), 463; (640), 320 on German immigrants in Brazil.

[17] Barker (18), 169f.

[18] Some exceptions are discussed in §4.32.

[19] See Barker (18) on the biculturality of children growing up in Tucson, Arizona.

Situations of congruent culture-and-language contact seem to invite interference of a lexical-cultural type (cf. pp. 56f.). The relationship of the cultures to
one another in a particular geographic habitat determines what one group learns
from the other and defines such gaps in the vocabulary of each group as may need
filling by borrowing. Even for extensive word transferring, large numbers of
bilingual speakers need not be involved and the relative size of the groups is
not necessarily a factor; after all, "there is no intrinsic reason [to assume] that,
when a large and a small group are brought into contact, the small group will
borrow more extensively than the large one. . . . A hundred individuals can learn
a new thing as readily as one."[20]

Culture contact naturally produces the diffusion of non-material as well as of
material culture elements. The non-material side of culture is particularly significant in explaining not only the borrowing of abstract vocabulary, but the
principles of selectivity and rejection of vocabulary. Cultural resistance long
delayed the adoption by Islam of gambling, insurance, or printing.[21] Resistance
of a similar type apparently led the Ashkenazic Jews to avoid the adoption from
medieval German of the word for 'Saturday'[22] (even though the names for the
other six days of the week were borrowed), and also to leave out from the large
German vocabulary they did accept such words as *tugent* 'virtue', *laster* 'vice',
buoʒe 'penance', and others with specifically Christian connotations.[23]

(4) RELIGION. One kind of cultural difference, namely a religious one, quite
often coincides—alone or in combination with others—with a mother-tongue
division. In many Ukrainian towns before World War I, for example, the mother-
tongue division between Ukrainian, Polish, and Yiddish coincided with the
religious division between Uniates, Catholics, and Jews. Similarly, for the Germans in the ethnic enclaves of Eastern Europe, the German mother-tongue and
the Lutheran religion "were the same thing."[24] In Switzerland, the author had
occasion to observe bilingual communities in which the mother-tongue division
coincides with no other cultural difference except the denominational one. Several villages around Murten, for instance, have German and French mother-
tongue groups which are exclusively Protestant and Catholic, respectively.
The religious division acts as an even greater barrier to the integration of the
communes than the linguistic one, so that in the bilingual but unireligious communes the contact of the two mother-tongue groups is considerably more intimate. A villager as a rule is more conscious of his neighbor's denomination than
of his mother-tongue. Not only is intermarriage quite rare, but everyday activities, too, are separated according to denominations. Thus, in the village of

[20] Linton (**312**), 499.
[21] Kroeber (**287**), 417f.
[22] German *Samstag* or *Sonnabend*, Yiddish *šabes*.
[23] Cf. M. Weinreich (**619**).
[24] Karasek-Lück (**258**), describing the Germans of Volhynia. In Catholic Brazil, according to Willems (**642**, 460), Protestant families are emotionally more attached to their German mother-tongue than Catholic German immigrants. See the special study on religion
and mother-tongue by Grentrup (**180**).

Courtaman there are two inns: a Protestant and a Catholic one. A surprising amount of linguistic self-sufficiency and unilingualism is possible in a denominationally divided bilingual village like Wallenried (pop. 265; 51% of French mother-tongue). Some children there grow up without having to learn the other language; as many as 41% of the native Schwyzertütsch speakers and 79% of the native French speakers were found to be unilingual in this village. While there are mixed play groups of pre-school age (the common language is French), the Protestants and Catholics have separate schools.[25] The contacts even within the village are thus quite restricted. The use of each language is rather specialized according to interlocutors, and in intergroup contact it is most restricted topically, but each language is used in all functions within the mother-tongue group. This considerably limits the possibilities of interference. The division of schools on linguistic-denominational lines exposes most children of both mother-tongues to the standardizing, conservatory influences on their language that emanate from the school as well as from the church. The results of any interference that does take place are thus additionally checked and eliminated.

The restricting effect on language contact and interference exercised by religious differences, especially in rural areas, should never be lost sight of. Some of the language borders in Europe which are more recent than religious borders represent lines where a language shift came to a standstill at a religious divide.[26] This phenomenon, too, can be observed in Switzerland at present. The Germanization of Romansh villages along the Rhine above Chur, originating from largely Protestant areas, has skipped the solidly Catholic Domat/Ems and Rhäzüns, but is engulfing such Protestant points as Trins, Flims, or Rothenbrunnen. On the contrary, the Protestantism of the Müstair Valley helps to protect it from the threat of Germanization proceeding from the neighboring Catholic valley of the Lower Engadine.[27] The denominational border is in both instances a barrier to the progress of the language shift.[28]

(5) RACE. The congruence of race and mother-tongue differences seems significant only to the extent that in some situations the racial division reinforces the bars to intermarriage and thus to the earliest and most intimate kind of home bilingualism. In Brazil, for example, the recognizable racial difference has prevented Brazilian-Japanese intermarriage much more effectively than Brazilian-German mixed marriages.[29]

(6) SEX. While certain differences in language style according to the sex of the speaker are not uncommon,[30] major language divisions coinciding with the sex difference are rare. The most famous case is probably the remnant of such a division in the Antilles which originated from the capture of Arawak-speaking

---

[25] Details in Weinreich (624), 233–5.

[26] See the special study by Cornish (107).

[27] Weinreich (624), 277; Gadola (155), 147; Waltershausen (606).

[28] The separatistic effect of religious differences is sometimes great enough to support the crystallization of new languages in contact situations; cf. §4.6.

[29] Willems (641), 105; (640), 451–61.

[30] Cf. Tagliavini (562); Jespersen (250), 237ff.

women by a predatory Carib-speaking tribe.[31] The contact between the sex
groups is of course so extensive that no such major difference can be long maintained. On the other hand, the tagging of selected speech features as feminine or
masculine makes them, in some cultures, highly immune to transfer to the speech
of the other sex.[32]

Occasionally one of the sexes may be more exposed to contact with a second
language. In Macedonia, for example, Aromunian women are reported to be
largely unilingual, while their husbands are bi- and multi-lingual.[33]

(7) AGE. A congruence between mother-tongue groups and age groups is the
synchronic manifestation of what is, diachronically seen, a language shift
(see also §4.7).[34]

A language shift is hardly ever so abrupt as to sever communication between
age groups. What appears like a discrete generational difference in mother-
tongues within a single family is a projection of a more gradual age-and-language
transition in the community.[35] It can be assumed that the same reasons that lead
an age group to shift to a new language usually compel its elders at least to
learn that language. Thus language shifts are almost invariably preceded by
widespread bilingualism. Whether they are also followed by bilingualism, i.e.
a lingering knowledge of the obsolescent language, seems to differ from case to
case. Unfortunately census evidence is usually only inferential. It is known, for
example, that among the descendants of German immigrants, the percentage of
American-born persons of American parentage who gave German as a mother-
tongue was 18.7% according to the 1940 census (587); among Swedish immigrants
the corresponding figure was only 4.1%. If there is a positive correlation between
the proportion of an ethnic group which passes on its language to its children
as a mother-tongue, and the total proportion which teaches its children the
language, then the knowledge of the obsolescent old-country language can be
assumed to have been about $4\frac{1}{2}$ times as widespread in the German group as
among the Swedish.

Whether the burden of bilingualism is borne by the group as a whole or to a
greater degree by one part of it seems to depend both on the suddenness of the
shift and the point to which it has progressed. In American immigrant families,
for example, the children usually learn English most rapidly and in the early
period it is they who switch back to the old-country tongue in communication
with their elders. A generation later the grandchildren are often unilingual

---

[31] Müller (379), II, 322–49; Jespersen (250), 237ff.

[32] See Jespersen, *ibid.*; Avanesov (13), 238; cf. also Capidan (90, 127–32) on the Rumanians
of Albania, whose unilingual women had somewhat different phonetics from those of the
plurilingual men; and Lévy (308) on certain lexical differences between men's and women's
speech in Yiddish.

[33] See Récatas (431).

[34] In the Swiss area of a Romansh-to-German shift, this author was able to establish
statistically the decreasing percentage of persons of Romansh mother-tongue in progressively lower age groups (624, 344–7).

[35] Selk (513) utilized the different language-usage habits of generations to measure the
process of Danish-to-German shift in Schleswig.

English and it is the parents and grandparents who must switch languages in deference to their interlocutors.

An obsolescent language seems destined to acquire peculiar connotations and to be applied in special functions even after it has lost its main communicative role. Under a rapidly progressing language shift it acquires a certain esoteric value.[36] On the other hand, the first generation to undergo the shift tends to learn enough of the obsolescent language to destroy this value; thus, many children of American immigrants "know" just enough of the old folks' language to understand what the parents mean to conceal. Obsolescent languages also easily develop comic associations. Patois columns in French Swiss newspapers or Pennsylvania-German sections in certain Pennsylvania journals are mainly restricted to humorous material. Among children of American immigrants, the mere utterance of a word in their parents' language easily evokes laughter.[37]

The stylistic specialization of an obsolescent language and the association of it with intimate childhood experiences is conducive to the borrowing of its lexical elements into the younger people's speech, especially in discourse that is informal and uninhibited by pretensions of high social status. Particularly apt to be transferred are colorful idiomatic expressions, difficult to translate, with strong affective overtones, whether endearing, pejorative, or mildly obscene.[38]

Correspondingly, the "new" language is likely to be viewed by members of the older age group as the epitome of fashion. This may lead, in turn, to heavy borrowing in the opposite direction designed to make utterances sound more youthful, modern, or elegant. In Brazil, for example, highly mixed speech has been found to be a phase in the transition of Germans from their native language to Portuguese.[39] It would be a worthwhile problem in sociolinguistics to determine the correlation between obsolescence of a language and the extent of interference in it.

(8) SOCIAL STATUS. While a difference in social status is often a concomitant of other group divisions (cultural, religious, indigenous vs. immigrant), situations of stable language contact in which the mother-tongue difference corresponds to a difference in the social status of two autochthonous groups, and to nothing else, are easier to imagine than to discover. One such case is reported from Java, where the nobility speaks Noko natively, while the commoners' mother-tongue is Kromo.[40] In Ireland, according to one opinion, Gaelic long

---

[36] A Swiss woman in an area that had shifted to French, when asked by an investigator to speak patois, said: "Why? Are there too many ears hearing us?" Cf. Gauchat (159), 25. See also Seliščev (509, 37) on the esoteric functions of Chuvash and Cheremis in areas where they are becoming obsolete.

[37] Related to this is the fact observed by Swadesh (558, 234) that "once the new language is widely adopted, there are certain groups and personalities that persist especially in retaining the old language."

[38] For Amer. Yiddish examples, see p. 35, footnote 21.

[39] Willems (640), 315. Rosenquist (453) notes similarly how Swedish in the United States, before being replaced, is influenced by English.

[40] Pieris (406), 330.

survived among the lower strata without appearing in the historical records produced by representatives of the autochthonous upper classes.[41]

In conditions of a language shift, however, some socially distinct groups often lead the rest of the population, so that a congruence between mother-tongue and social status can be traced, even if it is only transitional. Thus in many German cities and English rural areas all but the lowest stratum have shifted from the local dialects to the standard language.[42] Similarly, the shift to Portuguese among German immigrants in Brazil has been more rapid among the middle and upper classes than among the lowest.[43] Whether the determinant here is the greater cultural conservatism or the more limited social goals of some strata, a differentiated reaction to a new language is produced. As for socially differentiated resistance to a shift, cf. §4.42.

What the foreseeable linguistic effects of a stable status-and-language division are is difficult to say because of the scarcity of pertinent evidence, although it is to be expected that the familiar diffusion from the upper to the lower stratum accompanied by a trickling of slang expressions upward, which is characteristic of all linguistic innovations, will ensue. In situations of language shift, heavy interference as a forerunner of the shift is apparently so general (see p. 95) that it is hardly dependent on social differentiation. To subject a slow language shift, preferably in socially differentiated urban surroundings, to close sociolinguistic study seems a prerequisite to the elucidation of the phenomena involved.

. (9) OCCUPATION. Occasionally special occupational groups have languages of their own, e.g. the tailors of Saracatsana in Macedonia[44] or the Jewish cattle merchants of Alsace.[45] These are borderline cases, of course; it is not even always clear whether the special languages differ from the general language in more than certain sections of the vocabulary. Yet, because of the esoteric function of the special occupational languages, their value depends on the restriction of the group of initiates. Here, then, is a rare situation in which there is resistance to interference on the part of the speakers of the source language, a reluctance to "lend" rather than to borrow.[46] Only occasionally do individual words penetrate into general slang.

(10) RURAL vs. URBAN POPULATION. Among the non-linguistic groupings which sometimes coincide with mother-tongue differences in language contact situations, the urban-rural distinction perhaps deserves mention as a unique combination of social, occupational, and topographic differences. The linguistic diffusion proceeding from urban centers to the surrounding countryside has been

---

[41] Pokorny (412).

[42] Henzen (213), 182–6; Bloomfield (55), 51.

[43] Willems (642), 452f. See also Heberle (207).

[44] Capidan (91); Suli (555); Georgacas (165). Similar linguistic formations have been found by Keller (263a) in Ticino, Switzerland.

[45] Their cryptic language, an outgrowth of Western Yiddish, is called by them Lošlekoudeš. It will be described by this author in a forthcoming paper.

[46] In the field of acculturation, reluctance to "lend" due to the nature of the cultural item is illustrated by such phenomena as monopolies, patents, secret diplomacy; cf. Devereux and Loeb (119), 134f.

repeatedly demonstrated by dialectologists, especially the Marburg school of Wrede's (651) and by Frings (9). This diffusion would seem likely to take place not only when sporadic innovations are spread to similar dialects, but even when the city has shifted to a new language.

Rural populations sometimes develop a hostile attitude (or at least an ambivalent one) toward their urban centers; the effect of this on language shifts is mentioned in §4.71. Whether anti-urban attitudes can prevent the diffusion of linguistic interference phenomena short of a shift remains to be determined by empiric sociolinguistic investigation.

4.32 Lack of Congruent Non-Linguistic Divisions

There are some instances of language contact in which the language division does not correspond to any congruent non-linguistic divisions. A number of them are observable in Switzerland. After various culture patterns in their geographic distribution had been subjected to intensive study, little connection was found there between language and patterns of dress, food, games, or customs. On close scrutiny, such differences as exist, for example, between the spinning and weaving methods of the German and French Valais turn out not to be strictly congruent with the language frontier.[47] Switzerland generally has been discovered to be culturally divided not at the French-German language border, but by a line running further east through German-language territory, along the mountains Brünig and Napf and the rivers Reuss and Aare. While "it cannot be denied that individual, literary culture is associated for the most part with the geographic domains of the respective written languages . . . , folk culture often follows other divides—older ones, perhaps—than the ones between contemporary 'national' languages."[48] A preliminary examination by this author of unpublished materials of the Atlas of Swiss Folk Culture (160) failed to reveal any consistent cultural difference which could be connected geographically with the division between German and French or Romansh.

Again, in studying the status of the bilingual Swiss Raetoromans (i.e. Romansh speakers), this author tried to evaluate the content of the Raetoromans' group consciousness. It turned out that "ethnic" interpretations of the group's identity were secondary to linguistic considerations, if they entered the picture at all. A Raetoroman of German mother-tongue is impossible by definition. The Romansh as well as the Schwyzertütsch speakers consider themselves members of the Swiss nation (Volk or Nation; pievel, naziun), and more immediately of the Grison people (Bündnervolk, pievel grischun) and its culture. Only a few informants thought in terms of a Raetoroman Volk. In the struggle to resist the language shift, Raetoroman leadership hardly makes use of even the few existing differences in folkways, folk art, or folklore that could be emphasized to raise the Raetoromans' group solidarity. The competition between the languages has no overtones of an ethnic or social conflict.

A similar linguistically mixed area in Southern Hungary where the ethnic

[47] Bodmer (60), 96ff.
[48] Weiss (630), 154.

division between Germans, Hungarians, and Slovenes had become quite blurred was described by Werner (633). Other groups that have been characterized as ethnically indifferent are the inhabitants of Polesie, who called themselves neither Poles nor Russians, but merely *tutejsi* 'local people', and the "Blakkede" people in the German-Danish borderlands.[49]

The absence of socio-cultural divisions to reinforce the difference in mother-tongues is not only a factor facilitating language shifts but it probably also deters the development of resistance to linguistic interference, and is thus conducive to interlingual influence.

4.33 Conclusion

In the analysis of what makes one of two languages dominant for a bilingual individual, the multiplicity of contributing elements was pointed out (§3.38). The discussion of congruent linguistic and socio-cultural divisions in the preceding section of the present chapter underscores the difficulty of determining in some cases which language is "upper" or "dominant" in the bilingual community. The very breakdown of communities into mother-tongue groups gives rise to the question: Dominant for whom? Clearly each mother-tongue group can rate the two languages independently and with different results. It is doubtful altogether whether it is worth tagging two languages in contact as respectively "upper" and "lower" at any cost, since from the point of view of interference studies, various relations between mother-tongue groups are likely to have different characteristic effects on the languages in contact.

The difficulty of ranking two mother-tongue groups in hierarchical order is aggravated by the need to rank functions of the languages as well. It is therefore expedient, perhaps, to restrict the term DOMINANT to languages in contact situations where the difference in mother-tongues is coupled with a significant difference in social status (§4.36).[50] But this should not imply, of course, that even there the direction of interference is exclusively from the dominant language to the non-dominant one. In Southern Welsh dialects, for example, two phonemes, /ʉ/ and /i/, have been progressively merged (a case of underdifferentiation in the terminology of §2.21) despite the fact that the variety of the language which maintained the distinction was of "higher prestige."[51] Similarly, Baltic German, as noted in §2.21, was influenced by the socially lower Lettish and Estonian. In many contact situations the languages would have to be called neutral with respect to dominance or non-dominance.

[49] Selk (513). Cf. also Beck (35).

[50] The term would then be the counterpart to "prestige," i.e. the value of a language as a means of social advance (cf. p. 79, footnote 34). This terminology would accord with Bloomfield's distinction (55, 461) between "the UPPER or DOMINANT language, spoken by the conquering or otherwise more privileged group, and the LOWER language, spoken by the subject people, or, as in the United States, by humble immigrants." Needless to say, the implications drawn by Bloomfield from this distinction would be qualified by a more refined sociolinguistic analysis.

[51] Sommerfelt (533), 96.

The social functions of languages (§4.2) and the congruence of mother-tongue with non-linguistic group differences (§4.3) are worth describing not because they permit a simple ranking of the languages, but rather because the various *modi vivendi* create typical patterns of linguistic behavior and interference or resistance to interference.

4.4 The Standardized Language as a Symbol

4.41 Sources of Language Loyalty

The sociolinguistic study of language contact needs a term to describe a phenomenon which corresponds to language approximately as nationalism corresponds to nationality. The term LANGUAGE LOYALTY has been proposed for this purpose. A language, like a nationality, may be thought of as a set of behavior norms; language loyalty, like nationalism, would designate the state of mind in which the language (like the nationality), as an intact entity, and in contrast to other languages, assumes a high position in a scale of values, a position in need of being "defended." Language loyalty, like nationalism, can be "an *idée-force* which fills man's brain and heart with new thoughts and sentiments and drives him to translate his consciousness into deeds of organized action."[52] In response to an impending language shift, it produces an attempt at preserving the threatened language (cf. §4.7);[53] as a reaction to interference, it makes the standardized version of the language a symbol and a cause. Language loyalty might be defined, then, as a principle—its specific content varies from case to case—in the name of which people will rally themselves and their fellow speakers consciously and explicitly to resist changes in either the functions of their language (as a result of a language shift) or in the structure or vocabulary (as a consequence of interference). Thus in the field of sociolinguistics purism, standardization, language loyalty, and related defensive mechanisms are phenomena of major importance requiring systematic treatment, even if, for understandable reasons, they are considered irrelevant in descriptive structural linguistics.

What are the roots of language loyalty? One would suspect that a rudiment of this feeling is natural in every user of language, because the inescapable emo-

[52] Kohn (282), 19, in a reference to nationalism.

[53] Occasionally language loyalty can even be made subservient to aggressive purposes. Recent European history abounds in attempts to impose languages on populations by force. But there have also been grotesque attempts to modify languages (without displacing them) by ukase. The Russians have toyed with the idea of changing certain forms of Slavic languages in Soviet-occupied countries. For example, after invading Poland in 1939 they found the fact that 'Jew' was called in Polish *Żyd* distasteful, since *žid* in Russian is a term of contempt. Consequently, they ordered Polish newspapers to write *Jewrej*, coined on the model of the non-pejorative Russian *jevrej*. After World War II, the Russian occupation authorities in Poland again felt misgivings about the use of *pan* as a pronoun of polite address, since *pan* also means (in Russian as well as in Polish) 'squire', and was found to be an inappropriate remnant of feudalism in a People's Democracy; see Klemensiewicz (274).

tional involvement with one's mother-tongue as one learned it in childhood (§3.35) makes any deviation seem repugnant.[54] Differences in temperament may cause people to respond differently to this natural inertia. Beyond that, however, the extent of loyalty that is displayed varies with other socio-cultural factors from one contact situation to the next.

While the fact that languages can function as symbols of groups has been repeatedly noted in the literature,[55] little of a social-science nature has been done to analyze the symbolic association of a language as a standardized system with the group's integrity. The group involved is, of course, primarily the mother-tongue community, but frequently also some other congruent grouping; the nationality is a favorite. The correlation of language loyalty and nationalism is a significant sociological problem.[56] To be sure, "before the age of nationalism, . . . the spoken language . . . was in no way regarded as a political or cultural factor, still less as an object of political or cultural struggle."[57] But even in this age of nationalism, a group's language loyalty and nationalistic aspirations do not necessarily have parallel goals. As mentioned in §4.31, the Raetoromans, like the Italian Swiss, cultivate the fullest possible loyalty to their language without aspiring to such nationalistic goals as political independence. The "Yiddishist" movement in Eastern Europe before and after World War I similarly concentrated on a language program rather than on political organization. The connection is thus at least flexible and cannot be taken entirely for granted. Relations between language loyalty and group elans other than nationalistic also need to be investigated.

It is in a situation of language contact that people most easily become aware of the peculiarities of their language as against others, and it is there that the pure or standardized language most easily becomes the symbol of group integrity. Language loyalty breeds in contact situations just as nationalism breeds on ethnic borders.[58]

Even if not restricted to immediate situations of contact, loyalty sentiments probably bear some proportion to an actual or imagined threat to the language. As a reaction to a threat, manifestations of language loyalty might perhaps be viewed in a similar conceptual framework as those which anthropologists em-

---

[54] Similar statements can be made regarding non-linguistic aspects of culture. As Kroeber writes (287, 437), "people in growing up do get attached to the ways of their culture. . . . By the time they begin to age, their memories of the culture have got tinged with pleasurable nostalgic sentiments and assume a symbolic value."

[55] Cf. for example Sapir (471), 29.

[56] See Boehm (62), 235 f.; cf. also Vossler's eloquent, if uncritical, essay (603).

[57] Kohn (282), 6.

[58] As Boehm puts it (62, 234), "the national frontier . . . is the symbol of the territorial contiguity of nations and thus a particularly vital factor in modern nationalism. . . . Border populations are usually imbued with particularly militant nationalism, for here the contrast to an alien people and an alien culture is more generally apparent. . . . This 'pathos of the borderland' is the connecting link between the border regions and the capital city of a country . . ., the focal point for all the vital energies of a people. . . ." Pousland (418) notes a greater loyalty to pure French in Salem, Mass., and Canada than in France itself.

ploy in the study of nativism.[59] Linton, in his analysis of nativistic movements (313), classifies cultural groups in contact as objectively dominant or dominated and subjectively inferior or superior. It might be said accordingly that if a group considers itself superior but in practice has to yield to the other group in some of the functions of its language, or has to fill vocabulary gaps by borrowing from the other language, a resentful feeling of loyalty may be fostered. Thus language loyalty, like a nativistic movement, is "unlikely to arise in situations where both societies are satisfied with their current relationship."[60] It is rather frustrated superiority feelings that cause language loyalty to develop.[61]

The more "realistic" members of an objectively dominated group may attempt to better their lot by associating themselves with the dominant group. The sight of such "betrayals" invariably causes resentment among the more steadfast members of the dominated group, a resentment which brings with it unswerving language loyalty. Divergent reactions and the consequent resentful loyalty can be found in almost any type of group contact congruent with a mother-tongue division: ethnic and cultural contact, immigrant and indigenous populations, lower and higher social strata, rural and urban sections, old and young age groups. The way in which the dominated group splits can sometimes be explained by its internal makeup. As Linton puts it (313, 239), "... nativistic tendencies will be strongest in those classes of individuals who occupy a favored position and who feel this position threatened by culture change. This factor may produce a split in the society, the favored individuals or groups indulging in a rational nativism, ... while those in less favored positions are eager for assimilation. This condition can be observed in many immigrant groups in America where individuals who enjoyed high status in the old European society attempt to perpetuate the patterns of that society, while those who were of a low status do their best to become Americanized." While there is reason to doubt the universal applicability of this scheme, and while difference between individuals must be allowed for, one can say nevertheless that corresponding divergences in attitudes toward a language, and toward language norms as a group symbol, lend themselves to analysis according to similar criteria.

It is also pertinent to note that social action in the field of language has sometimes been based on a manipulation of language loyalty. Ordinarily, it is true, when a mother-tongue community exposed to contact splits on the point of loyalty to its language, the more loyal sector will resort to self-pity and exhortation of the less loyal. But occasionally leaders with more than usual insight will attempt to enhance the language loyalty of their fellow speakers by methodic,

[59] Kroeber defines nativism (287, 437) thus: "After two societies have come into sufficiently close contact for one to feel the other as definitely more populous, stronger, or better equipped, so that its own culture is in process of being supplanted by the other, a conscious preservation effort or defense is often produced. Such reactions have been called nativistic endeavors or revivals." The best survey of the problem seems to be Linton's (313).

[60] Linton (313), 234.

[61] Roberts (450) uses the term "counterprestige" for a reaction to prestige. Since "prestige" has been more narrowly defined in the present work, to adopt "counterprestige" in Roberts' sense would be misleading.

organized means. The reasoning behind such programs, their successes and
failures, also need to be studied for a fuller understanding of the interplay of
structural and socio-cultural factors in language development. One attempt to
create language loyalty was observed by this author in a Romansh section of
Switzerland.[62] A great deal of material concerning the more and less successful
revivals of half-"dead" languages (Hebrew, Irish), though easily available, has
not yet been utilized for sociolinguistic analysis. The creation of new standard
languages in the past century and a half is, by and large, also the record of the
organized buildup of language loyalty.[63]

4.22 Effectiveness of Standardization

In response to interference, language loyalty ordinarily concentrates on the
standardization of the language.[64]

Devotion to a standardized language is often thought to be an intellectualistic
affliction. In the speech of German immigrants to Brazil, for example, it has been
noted that Portuguese interference is most limited where there has been "an
influence of intellectuals from Germany."[65] Conversely, anti-purism sometimes
accompanies generally anti-intellectual, "slangy" behavior; "there are . . . areas
in our large cities where the young people deliberately refrain from speaking an
'unmixed' English lest their 'crowd' accuse them of being 'highhat.' "[66]

It is doubtful, nevertheless, whether intellectualistic motivations are the
ultimate determinant of a preoccupation with standardization. The Athabaskan
languages of America have displayed a marked resistance to loanwords, despite
varied cultural contacts,[67] apparently without the involvement of intellectualistic
motivations of an Occidental sort. This author has also observed Raetoroman
peasants artlessly attempting to speak a purer type of Romansh by avoiding
German loanwords. To be sure, the intellectual subgroup of a mother-tongue
group may have cause to be the most loyal to its language out of such considerations as Linton indicates (cf. p. 101); moreover, purism requires a degree of
concentration and self-consciousness which is best attainable in intellectual discourse (spoken and written). It would stand to reason, however, that the conscious resistance to interference on the principle of loyalty requires no greater
effort than the frequently observed conscious submission to interference which

[62] Weinreich (624, 360–405; also 621).

[63] See, for example, Kloss' sketchy but excellent review (275) of the development of a
dozen new Germanic standard languages.

[64] One type of reaction is PURISM, i.e. self-conscious resistance to all interference in the
name of a principle. But language loyalty is not necessarily puristic. In Hitlerite Germany,
where the symbolic values of the German language were so fully played upon, the purists
had to struggle for their cause as in the pre-Hitler years. In the Soviet Union, too, the
glorification of the "great and mighty" Russian language drowns out the occasional puristic
pronouncements.

[65] Willems (640), 305.

[66] Bossard (71), 701. Cf. also the heavy mixture in the slangy English-Spanish Pachuco
argot of the American Southwest, described by Barker (19), and the high percentage of
unetymologizable words in slangs generally.

[67] Sapir (472), 209.

takes place when the source language symbolizes high status. Whether this is actually so is a problem to be investigated.

For many decades now, dialectological as well as descriptive interests have made many linguists averse to problems of language standardization and have kept a damper on the potential development of sociolinguistic studies of the processes involved. However, if the social sciences were to be called upon to contribute more amply to the study of languages, the research problems concerning resistance to interference on the grounds of language loyalty could be formulated without much difficulty. They turned up in many spots in chap. 2 of the present study, and were summarized in the table on pp. 64f. It should be investigated what domains of language have been stressed in standardization programs (vocabulary, syntax, phonics), and the effectiveness of standardization in the various domains and under different historical conditions should be critically evaluated. Information is needed on how much socio-culturally induced resistance is needed to counteract structurally stimulated interference phenomena of various types. While there is little chance that such studies will reveal purism to have been a major factor even in the recent history of some languages, the net effect of standardizing tendencies might be assessed more correctly than heretofore. In such languages as Czech or Rumanian, for example, they did attain signal successes. A detailed sociolinguistic analysis of even the failures of standardization would shed light on the interplay of structural and non-structural factors that are involved in the regulation of interference.

4.5 Duration of Contact

The synchronic slant has been so dominant in descriptive linguistics that students of interference have generally overlooked the possibility of studying contact-induced progressive changes in a language against the time dimension.[68] Yet an attractive opportunity for short-term diachronic observation is offered by languages freshly brought into contact, as through migration.

The time factor in interference can be analyzed in two significant ways: first, through the relative chronology of the habitualization or elimination of interference features; and secondly, through the absolute time elapsed before this or that phenomenon of interference is habitualized or eliminated.

Some of the statements concerning the relative amounts of interference in various domains of language (phonetics, vocabulary, etc.; see §2.53) lend themselves to a chronological interpretation. Dauzat's assertion (113, 49–55), for example, that morphology is affected least implies that it is affected last; interference in vocabulary is asserted to be greatest, and, by implication, also takes

---

[68] In acculturation research, too, the time element has been widely neglected. Redfield, Linton, and Herskovits (432) did include "the factor of TIME elapsed since [the] acceptance [of a trait]" in their Memorandum, but Beals (33) notes that "field studies of acculturation frequently are essentially descriptive; we are given the results of acculturation rather than an attempt to discover its dynamics [p. 628]. . . . Dynamic situations, as the physicists have long recognized, require the use of time as a dimension. New techniques and standards are called for" (p. 638).

place first. But aside from the fact that such statements are theoretically untenable on the synchronic level (see p. 67), their validity as diachronic "laws" remains to be demonstrated. What is necessary is the close observation of a contact situation from its inception over a period of time, with the usual scientific controls, before anything factual can be said regarding either relative or absolute chronology.

The only real-life study of interference in time which this author is aware of is the dissertation by Sadlo (**459**), who actually retested the phonetics of the same subjects' speech after an interval. Among a group of children of emigrant Polish miners in France, Sadlo found that three years were sufficient to produce in their native Polish a merger of the palatal and hushing sibilants and affricates ($\acute{s} > \check{s}$, $\acute{z} > \check{z}$, $\acute{c} > \check{c}$). Other available evidence consists of educational progress measurements in second-language study. Although those are based on "artificial" classroom experience, they too may contain information relevant to the theory of interference. But such information still remains to be extracted.

Short-term empiric diachronic investigation may make it possible to clarify basic problems involving longer time spans as well. For example, according to an opinion current in Europe (the evidence remains to be presented in linguistically valid terms), immigrants acquire an American "accent" in their first-learned language after a few years' residence in the United States;[69] this would seem to show that mother-tongue phonetics are easily affected by bilingualism. On the other hand, it has been shown that phonic features of extinct languages can survive for many generations;[70] this has been cited as proof that a native phonetic system is, at bottom, extremely durable. Similar contradictory observations have been made on syntax. Detailed research must unravel these paradoxes. Perhaps the facts can be explained by the early establishment, and delayed persistence, of unified phonic or syntactic systems (cf. pp. 8f. above); other solutions, based on differences of socio-cultural setting and a neat distinction between phonemic and subphonemic features, or between relevant and redundant syntactic relations, ought not to be neglected either. The field is large and intriguing, and its implications for the understanding of "substratum" phenomena are obvious.

4.6 Crystallization of New Languages

Some situations of language contact have been productive of new, third languages, while others have not.[71] Some criteria for deciding whether or not a new

---

[69] Kock (**281**) states this about Swedish, Pap (**395**, 83) about Portuguese, Senn (**514**) about Lithuanian, Wechssler (**609**, 446) about other languages.

[70] Cf. Kessler (**266**) on remnants of Romansh sounds in one variety of Schwyzertütsch or Rosenquist (**453**) on the persistence of a Swedish "accent" in American English for generations (to quote but two of innumerable examples).

[71] The problem has been discussed in some detail by Loewe (**318**). Again, students of acculturation have had similar observations to make. In some situations of culture shift, it was noted, new marginal cultures have developed, but not in others. Thus, Willems reports (**640**, 186) that among some German immigrants in Brazil, the feelings of inferiority in rela-

language has developed out of the crossing of two others were discussed in §2.55. On that basis, trade languages like the Chinook Jargon, the creoles and pidgins, all undoubtedly deserve the appellations of new languages. On the other hand, such speech forms as often arise between dialects and their corresponding standard languages, e.g. the Greek *mikti*,[72] similar vernacular idioms in Upper Germany,[73] the "Halbdeutsch" of the Baltic countries,[74] the Hawaiian dialect of English,[75] or the Anglicized Italian of the United States[76] do not seem to have attained the stability of form, the breadth of function, or the distance from the stock languages, nor have they generated sufficiently separatistic subjective attitudes among their speakers, to be styled new languages in a valid sense of the term.

The nature of linguistic interference, it will be granted, is the same whether the interfered-with speech does crystallize into a new language or not. What are the factors, then, that do contribute to the development of a new language? The question can be examined according to the criteria outlined on p. 69.

(1) DEGREE OF DIFFERENCE. It takes the contact of two rather different languages to crystallize a new idiom sufficiently different from either of them to rate classification as a new language. On this point, therefore, the question of whether a third language does or does not emerge has a linguistic determinant, too. For example, the fact that Lower Germany has what is practically an intermediate language between the dialect and Standard German (the so-called Missingsch[77]), while Upper Germany does not, may, in part at least, be due to the fact that the dialect is considerably more unlike the standard language in Lower that in Upper Germany.

(2) STABILITY OF FORM. How firmly the patterns of interference become habitualized is already a matter beyond strictly linguistic causation. The relative stability of affected speech forms reflects rather the manner in which the two languages are learned by the bilinguals and the relative ineffectiveness of influences tending toward the elimination of interference (see pp. 87f.). It is significant that many of the new languages which have achieved some stability of form arose far from the centers of social control, "on very pronounced frontiers of culture. . . . Those [new languages] now extant are almost all closely connected with the great migrations of European peoples during the past four hundred

tion to both the German stock culture and the Luso-Brazilian culture are connected with the existence of a marginal, or intermediate, "Teuto-Brazilian" culture, which is a source of psychological compensations for the inferiority feelings (see also pp. 245–72, esp. 265ff.). Here Willems leans on the marginal culture theory, developed by Goldberg (171) as an antithesis to the marginal man theory. On the other hand, the Quechuan village of Nayón, Ecuador, is in the course of acculturation almost completely bypassing the intermediate stage of mestizo culture developed in other sections of the country; see Beals (34), 73.

[72] Intermediate between the *dimotiki* and the "pure" *katharevusa*; cf. Steinmetz (547).

[73] See Loewe (318).

[74] See Mitzka (370) on Latvia, Stammler (542) on Estonia.

[75] Described by Reinecke and Tokimasa (442); cf. also Reinecke (441), 118.

[76] Menarini (354), 159.

[77] Described in some detail by Borchling (69).

years."[78] They were crystallized, one might say, in conditions of "anti-prestige,"[79] or lack of sufficient "prestige" on the part of either language to promote it to the status of a norm.

(3) BREADTH OF FUNCTION. The crucial function which a regularly interfered-with type of speech must acquire in order to develop into full-fledged language is, it seems, use in the family. The socio-cultural settings in which a hybridized language can become the mother-tongue of a generation of children have been studied by Reinecke (**441**). "Very seldom," he found (p. 112), "does a trade language spontaneously become the mother-tongue of a group. Perhaps the only example in the literature is that of the Chinook Jargon, which is said to have been for a time the sole language of a few children of French Canadian *voyageurs* and squaws in Oregon Territory." Accordingly, Reinecke distinguishes trade jargons, which remain supplementary (i.e. the "other tongue" to all its speakers) from creole jargons, which develop into full-fledged mother-tongues.

The functions of a new language can be broadened by administrative fiat or other conscious efforts to include education, religion, and the like. In some cases, e.g. that of Papiamento in Curação or Haitian Creole, the new languages have been used in written form in the press and in literature, although long after contact with the African stock languages had been severed.[80] Such functional expansion naturally increases, in turn, both the stability of form and the subjective experience of the idiom as a separate language.

(4) SPEAKERS' OWN RATING. The development of an attitude among bilingual speakers in which their speech, a result of interference between two languages, is regarded as a new single language, again depends on various socio-cultural factors, such as the isolation of the group in contact from its unilingual hinterland, separatistic tendencies of an ethnic or political content, and so forth. The manner in which loyalty to a hybridized form of speech is generated and develops is an interesting sociolinguistic problem. In clarifying it, it may be useful to contrast the history of Yiddish with that of other Jewish languages. All of them represent unique fusions of various dialects of the stock languages (German, Spanish, Arabic, Persian, etc., as the case may be) with outside admixtures (Hebrew-Aramaic and Slavic, Turkish, etc., again as the case may be); but the language loyalty of the Yiddish-speaking community has not been equaled among the speakers of Dzhudezmo ("Judeo-Spanish") or other Jewish languages.

4.7 Language Shifts

4.71 Sociological Aspects

A language shift was defined (p. 68) as the change from the habitual use of one language to that of another. Whereas interference, even in its socio-cultural setting, is a problem in which considerations of linguistic structure enter, the

---

[78] Reinecke (**441**), 109. See also Schultze (**499**), whose study is superseded by the former.
[79] A term proposed by M. H. Roberts (**450**).
[80] Reinecke (**441**), 112, 117.

matter of language shifts is entirely extra-structural, since it can be taken for granted that the respective structures of two languages in contact never determine which language is to yield its functions to the other. Because there are no strictly linguistic motivations in language shifts, the matter need not be dealt with at length in the present study. But it may be useful to show at least how the framework established in §§4.2–4 for the sociolinguistic study of interference can be utilized to good advantage for the study of language shifts, too, if common oversimplifications are to be avoided.

First, language shifts should be analyzed in terms of the functions of the languages in the contact situation (cf. §4.2), since a mother-tongue group may switch to a new language in certain functions but not in others. For example, under a foreign occupation, or in migrating to a new country, the adult members of a mother-tongue group may come to use a new language in its dealings with governmental authorities, while the children use it in school; at the same time, the old language may live on in the homes and at informal gatherings of the group. In such a case we might speak of a PARTIAL rather than a TOTAL shift. While language shifts among urban immigrants in America are usually rapid and total, the language shifts among rural immigrant communities are often rather of a partial type for two or three generations, at least.[81]

It is a worthwhile further problem to investigate in what order languages are shifted in their several functions, and to what degree a shift in one function, e.g. in politics and education, necessarily brings about a shift in others. It would be interesting to study, too, whether standardized languages, applicable in all types of formalized communication (cf. p. 88), have a greater potential for displacing other idioms in a language shift than unstandardized languages. While this has often been supposed to be the case,[82] actual situations seem to vary. In East Prussia before World War I, many Lithuanians were highly conversant with Standard German, but it was only the Low German dialect, the knowledge of which spread rapidly among the postwar generation, that was able to displace Lithuanian.[83] In Switzerland, several generations of Raetoromans have known Standard German, but again it is the knowledge of unstandardized Schwyzertütsch which poses the threat of a substantial shift in some areas.[84] It would appear, then, that an unstandardized vernacular is sometimes more apt to be adopted than a standardized language whose functions do not include everyday speech.

Secondly, the nature of shifts should be studied in contact situations where the mother-tongue division is congruent with various other, non-linguistic divisions, in order to allow for a differentiated response to the new language among various subgroups. For instance, research on the shift to Portuguese among German

[81] See American Council of Learned Societies (3), no. 34, *passim*; cf. also Pihlblad (407) on conditions among the Swedes of Kansas.

[82] Cf. Hirt (220a), 252. Hall also writes (189, 19): "It is hard to think of any modern instance in which an entire speech community is under pressure to learn a substandard variety of a second language."

[83] Gerullis (167), 61f.

[84] Details described by Weinreich (624), 284–6.

immigrants in Brazil has shown various significant correlations.[85] The shift is a concomitant of the urbanization of the colonists; it progresses faster among the lowest social strata, but more rapidly among Catholics than among Protestants and faster among the better than the less well educated. It is most rapid in trilingual areas, where Portuguese makes headway as the common medium of communication.[86] The shift is also favored where non-linguistic forms of German culture are being abandoned simultaneously. In a Lithuanian village in East Prussia, it was observed that workers and artisans experienced considerably less embarrassment at shifting to German than did the more conservative farmers, hostile to urban innovations.[87] In the Hebrides, it is similarly reported, the Gaelic language survives in the countryside as a symptom of rural hostility to the Anglicized towns.[88]

Obviously, such differentiated situations cannot be subsumed under a simple statement as to which language has higher "prestige" or "social value." A study of one multilingual area in central Schleswig showed that Standard German —which many would readily call the socially "higher" idiom—displaced the Danish dialect totally, in all functions, but the Low German dialect only partially.[89] The configuration of dominance can be complicated, and oversimplifications must be guarded against no less that in considering the setting of interference (p. 98).

In general, the possible effects of language loyalty (cf. §4.4) in counteracting language shifts should be carefully sifted. Many languages with low "prestige" have been able to hold their own against threatening shifts for long periods. A peculiarly favorable socio-cultural setting, for instance, has enabled Schwyzertütsch to maintain itself against the onslaught of Standard German. Many "obsolescent" languages have received new leases on life through a rejuvenated language loyalty among their speakers[90] and have made the prediction of the death of languages a hazardous business.

Finally, language shifts, like interference, can and ought to be studied carefully against time. An outstanding research job on the "dynamics" of a language shift from Danish to Standard German in Schleswig has been contributed by

[85] Willems (642), 462ff.

[86] The effect of trilingualism is also discussed by Reinecke, who reports (441, 112): "Naturally, the more polyglot an area, the better the chance has a pidgin [or any other new language] to spread. . . . No jargon was able to gain more than a temporary foothold in Polynesia, the dialects of which are mutually intelligible or nearly so. But in Melanesia and the Papuan-speaking regions, where every village may speak a distinct language, Beach-la-mar English ran like wildfire. . . ."

[87] Gerullis (167), 64.

[88] C. A. Smith (526).

[89] See Selk (512) and Hahn's review (188).

[90] See Kloss' surveys of the Germanic field (275, 277), in which he also includes Yiddish. On Lallans (Scottish), see also Ziekursch (656) and Wagner (605). An excellent sociolinguistic analysis of the rise and decline of a Frisian-Dutch dialect is given by Hellinga (209). For Celtic parallels, see Rees (439), and also Weinreich (622) on Welsh. Details on Romansh are presented by Weinreich (624), 171-7, 363-83.

P. Selk (**513**). However, rather than examine the shift function by function, Selk concentrated on the family level and consequently reported only the total shift. In another time study of a total shift, Arsenian (**6**, 69), by correlating length of residence of parents in the United States with the bilinguality of their children, was able to measure quantitatively the progress of the language shift among Italian and Jewish immigrants.

4.72 Linguistic Implications

If the processes of interference and language shift are interconnected, the available evidence regarding one of them can be utilized in understanding the other. It has been suggested, for instance, that language shifts are characterized by word transfers, while loan translations are the typical mark of stable bilingualism without a shift.[91] Another hypothetical connection is that in a slow shift, the surviving language suffers less habitualized interference than in a rapid one.[92] Other correlates also have been proposed.

The crucial problems are these: Do the language shift and the processes of language influence take place in the same direction? Are their respective tempos correlated? Does a standstill in the language shift imply a standstill in interference, or, on the contrary, the crystallization of a new language?

That a language shift does not exclude linguistic influence in the opposite direction, i.e. interference in the "winning" language, is obvious from the survival of words from extinct languages in living ones; the way American English borrows words from receding immigrant languages is a case in point. But the conditions under which winning languages adopt more than loose lexical elements are still obscure.

Obviously it is a matter of socio-cultural conditions whether the speakers of the "losing" language learn the new language so well as to leave no trace on it, or whether they learn it in an imperfect manner, bequeathing the phonetic and grammatical peculiarities of their speech to future generations in the form of a substratum. Hence, in a language shift, the scholar must look not only for the pressures that determine the choice of language but also for those which decide the thoroughness with which the new language is learned and the flow of leveling, equalizing forces from the unilingual bulk which tend to eliminate traces of the old languages. The educational system, geographical accessibility, the rural or urban character of the shifting population are essential factors for the understanding of how substrata are formed. "It is generally believed," says Schuchardt (**498**, 528f.), "that the original language always 'protrudes' through the newly acquired one; but which of its sides, which part of it? We have to know the history of the people to decide whether AI is to be interpreted as A^i or I^a."

It has long been customary to use the evidence of cultural loanwords to reconstruct social, cultural, and political conditions under which the borrowings

---

[91] Willems notes, for example (**640**, 279), that in the German of Brazilian immigrants, loan translations are extremely rare.

[92] Seliščev (**509**), 38.

were made.[93] If the study of actual cases of language contact should show that
certain types of interference are habitualized under specific socio-cultural conditions, but not under others, then it may be possible to buttress the reconstruction
of social situations of the past with the help of linguistic evidence other than
cultural loanwords alone.

[93] Cf. Windisch (645) on the theoretical principles, and Mackenzie's coordination of
linguistics with history in Anglo-French relations (333). Seiler's 8-volume study of loanwords in German (507) is one of the crowning achievements of this approach.

5 Research Methods and Opportunities

5.1 Need for a Broad Approach

From the analysis of the mechanisms of linguistic interference, its structural causes, and its psychological and socio-cultural co-determinants, these basic problems emerge:

In a given case of language contact, which of the languages will be the source of what forms of interference? How thoroughly will the effects of interference be incorporated in the recipient language? How far in space will they be diffused?

Ever since the late nineteenth century there have been linguists interested in the concrete effects of language contact who endeavored to account for them by reference to the socio-cultural setting of the contact. After it had been demonstrated how the transfer of lexical material could be ascribed to cultural conditions,[1] it was attempted to apply similar methods to interference in the more highly structured parts of languages—sound systems and grammar. The classic paper by Hempl (**210**), for example, written in 1898, divided language contacts according to the demographic and cultural characteristics of the communities in which they occurred, showing that the stabilization or elimination of effects of interference varied with many external circumstances. Thinking along these lines would hardly meet with any opposition today. But arguments such as Hempl's, while they offered a partial explanation of the direction of interference and perhaps its depth of penetration, did little to account for the principles of selectivity according to which this or that concrete instance of interference was established or eliminated in the recipient language. It is surprising that social scientists concerned with language have done so little to apply the findings and methods in their general field of work to the problems that have been discussed here.

A radically different approach to these problems was offered by twentieth-century descriptive linguistics when the Prague phonologists, in the late twenties and early thirties, tackled the matter of interference from the structural side. They held the view that the spread of linguistic features from one language to another was but an extension of linguistic change in general, since, as Jakobson (**241**, 193) put it, "differences of language are no hindrance to the diffusion of phonemic or grammatical devices."[2] The selection of new traits for adoption by another language, as they saw it, is governed by the structure of the recipient language, just as diffusion within a single language is governed by its structure. What is amenable to the recipient structure is taken over from the modified

[1] Cf. the essay by E. Windisch (**645**), published in 1897, and frequently quoted, and the paper by Wackernagel (**604**). Schuchardt, of course, anticipated these by his unexcelled *Slawo-deutsches und Slawo-italienisches* (**496**) of 1884.

[2] See also the subsequent statement of this theory by Martinet (**344**), 24ff.

speech of bilinguals; the rest is ignored.[3] Accordingly, every language is to be regarded as constantly exposed to potential interference stemming from its neighboring languages. On this premise, the Prague school proceeded to set up "phonological areas in which genetically different or divergent languages show similar phonological features."[4]

The new approach produced a number of studies on the sharing of structural features, or the diffusion of structural changes—mostly phonemic[5]—among adjacent non-related languages.[6] Its followers found themselves in sympathy, too, with parallel efforts of other schools, e.g. the work on American linguistic areas by Boas (**56**), Sapir (**473**), and their students.[7] There were also interesting attempts made to determine what geographic conditions are conducive to the diffusion of linguistic innovations and the formation of linguistic areas.[8] To be sure, the new discoveries were at first characterized by a strong emphasis on structural considerations, while the social setting of language contact was left in the background. In recent publications, however, a more equal balance between the various factors seems to have been struck. A combination of socio-cultural and structural approaches was used, for example, by Martinet (**346**) on problems which did not seem soluble by either method alone.[9] Thus, the replacement of F by *h* in Spanish as a result of Basque influence had previously been attributed to the "acoustic equivalence" of these sounds. Martinet demonstrated the untenability of this controversial argument and proposed a far more convincing solution based on an examination of the total phonemic structure of Old Basque (141–3). He then took up the socio-cultural conditions under which this Basque interference must have occurred. Some students of the problem had found it difficult to visualize the replacement process ($h \rightarrow$ F) in view of the lowly social status of Basque compared to Latin; but as Martinet was able to show (143–5), a more differentiated consideration of the socio-cultural setting, reckoning with the conversion of Castile from a remote frontier province of the Romania to a position of political and cultural supremacy, makes the postulated phonic development entirely plausible.[10]

It has been the purpose of the present study to show the promise of such a twin approach by exploring the great variety of factors, both structural and socio-cultural, on which the effects of language contact may depend. If but few

---

[3] Jakobson (**244**).

[4] Martinet (**344**), 26. The first proposed definition of a *Sprachbund*, or language "affinity," was presented by Troubetzkoy (**582**) in 1928.

[5] Recently there has been a revival of interest in grammatical areas as well; see Martinet (**340**).

[6] Jakobson (**242**); van Wijk (**639**); Havránek (**205**); Tesnière (**569**).

[7] Cf. Jakobson (**241**).

[8] Savickij (**475**).

[9] The basic principles are discussed by Martinet (**346**), especially p. 155. See also Vogt (**599**), 32.

[10] A number of other instances of sound change specifically attributable to foreign influence have been analyzed in the combined framework of structure¦ and socio-cultural setting by Martinet in another study (**342**).

final conclusions on matters of principle or solutions to concrete problems have been offered, it is because the prime goal of the study has been the formulation of research objectives and a discussion of methods.

5.2 Multiple Language Contacts as a Favorable Field of Study

The theory of interference as well as the methodology of studying it can profit substantially from investigations of multiple language contact, that is, of cases in which the same language has been in contact with two or more others. With the structure of that one language constant, the mutual influences of it on the others, and vice versa, can be described in fully comparable terms, and the likelihood of chance convergence or of similarity due to other uncontrollable causes[11] is considerably reduced.

Some parts of the world have traditionally formed linguistic whirlpools, and some languages have been exposed more than others to linguistic cross currents.

One famous area of multiple language contact has been the Balkan peninsula. It has fascinated students of interference for decades; since Schuchardt (**496**), it has served as a storehouse of standard examples for practically every type of interference. Special periodicals devoted to Balkanology have explored the problems of common linguistic and cultural features of the area, and numerous separate studies have been published on the subject.[12]

A language which has, in the course of its history, experienced particularly multifarious and intimate contacts with others is Yiddish. The Yiddish language grew up on German dialect territory. One branch of it matured in Germany proper, a larger one in a Slavic environment; still others developed in contact with Rumanian, Hungarian, Lithuanian, and I ettish. In Alsace and Lorraine, Yiddish evolved on the fringes of French-speaking territory. During the late nineteenth and early twentieth century, large segments of the Yiddish language community were withdrawn from the Slavic and other Old-World spheres of influence and brought into fresh contact with English, Spanish, and Portuguese in the Americas. One finds, accordingly, in the history of Yiddish a certain basic structure now maintaining itself, now submitting to some outside interference only to integrate the effects of this interference into a new, unique whole—depending on the specific historical circumstances. Such structural features in Yiddish as the opposition between some palatal and non-palatal consonants, for example, or that between perfective and non-perfective verbs, were at least partly acquired from, and supported by, contact with Slavic languages. In America, where this support has been discontinued, one can observe an incipient blurring of these distinctions and the acquisition of new patterns. In this connection, it is also relevant to contrast structural features of various dialects of Old-World Yiddish. They differ, for example, in their treatment of external

---

[11] Martinet (**346**), 156.

[12] Cf. Skok and Budimir's fascinating introduction (**523**) to the *Revue internationale des études balkaniques*. Sandfeld's celebrated works are listed in the bibliography (**465–470**). See also the series by Šufflay (**554**) and Barić (**17**), and the study on Balkan folklore by Schneeweiss (**495**).

sandhi. The eastern dialects seem to follow the Belorussian-Russian system, while the central dialects of Poland agree rather with the patterns of (Eastern) Poland.[13] In the Yiddish field, it is therefore possible to study the problem of congruence or non-congruence of structural isoglosses in coterritorial languages on a grand scale.[14]

The structural variety of outside influences in different socio-cultural settings thus commends languages like Yiddish and areas like the Balkans to the attention of students of interference.

In developing the theoretical and practical tools of interference study, there are certain additional advantages in selecting for analysis cases of language contact which are accessible to observation by direct field techniques and can consequently be described according to the most rigorous standards. In that way some of the risks inherent in reconstructing both structural and socio-cultural situations of the past can be avoided. The insights acquired and procedures developed from synchronic studies can then be applied to the solution of problems of diachronic structural linguistics. For this reason, the multiple language contacts taking place at present in countries like India or Israel represent attractive fields of investigation. Especially promising opportunities for research offer themselves in the Americas. It would be a pity if all these highly accessible but almost unexplored linguistic "super-Balkans" were to be overlooked.

To take the American scene: Even in the study of native Indian languages, the problems of multiple contact might be made a frutiful new point of departure.[15] But perhaps even more enticing is the analysis of American immigrant speech.[16] Dozens of European and several Asian languages are here represented by a total of tens of millions of speakers. The languages—some of them comprising several distinct dialects—are of the most different structures, and the socio-cultural relations between the various language communities run the gamut, in North America alone, from the firmly entrenched position of French in Canada, through the respectable obsolescence of a Scandinavian language in a Middle Western farm area, to the lowly status of an East European language in a large metropolis or an Indian language in the vicinity of a reservation. The American field provides a further opportunity to investigate language communities (e.g. the Yiddish group) which were already bilingual in the Old World but were withdrawn from contact with one language and brought into contact with English or Spanish on this side of the ocean.

In the United States, at least, the subject of language contact was "for many years markedly neglected. . . . Just as the bilingual himself often was a marginal personality, so the study of his behavior was a marginal scientific pursuit."[17]

---

[13] Gutmans (184).

[14] See Weinreich (624a). In the majority of language areas, overlappings with other languages are marginal at best. Cf. the discussion of Polish-German coterritorial dialectology by Mitzka (369), 87–91.

[15] Voegelin (597), 58.

[16] Cf. Meillet (350a), 114–6.

[17] Haugen (202), 272.

A turn for the better took place when the Committee on American Speech of the American Council of Learned Societies raised the problem of non-English speech in the United States.[18] Cognizant of the fact that research on minority languages "is of importance . . . for general linguists,"[19] the Committee tried to summarize descriptive work done in the field and to establish contacts between interested scholars. Pertinent books and articles have since been appearing in increasing numbers,[20] each containing important and useful data. Yet no two studies are thoroughly comparable, because the linguistic techniques employed and the sociological orientations, if any, on which they are based have been so different from one case to the next. It is consequently a major task in research planning to promote the coordination of studies in this field by drawing up general canons of description. New research will then become more systematic and the results more fully comparable. This, in turn, will increase their usefulness for diachronic investigation as well.

It is the hope of the author that the present study will stimulate the coordination of research into language contact on the broad linguistic and social-science foundations which have already been laid for it in various parts of the world.

[18] The proceedings of its 1940 conference were published by the Council in its *Bulletin* (3), no. 34. See also the Council's *Bulletin* (3), no. 40, p. 29; no. 43, p. 35.

[19] Hans Kurath in his final report (3, no. 43, p. 35).

[20] See Index (pp. 147f.) under Canada and United States.

Appendix

Effects of Bilingualism on the Individual

From the point of view from which language contact and interference are considered in the main body of this book, the effects of bilingualism on non-linguistic behavior are a rather secondary issue. However, this aspect of bilingualism has probably received more attention than any other in the literature.[1] Indeed, any correlation. between bilingualism and intelligence or character traits would have serious social, if not linguistic, implications. If one were to believe such writers as Weisgerber (**627**), bilingualism is capable of impairing the intelligence of a whole ethnic group and crippling its creative abilities for generations. Because of the importance of the problem, the present appendix surveys what evidence there is concerning the effect of bilingualism on mental development and on emotional adjustment.

1. Effects on Intelligence[2]

Among the pioneer experimental works on the intelligence of bilinguals was the investigation by D. J. Saer (**460**), who tested about 1,400 children in five rural and two urban districts in Wales. The tests revealed the following IQs:

	Urban	Rural
Monoglot	99	96
Bilingual	100	86

Saer explains the inferiority of rural children by the fact that the city child resolves the conflict between Welsh and English at an early age, before entering school, while the rural child meets the conflict between its "positive self-feeling" and its "instinct for submission" later, when it can no longer take it in its stride.[3]

In a study of Canadian Indians in 1928, Jamieson and Sandiford (**249**) found monoglots to surpass bilinguals in intelligence in three tests out of four. In the investigation made by Davies and Hughes (**116**) of the comparative intelligence of Jewish and non-Jewish children in London, England, the former, presumably bilingual, achieved higher scores.

In summarizing 32 studies carried out in the United States, Arsenian (**6**) notes that 60% of them brought out a handicap induced by bilingualism; 30% considered the handicap, if any, to be unimportant; 10% produced no conclusive evidence of any such handicap. This wide divergence in results is ascribed by Arsenian to methodological deficiencies. The inconclusive character of so much previous work prompted Arsenian to make his own study, based on a better

---

[1] See the bibliographies by Schliebe (**485**) and Arsenian (**6, 7**).

[2] The study by Darcy (**111a**), which unfortunately appeared too late to be utilized here, represents the best up-to-date survey of the problem.

[3] Arsenian (**6**) strongly doubts the validity of these results because of deficiencies in Saer's method, e.g. the assumption of constancy in factors which are really variable.

theoretical preparation, larger samples, more careful methods, and the use of a finer tool in the form of Hoffman's Bilingual Schedule (**224**). After correlating the mental ability, age-grade status, and socio-economic background of 1,152 Italian and 1,196 Jewish American-born children, aged 9 to 14, of Brooklyn, N.Y., with their bilingual background, Arsenian found no significant impact of bilingualism on intelligence for the groups as a whole or for any socio-economic sector of it. In comparing "highly bilingual" and "low bilingual" children with respect to mental development, Arsenian again obtained no significant difference. A supplementary study by Arsenian in collaboration with Pintner (**408**) only supports the finding of a 0-correlation between bilingualism and verbal intelligence as well as school adjustment.

W. Toussaint (**575**), in a study made in Belgium in 1938 (not included in Arsenian's survey), tried to compare the intellectual and moral development of unilingual and bilingual Flemish and Walloon children on the basis of written examinations of about 40 children of each kind. His findings were that bilingualism affected the intellectual performance of primary-school children negatively. Stecker (**545**), on the contrary, reported no detrimental effects of bilingualism on the intelligence of South American children.

The South African Bilingual Survey (**335,** 70) showed that "children from more or less bilingual homes are, on the whole, more intelligent than children from purely unilingual homes, whether English or Afrikaans. . . . This superiority in intellectual development . . . is probably due largely to selective factors of a social nature which operate in South African society," and which are still to be investigated. In any case, there was no discrepancy with Arsenian's conclusions.

D. T. Spoerl (**540**) found that her bilingual subjects equaled the unilinguals in verbal intelligence, surpassed the latter slightly in the level of their vocational plans, and excelled them significantly in academic work.

In 1951, Jones and Stewart (**254**) again found unilinguals to surpass bilinguals in intelligence in both verbal and non-verbal tests. Thus the majority of experimenters deny the allegedly evil effects of bilingualism on mental development, although the contrary results obtained by Saer, Jamieson and Sandiford, Toussaint, and Jones and Stewart must still be accounted for.[4]

2. Effects on Group Identification

The structure of a language group belongs primarily to sociology, but the allegiance problems of the bilingual who potentially belongs to two language communities can also be formulated in terms of individual psychology.

The most active interest in this question was displayed by German scholars of the Hitler era, who were preoccupied with the assimilation and "transethnization" (*Umvolkung*) of *Volksdeutsche* (ethnic Germans). In their view the focal question for research on bilingualism was "the psychological comportment of

---

[4] Cf. Bovet (**73**). Arsenian's studies have not been recognized as final for all phases of the problem; in 1945, Darcy's thesis at Fordham University investigated bilingualism of pre-school children (**111**).

the bi- or multilingual in relation to the problems of ethnic politics and of ethnic and cultural biology, such as 'deëthnization' [*Entvolkung*], intermarriage, etc."[5] The writings of this school of thought, however, comprise schematic plans of work rather than description, not to speak of experimentation. Schmidt-Rohr (**491, 493,** and **490,** 178–92) discusses the logical connection between bilingualism and ethnic shift. Beyer (**43**), Beck (**36**), and Meiching (**349**) explore the psychological aspects of ethnic shifts. Loesch includes among his research problems the effects of a language shift on individuals (**316,** 164); in another paper (**315,** 229) he correlates stages of linguistic and ethnic assimilation of Germans in the United States. Heberle (**207**) disputes the claim that the more educated Germans in the United States retain their mother-tongue longer. Vasterling (**590**) discusses the deëthnization of adolescents; Geissler sets up a scheme of assimilation in several steps on the basis of his observations in Yugoslavia (**163,** 97 ff.). Kroh (**288**) has been more careful than the others; "the relation between bilingualism and 'transethnization,' " he says, "follows no fast rules, and differs so widely with the structure of the personality or the ethnic group that a large number of detailed studies will be necessary before general principles can be formulated."

In the United States, where language shifting is such a common constituent of the acculturation of immigrants, the problem of group identification of bilinguals has not found the attention it deserves. Fishman's experiment (**148**) on the group identification of bilingual Jewish children, showing that Yiddish-English bilingualism is not correlated with self-identification as an "American," is a pioneer undertaking with profound implications for the future study of American culture.[6] Barker's analysis (**19**) of the social disorientation of those elements of the population of Tucson, Arizona, who speak the *pachuco* argot is also exemplary in its field.

The common view of a bilingual hovering between two social systems as a "marginal man" has been thoroughly criticized by Goldberg (**171**). The marginal area is but a type of culture area, he argues; its content may be as much of a unity as the content of any other culture.

> If (1) the so-called "marginal" individual is conditioned in his existence on the borders of two cultures since birth, if (2) he shares this existence and conditioning process with large numbers of individuals . . ., if (3) his years of early growth . . . find him participating in institutional activities manned largely by other "marginal" individuals like himself, and, finally, if (4) his marginal position results in no major blockages or frustrations, . . . then he is not a true "marginal" individual . . . but a participant member of a marginal culture,[7] [which is]

a psychologically quite different experience. Pieris has shown (**406**) that in some

---

[5] Schliebe (**486**).

[6] Also in 1949, Johnson, in his Colorado University thesis, dealt with the relation of bilingualism to the formation of racial attitudes (**251**).

[7] Goldberg (**171,** 53). The distinction between merged and coexistent cultures in a single area recalls the theoretical problem of languages in contact; cf. §2.12.

cases bilingualism indicates cultural marginality, as among English speakers in Ceylon; in other situations, both languages are part of the same culture; e.g. Noko and Kromo, spoken respectively by Javanese noblemen and commoners. It has been this author's observation in Switzerland that Romansh-German bilingualism involves no social or cultural marginality; the negligibly small content of the ethnic designations "Raetoroman" and "German" is one of the main facilitating factors in the language shift.[8]

3. Effects on Character Formation

The contention that bilingualism causes emotional difficulties was already implicit in early writings such as Epstein's (**138**) and Blocher's (**54**). Ries went even further (**448, 449**) by attempting explicitly to ascribe the allegedly second-rate character of the Luxembourger to his bi- or tri-lingualism. "The temperament of the Luxembourger is rather phlegmatic. . . . We have none of the German sentimentalism [*Gemüt*], and even less of French vivacity. . . . Our bilingual eclecticism . . . prevents us from consolidating our conception of the world and from becoming strong personalities. . . . We are condemned to having our wings cut by skepticism and the dread of responsibilities . . ." and so on (**448,** 17 f.). Obviously, evidence of this kind cannot be used in studying the effects of bilingualism, although Toussaint (**575**, 89) took it quite seriously.

Gali (**156**) has suggested that bilingual persons may be morally depraved because they do not receive effective religious instruction in their mother-tongue in childhood.[9]

Pauly (**398**) has studied the handwriting of bilinguals in various scripts.

The preoccupation of German scholars with the effects of bilingualism on character has been noted above.[10] Henss (**211**), assuming a correlation between stuttering,[11] left handedness, and bilingualism, also concludes that it is an evil. A bilingual child, he contends, especially one that is away from its native land, "early begins to brood over its own peculiarities and its difference from the surrounding world; it becomes subject to an inner split [*Zerrissenheit*] and starts a fight for clarification, a struggle for becoming whole [*Ganzwerdung*]," which in turn leads to intellectual and moral deterioration. "Bilingualism is always connected with hybrid culture and its consequences," including attendant evils such as those "demonstrated" by Ries.

Michaelis (**358**) has claimed that the bilingual children of German merchants in the Near East suffer from "poverty of concepts," superficiality, laziness, and a definitely materialistic character. Sander (**464**), another German writer, declares:

Bilingualism leads not only to harmless speech errors, but it goes deeper, especially when it is imposed by force in early childhood, and endangers

---

[8] See §4.32 above.

[9] Cf. also Dahlem (**110**).

[10] Cf. also Sander (**463**).

[11] A significantly higher incidence of stutterers among bilinguals was statistically established by Travis, Johnson, and Shover (**579**).

the closed and self-centered wholeness of the developing structure. . . .
Every language establishes, as an articulated [*gegliedert*] system, a very
definite, relatively uniform and closed orientation of perception, feeling,
and thinking in those who speak it. The consequence [of bilingualism in
children] is that the inner attitudes which are conditioned by language
will not stand unconnectedly beside one another, but will enter into conflicting tensions in the child's soul. . . . This functional opposition of two
language formations can lead to shake-ups of the structure.

Conceding that bilingualism may favor one's analytic abilities, he feels nevertheless that it handicaps the more important ability to synthetize. He then
goes on to the "bilinguality of feelings" and the moral inferiority, the "mercenary
relativism" of bilingual persons, who switch principles according to the exigencies of a situation just as they switch languages according to their interlocutors.

K. Müller (**380**) claims to have shown how a particularly vicious kind of
bilingualism has made the population of Upper Silesia inferior in its capacity
to think and feel.

Weiss (**629**) scoffs at such speculations, arguing that the "psychological wholeness of the bilingual person suffers not at the clash of linguistically fixed concept
systems, but from the insecurity of his external life conditions." This line of
thought is an attempt to reintroduce scholarly sanity into political speculation
on a psychological problem.

A number of American writers have expressed themselves on the alleged
dangers of culture conflict inherent in bilingualism. Raubicheck (**426**) and
Levy (**309**) have discussed personality difficulties arising out of the intolerant
and often cruel attitude of the American environment toward non-English-
speaking children.[12] Bossard (**71**), from an examination of 17 case documents,
inferred that bilinguals are forced to develop a number of "protective" devices,
such as a restrained manner of speaking, inconspicuous behavior, home avoid-
ance, and meticulous English.

Spoerl's study (**539**) distinguishes itself from all the preceding speculation
by its sound experimental basis. To explore "the various emotional factors
which result, at the college level, from the experience of having been brought
up through childhood in a bilingual environment," Spoerl tested a group of 101
college freshmen according to various symptoms of maladjustment. She arrived
at the conclusion that it is the higher frequency and intensity of family conflicts
in bilingual homes—not the child's "mental conflict" resulting from speaking
two languages—which produces maladjustment.[13] Thus bilingualism and its

[12] Cf. also Haught (**204**). As Hall puts it (**189**, 16), the effects of the condemnation of a
language as inferior "in social or educational situations can be traumatic in the extreme."
[13] The only direct symptom of language difficulty appeared in a word-association test
in which bilinguals associated the word *language* with speaking, while unilingual students
were more prone to associate it with some specific foreign language; this, according to
Spoerl, is a remnant of greater speech difficulties in childhood.

effects function as a culture-complex pattern and not as a direct handicap against the individual.

Fishman (148) tested a group of children for a correlation between the degree of their bilinguality and their friendship and leisure habits, without finding any significant correlation.

Of course, a great deal may depend on the relations between the two language communities. Bossard (71) mentioned the special handicap of bilingualism when the second language is one of a hostile nation. "A war will often afflict a bilingual person particularly severely because it may be to him almost a civil war."[14] But the experimental evidence so far, offered by Spoerl and Fishman, on the whole disproves the alleged detrimental effects of bilingualism on emotional life. If such an effect were real, then a bilingual population would be more stupid, less practical, less well-adjusted than unilingual societies;[15] this has never been proved. On the other hand, the difficulties of bilinguals induced by the more complex cultural situation in which they live need to be elucidated.

4. Educational Problems Related to Bilingualism

In the many areas of the world where people with different languages live within the same territories it is not always possible to concentrate the children of each language group in separate schools, especially in small communities. It is therefore inevitable, even where there is no intention of imposing the state language upon the minority, that some children receive their instruction in a language other than their mother-tongue. Not only does this retard the children's education, but their knowledge of their own language suffers, and its cultivation is neglected. It has been contended, furthermore, that in segregated ("single-medium") schools, or even in segregated classes of the same ("parallel-medium") schools, intolerant attitudes toward the other language and its speakers are fostered, and thereby the sound civic life of a bilingual country is endangered.

The basic educational problems with regard to bilingualism are the organization of schools in bilingual areas and the best pedagogical methods for teaching two languages. Of all questions relating to bilingualism, these were probably the first to receive systematic attention. As early as 1910, Ghibu (168) was able to list almost a hundred items of bibliography on bilingual schools in German, French, Hungarian, and Rumanian.[16] An attempt to coordinate and systematize research on bilingualism was made by the Geneva International Bureau of Education by convening in the spring of 1928 the Luxembourg Conference on Bilingualism and Education (86). The conference received reports on condi-

---

[14] Christophersen (101), 9f.

[15] Paraphrasing Lehrer (300), 305.

[16] Cf. also the bibliographies by Blocher (54) and, quite recently, Leopold (303). Between 1893 and 1903, a special periodical, *Die zweisprachige Volksschule*, appeared in Breslau, Germany. Hall (189) gives a sketchy survey of some educational questions.

tions in Wales, Belgium, Bengal, Switzerland, and Czechoslovakia and discussed various theoretical and methodological questions. The world conferences of the New Education Fellowship have devoted increasing attention to bilingualism (**384**). At a special conference in Stuttgart in 1938, German educators and *Kulturpolitiker* also urged the development of further research.

A detailed discussion of the educational difficulties would lead too far afield. Some of the works listed in the bibliography are concerned with bilingual education in specific areas. Many of them also deal with principles.

Bibliography

The listing which follows includes all sources referred to in the text of the study as well as selected additional references on subjects discussed in the present work.

In the transliteration of titles from languages using the Cyrillic script, *c* corresponds to ц, *j* to й or the first element of я, ю, and initial e; *x* stands for x, *y* for ы (Ukrainian и), and ' for ь. Yiddish titles are cited in the widely accepted transliteration system of the Yiddish Scientific Institute—Yivo, in which *sh* = [š], *kh* = [x], *y* = [j].

Titles preceded by ° were inaccessible to this author.

The index on pp. 147f. groups the titles according to subjects.

1 AGARD, FREDERICK B. and DUNKEL, HAROLD B.: *An Investigation of Second-Language Teaching*, Boston—New York, 1948.

2 ALBERT, HERMANN: *Mittelalterlicher englisch-französischer Jargon* (= *Studien zur englischen Philologie* 63), Halle, 1922.

3 AMERICAN COUNCIL OF LEARNED SOCIETIES: *Bulletin* nos. 40 (1948), 43 (1950); and especially no. 34 (= *Conference on Non-English Speech in the United States*), March, 1942.

4 AMMENDE, EWALD (ed.): *Die Nationalitäten in den Staaten Europas*, Vienna, 1931.

5 ARON, A. W.: The Gender of English Loan-Words in Colloquial American German, *Curme Volume of Linguistic Studies* (= *Language Monographs* 7), Baltimore, 1931.

6 ARSENIAN, SETH: *Bilingualism and Mental Development*, New York, 1937.

7 ——: Bilingualism in the Post-War World, *Psychological Bulletin* 42.65–86 (1945).

8 ATHANASIADÈS, GEORGES: *Le bilinguisme dans les écoles grecques*, Geneva, 1940.

9 AUBIN, HERMANN; FRINGS, THEODOR, and MÜLLER, JOSEF: *Kulturströmungen und Kulturprovinzen in den Rheinlanden*, Bonn, 1926.

10 AUCAMP, A[NNA] J.: *Bilingual Education and Nationalism With Special Reference to South Africa*, Pretoria, 1926.

11 AUERHAN, JAN: *Die sprachlichen Minderheiten in Europa*, Berlin, 1926.

12 *Auslandsdeutsche Volksforschung*, Stuttgart 1— (1937ff.).

13 AVANESOV, R. I.: *Očerki russkoj dialektologii* I, Moscow, 1949.

14 BÄHLER, [E.] L.: *Die Organisation des öffentlichen Schulwesens der schweizerischen Kantone; Mannigfaltigkeit in der Einheit* (= *Archiv für das schweizerische Unterrichtswesen* 33), 1947.

15 BANGERTER, ARNOLD: *Die Grenze der verbalen Pluralendungen im Schweizerdeutschen* (= *Beiträge zur schweizerdeutschen Mundartforschung* 4), Frauenfeld, 1951.

16 BARBEAU, VICTOR: *Le ramage de mon pays; le français tel qu'on le parle au Canada*, Montreal, 1939.

17 °BARIĆ, HENRIK: *O uzajamnim odnosima balkanskih jezika*, Belgrade, 1937.

18 BARKER, GEORGE C.: Growing Up in a Bilingual Community, *The Kiva* 17.17–32 (1951).

19 ——: Pachuco: An American-Spanish Argot and Its Social Functions in Tucson, Arizona, *University of Arizona Bulletin* XXI, 1 (= *Social Science Bulletin* 18), 1950.

20 ——: Social Functions of Language in a Mexican-American Community, *Acta Americana* 5.185–202 (1947).

21 BARNOUW, ADRIAAN J.: *Language and Race Problems in South Africa*, The Hague, 1934.

22 BARON, SALO W.: *Nationalism and Religion*, New York, 1947.

22a BARTOLI, MATTEO: Per la storia della lingua italiana, *Archivio glottologico italiano* 21.72–107 (1927).

23 BÄSCHLIN: Die freien evangelischen Schulen in der Schweiz, *Archiv für das schweizerische Unterrichtswesen* 24.292ff. (1938).

24 BASTIEN, HERMAS: *Le bilinguisme au Canada*, Montreal, 1938.

25 BATEMAN, W. G.: A Child's Progress in Speech, With Detailed Vocabularies, *Journal of Educational Psychology* 5.307–20 (1914).

26 °BAUER, B.: *Die Sprachenfrage im Volksschulwesen Elsass-Lothringens*, 1938.

27 BAUER, HANS: *Zur Frage der Sprachmischung im Hebräischen*, Halle, 1924.

28 BAUER, ROBERT: Ein Volk ohne Sprache—die Iren, *Nation und Staat* 10.506–13 (1937).

29 BAUMGARTNER, HEINRICH: Das Verhältnis des deutschsprechenden Bielers zu seiner Mundart, zur Schriftsprache und zum Französischen, *Bieler Jahrbuch* I (1927), 61–88.

30 ——: Ein zweisprachiges Gymnasium, *Bieler Jahrbuch* VI (1932).

31 °BAUWENS, L.: *Régime linguistique de l'enseignement primaire et de l'enseignement moyen*, Brussels, 1933.

32 BAZELL, C. E.: [Reply to Question IV], in INTERNATIONAL CONGRESS OF LINGUISTS, 6TH (231), 303.

33 BEALS, RALPH: Acculturation, in *Anthropology Today* (ed. A. L. Kroeber), Chicago, 1953, 621–41.

34 ——: Acculturation, Economics, and Social Change in an Ecuadorean Village, in INTERNATIONAL CONGRESS OF AMERICANISTS, 29TH (228), 67–73.

35 °BECK, ROBERT: *Schwebendes Volkstum im Gesinnungswandel*, Stuttgart, 1938.

36 ——: Zur Psychologie der Umvolkung, *Baltische Monatshefte* 1938, 41–8.

37 °BECKMAN, NAT[ANAEL]: *Västeuropeisk syntax; några nybildnungar i nordiska och andra västeuropeiska språk*, Göteborg, 1934.

38 BELIĆ, A.: [Reply to Question IV], in INTERNATIONAL CONGRESS OF LINGUISTS, 6TH (231), 304.

39 BENARDETE, DOLORES: Immigrant Speech—Austrian-Jewish Style, *American Speech* 5.1–15 (1929/30).

40 BERGER, MARSHALL D.: The American English Pronunciation of Russian Immigrants, Unpublished Doctoral Dissertation, Columbia University, 1951; available on microfilm; summarized in *Dissertation Abstracts* 12.417 (1952).

41 BETZ, WERNER: *Deutsch und Lateinisch; die Lehnbildungen der althochdeutschen Benediktinerregel*, Bonn, 1949.

42 ——: Zur Erforschung des "inneren Lehnguts," in INTERNATIONAL CONGRESS OF LINGUISTS, 5TH (230), 33–5.

43 BEYER, HANS JOACHIM: Zur Frage der Umvolkung, *Auslandsdeutsche Volksforschung* 1.361–86 (1937).

44 °BIKČENTAJ, YROGLO and LAVROVA-BIKČENTAJ: *Myšlenije na rodnom i čužom jazykax*, Moscow, 1929; quoted by WEINREICH (618).

45 BIRNBAUM, SALOMO: *Das hebräisch-aramäische Element in der jiddischen Sprache*, Leipzig, 1922.

46 BJERRUM, ANDERS: Über die phonematische Wertung der Mundartaufzeichnungen, *Bulletin du Cercle Linguistique de Copenhague* 5.29–51 (1938/39).

47 °BJÖRKMAN, E.: Blandspråk och lånord, *Förhandlingar vid sjätte nordiska filologmötet i Uppsala*, 1902, 145–61.

48 °BLANKEN, GERARD HENDRIK: *Les Grecs de Cargese*, Leyden, 1951.

49 °BLIJDENSTEIN, G. F.: Zeichnen im zweisprachigen Unterricht, *Deutsche Schule im Ausland* 1935, 272ff.

50 BLOCH, OSCAR: *La pénétration du français dans les parlers des Vosges Méridionales* (= *Bibliothèque de l'École des Hautes Études* 232), Paris, 1921.

51 BLOCHER, EDUARD: *Die deutsche Schweiz in Vergangenheit und Gegenwart* (= *Schriften des Deutschen Ausland-Instituts* 8), Stuttgart, 1923.

52 ——: *Rückgang der deutschen Sprache in der Schweiz*, n.d.

53 ——: Vom Zerfall der Mundart, *Jährliche Rundschau des Deutschschweizerischen Sprachvereins* 1916.

54 ——: *Zweisprachigkeit: Vorteile und Nachteile* (= *Pädagogisches Magazin* 385), Langensalza, 1909.

55 BLOOMFIELD, LEONARD: *Language*, New York, 1933.
56 BOAS, FRANZ: On Alternating Sounds, *American Anthropologist* 2.47–53 (1889).
57 ——: The Classification of American Languages, *American Anthropologist* n.s. 22.367–76 (1920).
58 BOCK, KARL N[IELSEN]: Grænseegnenes Sprog: Mellemslesvigs Sprogforhold, *Haandbog i det slesvigske Spørgsmaals Historie, 1900–1937* (ed. Franz v. Jessen), Copenhagen, 1938, III, 615–84.
59 ——: *Niederdeutsch auf dänischem Substrat* (= *Deutsche Dialektgeographie* 34), Copenhagen, 1933.
60 BODMER, ANNEMARIE: *Spinnen und Weben im französischen und deutschen Wallis* (= *Romanica Helvetica* 16), Geneva—Zurich, 1940.
61 BOEHM, MAX HILDEBERT: *Das eigenständige Volk*, Göttingen, 1932.
62 ——: Nationalism, in *Encyclopedia of the Social Sciences*, XI, New York, 1933, 231–40.
63 BOGORODITZKIJ, V. A.: Über Sprachfehler der Deutschen im Russischen und der Russen im Deutschen, *Archiv für slavische Philologie* 41.1–13 (1927).
64 ——: *Očerki po jazykovedeniju i russkomu jazyku*, 1910.
65 °——: Nepravil'nosti russkoj reči u čuvaš, *Etjudy po tatarskomu i tjurkskomu jazykoznaniju*, Kazan', 1933, 106–12.
66 °BOILEAU, L.: Le problème du bilinguisme et la théorie des substrats, *Revue des langues vivantes* 12.113–25, 169–93, 213–24 (1946).
67 *Bol'šaja sovetskaja enciklopedija*, 1st ed., vol. S.S.S.R., Moscow, 1946.
68 BONFANTE, G.: [Reply to Question IV], in INTERNATIONAL CONGRESS OF LINGUISTS, 6TH (231), 304.
69 BORCHLING, CONRAD: Sprachcharakter und literarische Verwendung des sogenannten "Missingsch," *Wissenschaftliche Beihefte* (no. 37) *zur Zeitschrift des Allgemeinen Deutschen Sprachvereins* 5.193–221 (1916).
70 BORN, ERIC FREIHERR VON: Schwedisch und Finnisch in Finnland, *Baltische Monatsschrift* 60.359–66 (1928).
71 BOSSARD, JAMES H. S.: The Bilingual Individual as a Person—Linguistic Identification With Status, *American Sociological Review* 10.699–709 (1945).
72 BOUDA, KARL: Zur Sprachmischung, *Zeitschrift für Phonetik und allgemeine Sprachwissenschaft* 1.65–7 (1947).
73 BOVET, PIERRE: *Bilinguisme et éducation*, [Geneva, 1932].
74 ——: Les problèmes scolaires posés par le bilinguisme, *Schweizer Erziehungsrundschau* 1/1935.
75 BRANDENSTEIN, W.: Substrato, Superstrato, Adstrato, in INTERNATIONAL CONGRESS OF LINGUISTS, 5TH (230), 48.
76 BRANDSTETTER, RENWARD: *Das schweizerdeutsche Lehngut im Romontschen*, Lucerne, 1905.
77 BRAUN, MAXIMILIAN: Beobachtungen zur Frage der Mehrsprachigkeit, *Göttingische gelehrte Anzeigen* 199.115–30 (1937).
78 BRAUNSHAUSEN, NICOLAS: Le bilinguisme et la famille, in BUREAU INTERNATIONAL D'ÉDUCATION (86), 87–94.
79 ——: *Le bilinguisme et les méthodes d'enseignement des langues étrangères* (= *Cahiers de la Centrale du P.E.S. de Belgique* VII), Liége, 1933.
80 BRÉAL, MICHEL: Le mécanisme grammatical peut-il s'emprunter? *Mémoires de la Société Linguistique de Paris* 7.191f. (1892).
81 BROCH, OLAF: Russenorsk, *Archiv für slavische Philologie* 41.209–62 (1927).
82 BRUCKNER, W[ILHELM]: Die Bedeutung der Ortsnamen für die Erkenntnis alter Sprach- und Siedlungsgrenzen in der Westschweiz, *Vox Romanica* 1.235–65 (1936).
83 BUDIMIR, MILAN: Pathologische Lauterscheinungen in der Alloglottie, in Third International Congress of Linguists (1933), *Atti*, Rome, 1935, 54–8.
84 BUFLINGTON, A. F.: English Loan Words in Pennsylvania German, *Studies in Honor of Albrecht Walz*, Lancaster (Pa.), 1941

84a *A Bulletin of Bilingual Studies,* Published by the Bilingualism Committee of the University of Wales; no. 1, October, 1936 (mimeographed); no. 2, June, 1938; no. 3, June, 1939.

85 °BUNSEN, MARIE VON: *Die Welt, in der ich lebte,* Leipzig, [1929].

86 BUREAU INTERNATIONAL D'ÉDUCATION: *Le bilinguisme et l'éducation,* Travaux de la conférence internationale [sur le bilinguisme] tenue à Luxembourg . . . , Geneva—Luxembourg, 1928; Spanish edition: *El bilingüismo y la educación,* Madrid, 1932.

87 BUROS, OSCAR KRISEN (ed.): *Third Mental Measurements Yearbook,* New Brunswick (N. J.), 1949.

88 BYCHOWSKI, Z.: Über die Restitution der nach einem Schädelschuss verlorenen Umgangssprache bei einem Polyglotten, *Monatschrift für Psychiatrie und Neurologie* 45.183–201 (1919).

88a CALIFORNIA, DEPARTMENT OF EDUCATION: *Teacher's Guide to the Education of Spanish-Speaking Children* (= *Bulletin* 21, no. 4), 1952.

89 °CANADA, DEPARTMENT OF EDUCATION: *Report of the Committee Appointed to Enquire into the Conditions of the Schools Attended by French-Speaking Pupils,* 1927.

90 °CAPIDAN, TH.: *Fărşeroţii, studiu linguistic asupra Românilor din Albania,* Bucharest, 1931.

91 ——: Le bilinguisme chez les Roumains, *Langue et littérature* (Bulletin de la section littéraire de l'Académie Roumaine) 1.73–94 (1941).

92 ——: Les éléments des langues slaves du sud en roumain et les éléments roumains dans les langues slaves méridionales, *Langue et littérature* (cf. **91**) 1.199–214 (1941).

93 ——: *Meglenoromânii I: istoria şi graiul lor* (= *Academia Română, Studii şi cercetări* 7), Bucharest, 1925.

94 ——: Une suffixe albanais en roumain, *Revue internationale des études balkaniques* 2.130–6 (1936).

95 CAPLOW, THEODORE: The Modern Latin American City, in INTERNATIONAL CONGRESS OF AMERICANISTS, 29TH (**228**), 255–66.

96 CARR, DENZEL: Comparative Treatment of Epenthetic and Paragogic Vowels in English Loan Words in Japanese and Hawaiian, *Semitic and Oriental Studies* . . . [*for*] *William Popper* (= *University of California Publications in Semitic Philology* 11), 1951, 13–26.

97 CASAGRANDE, JOSEPH BARTHOLOMEW: Comanche Linguistic Acculturation: a Study in Ethnolinguistics, Unpublished Dissertation, Columbia University, 1951; available on microfilm; summarized in *Microfilm Abstracts* 4.811f. (1951).

98 CEBOLLERO, PEDRO A.: *A School Language Policy for Puerto Rico,* San Juan (P. R.), 194[5?].

99 °CHEN, ELINOR YUK LIN: A Study of Sentences by the Bilingual Child of Chinese Ancestry, Unpublished M.A. Thesis, Honolulu, 1935.

100 °CHOKSI, M.: The Problem of Teaching English in Bombay Schools, *Teaching* 20.112-5 (1948).

101 CHRISTOPHERSEN, PAUL: *Bilingualism,* London, 1948.

102 °CHURCH, ALFRED M.: The Standardized Testing Program Summary Report, 1947, *Hawaii Educational Review* 36.53–8 (1947).

103 CLERC, CHARLY: Il ne s'agit pas d'être bilingues, mais . . . [*sic*], *Die Schweiz* XIV (1943), 148–52.

104 COALE, WILLIS BRANSON: *Successful Practices in the Teaching of English to Bilingual Children in Hawaii* (= *U. S. Department of the Interior, Office of Education, Bulletin 1937,* 14), Washington, 1938.

105 °COLLINDER, BJÖRN: *Språkstrid och nationalitetskamp i Finland,* Stockholm, 1935.

106 CORNIOLEY, HANS: *Muttersprachliche Zerfallserscheinungen beim Aufenthalte in fremdem Sprachgebiet,* Berne, 1936.

107 CORNISH, VAUGHAN: *Borderlands of Language in Europe and Their Relations to the Historic Frontier of Christendom,* London, 1936.

108 ČOUKA, FR.: Über die Sprache tschechischer Kinder in einer deutschen Schule, in BUREAU INTERNATIONAL D'ÉDUCATION (86), 157–71.

109 °DĄBROWSKI, CZ.: Ze słownictwa i gramatyki języka ludności polskiej na Białorusi sowieckiej, Minsk, 1932.

110 °DAHLEM, HANS-JOACHIM: Die Zwei- und Mehrsprachigkeit in ihrer Bedeutung und ihren Folgen für die deutschen Volkskirchen Ost- und Südeuropas, Auslandsdeutschtum und evangelische Kirche 1935.

111 °DARCY, N. T.: The Effect of Bilingualism Upon the Measurement of the Intelligence of Children of Preschool Age, Unpublished Doctoral Dissertation, Fordham University, 1945.

111a ——: A Review of the Literature on the Effects of Bilingualism Upon the Measurement of Intelligence, Journal of Genetic Psychology 82.21–57 (1953).

112 DAUZAT, ALBERT: Le déplacement des frontières linguistiques du français de 1806 à nos jours, La Nature 55.ii.529–35 (1927).

113 ——: Les patois, Paris, 1927.

114 °DAVIAULT, SUZANNE: L'enseignement du français en pays bilingues, Cannes, 1951.

115 °DAVID, HENRY: Bilingualism, Dissertation in Preparation, New York University, 1951; reported in Publications of the Modern Language Association of America 67 (1952), no. 3, 128.

116 DAVIES, M. and HUGHES, A. G.: An Investigation into the Comparative Intelligence and Attainments of Jewish and Non-Jewish Children, British Journal of Psychology (General Section) 18.134–46 (1927).

117 DEETERS, GERHARD: Armenisch und Südkaukasich; ein Beitrag zur Frage der Sprachmischung, Caucasica 3.57–82 (1926).

118 DEVEREUX, GEORGE: Mohave Voice and Speech Mannerisms, Word 5.268–72 (1949).

119 —— and LOEB, EDWIN M.: Antagonistic Acculturation, American Sociological Review 8.133–47 (1943).

120 DHONDT, J.: Essai sur l'origine de la frontière linguistique [en Belgique], L'Antiquité classique, 16.261–86 (1947).

121 DILLON, MYLES: Linguistic Borrowing and Historical Evidence, Language 21.12–7 (1945).

122 DIRR, A.: Linguistische Probleme in ethnologischer, anthropologischer und geographischer Betrachtung, Mitteilungen der Anthropologischen Gesellschaft in Wien 39.301–20 (1909), 40.22–43 (1910).

123 °DMITRIJEV, N. K. and ČISTJAKOV, V. M. (eds.): Voprosy metodiki prepodavanija russkogo jazyka v nerusskoj škole, Akademija Pedagogičeskix Nauk R.S.F.S.R., Moscow—Leningrad, 1948.

124 DODD, STUART C.: On Measuring Languages, Journal of the American Statistical Association 44.77–88 (1949).

125 DOROSZEWSKI, WITOLD: Język polski w Stanach Zjednoczonych A.P., Warsaw, 1938.

126 DRAYE, H.: De gelijkmaking in de plaatsnamen, Bulletin de la Commission Royale de Toponymie et Dialectologie [Belge], 15.357–94 (1941), 16.43–63 (1942), 17.305–90 (1943).

127 °——: De studie van de vlaamsch-waalsche taalgrens in België, Brussels, 1945.

128 °——: De studie van de vlaamsch-waalsche taalgrenslijn in België geduurende de Hedendaagsche Periode, Leuvensche Bijdragen 33.61–112 (1941), 34.1–37 (1942).

129 °DREHER, JOHN JAMES: A Comparison of Native and Acquired Intonation, Unpublished Doctoral Dissertation, University of Michigan, 1951; available on microfilm; summarized in Microfilm Abstracts 11.461 (1951).

130 DUDEK, J. B.: The Bohemian Language in America, American Speech 2.209–311 (1926/27).

131 ——: The Americanization of Czech Given Names, American Speech 1.18–22, 161–6 (1926).

132 DUFRENNE, JEAN MARC: Les anglicismes dans le parler canadien-français, Idées 6.257–79 (1937).

133 EIKEL, FRED, JR.: The Use of Cases in New Braunfels [Texas] German, *American Speech* 24.278–81 (1949).

134 EISEMANN, KARL ERWIN: *Das alemannische Lehngut in der ostfranzösischen Mundart von Schnierlach (Lapoutroie) in den Vogesen* (= *Leipziger romanistische Studien, Sprachwissenschaftliche Reihe* 20), 1939.

135 °EISERMANN, WALTER: Beobachtungen zur Ein- und Zweisprachigkeit niederdeutscher Kinder, Dissertation in Preparation at University of Hamburg, 1950; reported in *Publications of the Modern Language Association of America* 55 (1950), no. 3, 227.

136 EMRICH, LENNA: Beobachtungen zur Zweisprachigkeit in ihrem Anfangsstadium, *Deutschtum im Ausland* 21.419–24 (1938).

137 ENCICLOPEDIA ITALIANA, 1933, *s.v.* Italia, vol. xix, 928–32.

138 EPSTEIN, IZHAC: *La pensée et la polyglossie*, Paris, [1915].

139 ERBE, H.: *Die Hugenotten*, Essen, 1937.

140 ESPER, ERWIN ALLEN: *A Technique for the Experimental Investigation of Associative Interference in Artificial Linguistic Material* (= *Language Monograph* 1), Baltimore, 1925.

141 ESPINOSA, AURELIO M.: *Estudios sobre el español de Nuevo Méjico*, Buenos Aires, 1930.

142 FABRYKANT, I.: Galitsizmen in yidish, *Yidishe shprakh* 7.47–59 (1947).

143 FAINE, J.: *Le créole dans l'univers*, Port-au-Prince, 1939.

144 FANO, R. M.: The Information Theory Point of View in Speech Communication, *Journal of the Acoustical Society of America* 22.691–6 (1950).

145 FAUSEL, ERICH: Eine deutsch-brasilianische Wortsammlung, *Auslandsdeutsche Volksforschung* 1.308–11 (1937).

146 FEIST, ROBERT: *Studien zur Rezeption des französischen Wortschatzes im Mittelenglischen*, Leipzig, 1934.

147 FELTES, J.: Les efforts phonétiques d'un petit peuple trilingue, Third International Congress of Phonetic Sciences, *Proceedings*, 1938, 924–6.

148 FISHMAN, JOSHUA A.: Tsveyshprakhikayt in a yidisher shul: eynike korelatn un nitkorelatn, *Bleter far yidisher dertsiung* 1951, no. 4, 32–42.

149 ——: Degree of Bilingualism in a Yiddish School and Leisure Time Activities, *Journal of Social Psychology* 36.155–65 (1952).

150 FLOM, GEORGE T.: English Elements in Norse Dialects in Utica, Wisconsin, *Dialect Notes* 2.257–68 (1900/01).

151 ——: English Loanwords in American Norwegian, As Spoken in the Koshkonong Settlement, Wisconsin, *American Speech* 1.541–8 (1925/26).

152 ——: The Gender of English Loanwords in Norse Dialects in America; a Contribution to the Study of the Development of Grammatical Gender, *Journal of English and Germanic Philology* 5.1–31 (1903/05).

153 FREY, J. WILLIAM: The Phonemics of English Loan Words in Eastern York County Pennsylvania Dutch, *American Speech* 17.94–101 (1942).

154 FRIES, CHARLES C. and PIKE, KENNETH L.: Coexistent Phonemic Systems, *Language* 25.29–50 (1949).

155 GADOLA, GUGLIELM: Domat ed il Romontsch, *Igl Ischi* 33.146–58 (1947).

156 GALI, ALEXANDRE: Comment mesurer l'influence du bilinguisme, in BUREAU INTERNATIONAL D'ÉDUCATION (86), 123–36.

156a ——, and G.: Quelques données sur le bilinguisme, in NEW EDUCATION FELLOWSHIP (384).

157 GARVIN, PAUL: Distinctive Features in Zoque Phonemic Acculturation, *Studies in Linguistics* 5.13–20 (1947).

158 °GATENBY, E. V.: Second Language in the Kindergarten, *English Language Teaching* 1 (1947).

159 GAUCHAT, LOUIS: L'état actuel des patois romands, *Der Geistesarbeiter* 21.21–8 (1942).

160 GEIGER, PAUL and WEISS, RICHARD, eds.: *Atlas der schweizerischen Volkskunde*, Zurich, 1950ff.

161 °GEISSLER, B.: Von der Sekundärsprache und ihrer Bedeutung im religiös-kirchlichen Leben, *Franz Rendtorff-Festschrift*, 1930.

162 GEISSLER, HEINRICH: Umvolkungserscheinungen bei Jugendlichen in der fremd-völkischen Großstadt, *Auslandsdeutsche Volksforschung* 2.358–65 (1938).

163 ——: *Zweisprachigkeit deutscher Kinder im Ausland*, Stuttgart, 1938.

164 °GENELIN, PLACI: Germanische Bestandteile des rätoromanischen (surselvischen) Wortschatzes, *Programm der k. k. Oberrealschule in Innsbruck* 1899/1900.

165 °GEORGACAS, DEMETRIUS JOHN: Peri tēs katagōgēs tōn Sarakatsanaiōn kai tou ono-matos autōn, *Archives of the Thracian Language and Folklore Thesaurus* 12.65–128 (1945/46), 14.193–270 (1948/49).

166 °GEORGEVSKIJ, A. P.: Russkije govory Primorja, *Trudy gosudarstvennogo dal'ne-vostočnogo universiteta* III, no. 7, 1928.

167 GERULLIS, GEORG: Muttersprache und Zweisprachigkeit in einem preussisch-litauischen Dorf, *Studi baltici* 2.59–67 (1932).

168 GHIBU, ONISIFOR: *Der moderne Utraquismus* (= *Pädagogisches Magazin* 414), Langen-salza, 1910.

169 GILLOUIN, RENÉ: *De l'Alsace à la Flandre; le mysticisme linguistique*, Paris, 1930.

170 GÖBL-GALDI, L.: Ésquisse de la structure grammaticale des patois français-créoles, *Zeitschrift für französische Sprache und Literatur* 58.257–95 (1934).

171 GOLDBERG, MILTON M.: A Qualification of the Marginal Man Theory, *American Socio-logical Review* 6.52–8 (1941).

172 GOLDSTEIN, KURT: *Language and Language Disturbances*, New York, 1948.

173 —— and KATZ, S. E.: The Psychopathology of Pick's Disease, *Archiv für Neurologie und Psychiatrie* 38.473–90 (1937).

174 GRAUR, A.: Désinences pour mots étrangers, *Faculté des Lettres de Bucarest, Bulletin linguistique* 2.238–41 (1934).

175 ——: Langues mêlées, *Faculté des Lettres de Bucarest, Bulletin linguistique* 15.8–19 (1947).

176 ——: Notes sur le bilinguisme. *Faculté des Lettres de Bucarest, Bulletin linguistique* 7.179f. (1939).

177 GREAT BRITAIN, MINISTRY OF EDUCATION, WELSH DEPARTMENT: *Language Teaching in Primary Schools* (= *Pamphlet* 1), London, 194[6?].

178 ——: *Bilingualism in the Secondary School in Wales; Y Broblem Ddwyieithog yn yr Ysgol Uwchradd yng Nghymru* (= *Pamphlet* 4), London, 1949.

179 GREENBERG, JOSEPH H.: Some Aspects of Negro-Mohammedan Culture Contact Among the Housa, *American Anthropologist* n.s. 43.51–61 (1941).

180 GRENTRUP, THEODOR: *Religion und Muttersprache* (= *Deutschtum im Ausland* 47/9), Münster (Westfalen), 1932.

181 GROOS, W.: *Wanderfahrten längs der Sprachgrenze in der Schweiz* (= *Schriften des allgemeinen deutschen Schulvereins zur Erhaltung des Deutschtums im Auslande* 6), Berlin, 1908.

182 GROOTAERS, L.: Tweetaligheid, *Album Frank Baur* I, Antwerp, 1948, 291–6.

183 GRÜNBAUM: *Mischsprachen und Sprachmischungen* (= *Sammlung gemeinverständlicher Vorträge* XX, 473), Berlin, 1885.

184 GUTMAN[s], TEODOR: Di konsonantn-asimilatsye in zats, *Filologishe shriftn fun Yivo* II (1928), 107–10.

185 °GYSSELING, M.: Le Namurois, région bilingue jusqu'au 8e siècle, *Bulletin de la Com-mission de Toponymie et Dialectologie* 21.201–9 (1948).

186 HAAS, H.: Meine Sprachgeschichte, *Bieler Jahrbuch* III (1929), 45–55.

187 HAAS, MARY R.: Interlingual Word Taboos, *American Anthropologist* n.s. 53.338–44 (1951).

188 HAHN, W. VON: Review of SELK (512) in *Wörter und Sachen* n.s. 2.93f. (1939).

189 HALL, ROBERT A., JR.: Bilingualism and Applied Linguistics, *Zeitschrift für Phonetik und allgemeine Sprachwissenschaft* 6.13–30 (1952).

190 HALLOWELL, A. IRVING: Cultural Factors in the Structuralization of Perception, in *Social Psychology at the Crossroads* (ed. J. H. Rohrer and M. Sherif), New York, 1951, 164–95.

191 ——: Ojibwa Personality and Acculturation, in INTERNATIONAL CONGRESS OF AMERICANISTS, 29TH (228), 105–12.

192 ——: Sociopsychological Aspects of Acculturation, in *The Science of Man in the World Crisis* (ed. R. Linton), New York, 1945, 171–200.

193 *Handwörterbuch des Grenz- und Auslanddeutschtums* (ed. Carl Petersen and others), Breslau, 3 vols., 1933–38.

194 HARDIE, D. W. F.: *A Handbook of Modern Breton (Armorican)*, Cardiff, 1948.

195 HARDY, G.: Le problème de la langue véhiculaire dans l'enseignement colonial, *International Education Review* 1.442–9 (1931).

196 HARRIS, JESSE W.: German Language Influences in St. Clair County, Illinois, *American Speech* 23.106–10 (1948).

197 HARTEN-HOENCKE, TONI: Dichten in fremder Sprache, *Die Literatur, Monatsschrift für Literaturfreunde* 29.321–4 (1927).

198 HAUDRICOURT, A.-G., and MARTINET, ANDRÉ: Propagation phonétique ou évolution phonologique? Assourdissement et sonorisation d'occlusives dans l'Asie du Sud-est, *Bulletin de la Société de Linguistique de Paris* 43.82–92 (1946).

199 HAUGEN, EINAR: Language and Immigration, *Norwegian-American Studies and Records* 10.1–43 (1938).

200 ——: Om en samlet fremstilling av norsk-amerikansk sprogutvikling, *Avhandlinger utgitt av det Norske Videnskaps-Akademi i Oslo*, II Kl., 1938, no. 3.

201 ——: Phonological Shifting in American Norwegian, *Language* 14.112–20 (1938).

202 ——: Problems of Bilingualism, *Lingua* 2.271–90 (1950).

203 ——: The Analysis of Linguistic Borrowing, *Language* 26.210–31 (1950).

203a ——: The Impact of English on American-Norwegian Letter Writing, *Studies in Honor of Albert Morey Sturtevant*, Lawrence (Kan.), 1952, 76–102.

204 HAUGHT, B. F.: The Language Difficulty of Spanish-American Children, *Journal of Applied Psychology* 15.91–5 (1931).

205 HAVRÁNEK, BOHUSLAV: Zur phonologischen Geographie; das Vokalsystem des balkanischen Sprachbundes, *Archives néerlandaises de phonétique expérimentale*, 8/9.119–25 (1933).

206 HAYES, FRANCIS C.: Anglo-Spanish Speech in Tampa, Florida, *Hispania* 32.48–52 (1949).

207 HEBERLE, RUDOLF: Auslandvolkstum; soziologische Betrachtungen zum Studium des Deutschtums im Auslande (= *Beiheft 2 zum Archiv für Bevölkerungswissenschaft und -politik* VI), Leipzig, 1936.

208 HEGNAUER, CYRIL: *Das Sprachenrecht der Schweiz*, Zurich, 1947.

209 HELLINGA, W. Gs.: Het Stadtfries en de problemen van taalverhoudingen en taalinvloed, *Tijdschrift voor Nederlandsche Taal- en Letterkunde* 59.19–52, 125–58 (1940).

210 HEMPL, G.: Language-rivalry and Speech-differentiation in the Case of Race-mixture, *Transactions of the American Philological Association* 29.31–47 (1898).

211 HENSS, WILHELM: Erziehungsfragen der fremden Minderheiten, in BUREAU INTERNATIONAL D'ÉDUCATION (86), 69–86.

212 ——: Zweisprachigkeit als pädagogisches Problem, *Ethnopolitischer Almanach* II (1931), 47–55.

213 HENZEN, WALTER: *Schriftsprache und Mundarten*, Zurich—Leipzig, 1938.

214 HERMAN, LEWIS and MARGUERITE S.: *Manual of Foreign Dialects for Radio, Stage, and Screen*, Chicago—New York, 1943.

215 °HERRMAN, G. and PÖTZL, O.: Bemerkungen über Aphasie der Polyglotten, *Neurologisches Centralblatt*, 1920.

216 HERSKOVITS, MELVILLE J.: *Acculturation; the Study of Culture Contact*, New York, 1938.

217 ——: *Man and His Works*, New York, 1948.

218 ——: Some Comments on the Study of Culture Contact, *American Anthropologist* n.s. 43.1–10 (1941).

219 ——: Introduction to INTERNATIONAL CONGRESS OF AMERICANISTS, 29TH, (228), 48–63.

219a HERZOG, GEORGE: Culture Change and Language: Shifts in the Pima Vocabulary, *Culture, Language, and Personality*, Menasha (Wis.), 1941, 66–74.

220 HEUVERSWYN, A. and TH. VAN: *Eene vreemde spraak als voertal van 't onderwijs*, Ghent, 1899.

220a HIRT, HERMANN: *Geschichte der deutschen Sprache*, Munich, 1919.

221 HJELMSLEV, LOUIS: Caractères grammaticaux des langues créoles, 2ᵉ Congrès International des Sciences Anthropologiques et Ethnologiques (2nd Session), *Comptes rendus*, Copenhagen, 1938, 373f.

221a HOARDE, LUCY CLAIRE: *Teaching English to Spanish-Speaking Children in the Primary Grades*, El Paso (Tex.), 1936.

222 °HOCHE, A.: *Das träumende Ich*, Jena, 1927.

223 HOFFMAN, HUGO: Einfluss des Polnischen auf Aussprache, Schreibung und formale Gestaltung der deutschen Umgangssprache in Oberschlesien, *Zeitschrift für deutsche Mundarten* 1909, 264–79.

224 HOFFMAN, MOSES NAPHTHALI HIRSCH: *The Measurement of Bilingual Background*, New York, 1934.

225 HOIJER, HARRY: Linguistic and Cultural Change, *Language* 24.335–45 (1948).

226 HUBBELL, ALLAN FORBES: *The Pronunciation of English in New York City; Consonants and Vowels*, New York, 1950.

227 HUSCHER, H.: Das Anglo-Irische als Ausdrucksmittel, *Englische Kultur in sprachwissenschaftlicher Deutung, Max Deutschbein zum 60. Geburtstage*, Leipzig, 1936.

228 INTERNATIONAL CONGRESS OF AMERICANISTS, 29TH: *Proceedings*, vol. 2: *Acculturation in the Americas* (ed. Sol Tax), Chicago, 1952.

229 INTERNATIONAL CONGRESS OF LINGUISTS, 4TH: *Actes*, Copenhagen, 1938.

230 ——, 5TH: *Réponses au questionnaire*, Brugge, 1939.

231 ——, 6TH: *Actes*, Paris, 1949.

232 ——, 7TH: *Preliminary Reports*, London, 1952.

233 IORGA, N.: Ce que vaut le vocabulaire, *Mélanges . . . P. M. Haškovec*, Brno, 1936, 185ff.

234 °ISBERT, OTTO A.: Die Psychologie der Madjarisierung, *Deutsches Grenzland* 1936, 59–71.

235 ITTENBACH, MAX: Zweisprachigkeit und organischer Grundbegriff, *Auslandsdeutsche Volksforschung* 1.420–3 (1937).

236 JABERG, KARL: Considérations sur quelques caractères généraux du romanche, *Mélangues Bally*, Geneva, 1939, 283–92.

237 ——: [Discussion of SANDFELD (466)], in INTERNATIONAL CONGRESS OF LINGUISTS, 4TH (229), 65.

238 ——: *Sprachwissenschaftliche Forschungen und Erlebnisse* (= *Romanica Helvetica* 6), 1937.

239 JAFFE, JUDAH A.: Yidish in Amerike, *Yivo-Bleter* 10.127–45 (1936).

240 JAKOBSEN, JAKOB: *Det norrøne Sprog på Shetland*, Copenhagen, 1897.

241 JAKOBSON, ROMAN: Franz Boas' Approach to Language, *International Journal of American Linguistics* 10.188–95 (1944).

242 ——: *K xarakteristike jevrazijskogo jazykovogo sojuza*, Paris, 1931.

243 ——: Prinzipien der historischen Phonologie, *Travaux du Cercle Linguistique de Prague* 4.247–67 (1931); republished in French as an appendix to TROUBETZKOY (583), 315–36.

244 ——: Sur la théorie des affinités phonologiques des langues, in INTERNATIONAL CONGRESS OF LINGUISTS, 4TH (229), 48–59; reprinted as an appendix to TROUBETZKOY (583), 367–80.

245 ——; FANT, C. GUNNAR M., and HALLE, MORRIS: *Preliminaries to Speech Analysis*

(= *Massachusetts Institute of Technology, Acoustics Laboratory, Technical Report* 13),
²1952.

246 JAKUBINSKIJ, LEV: O dialektologičeskoj reči, *Russkaja reč* 1.96–194 (1923).

247 ——: Neskol'ko zamečanij o slovarnom zaimstvovanii, *Jazyk i literatura* 1.1–19
(1926).

248 JAKUBOWSKI, WIKTOR: Uwagi o językowej stronie przekładów z języka rosyjskiego na
polski, *Język polski* 29.155–67 (1949).

249 JAMIESON, ELMER, and SANDIFORD, PETER: The Mental Capacity of Southern Ontario
Indians, *Journal of Educational Psychology* 19.313–28 (1928).

250 JESPERSEN, OTTO: *Language, Its Nature, Development, and Origin*, London, 1922.

251 JOHNSON, GRANVILLE B., JR.: The Relationship Existing Between Bilingualism and
Racial Attitudes, *Journal of Educational Psychology* 42.357–65 (1951).

251a ——: Bilingualism As Measured by a Reaction-Time Technique and the Relationship
Between a Language and a Non-Language Intelligence Quotient, *Journal of Genetic
Psychology* 82.3–9 (1953).

252 JOHNSON, JEAN BASSETT: A Clear Case of Linguistic Acculturation, *American Anthropologist* n.s. 45.427–34 (1943).

253 JONES, W. R.: Attitude Towards Welsh as a Second Language; a Preliminary Investigation, *British Journal of Educational Psychology (General Section)* 19.44–52 (1949).

254 ——, and STEWART, W. A. C.: Bilingualism and Verbal Intelligence, *British Journal of
Psychology (Statistical Section)* 4.3–8 (1951).

255 JUTZ, LEO: Sprachmischung in den Mundarten des Vorarlbergs, *Germanisch-Romanische
Monatsschrift* 14.256–68 (1926).

256 KAINZ, FRIEDRICH: *Psychologie der Sprache*, Stuttgart, 1943.

257 KAISIG, K.: Zur Frage der oberschlesischen Mundart, *Muttersprache* 48.220–3 *(Beilage;*
1933).

258 KARASEK-LÜCK, K.: *Die deutschen Siedlungen in Wolhynien* (= *Deutsche Gaue im Osten*
3), Plauen, 1931.

259 KARSTEN, J. E.: Eine vielsprachige Bauernbevölkerung, *Donum Natalicum Schrijnen*,
Nijmegen, 1929, 76–8.

260 ——: Mélange des langues et emprunts, *Scientia* 58.182–92 (1935).

261 KÄSTNER, WALTER: *Die deutschen Lehnwörter im Polnischen* I, Berlin, 1939.

262 °KAUDERS, O.: Über polyglotte Reaktionen bei einer sensorischen Aphasie, *Zeitschrift
für die gesamte Neurologie und Psychiatrie* 122.651–66 (1929).

263 KAUFMANN, EUGEN: Der Fragenkreis ums Fremdwort, *Journal of English and Germanic
Philology* 38.42–63 (1939).

263a KELLER, O.: Die Geheimsprache der wandernden Kesselflicker der Val Colla, Tessin,
Volkstum und Kultur der Romanen 7.55–81 (1934).

264 KENYÈRES, ADÈLE: Comment une petite Hongroise de sept ans apprend le français,
Archives psychologiques 26.321–66 (1938).

265 KERCHEVILLE, F. M.: A Preliminary Glossary of New Mexican Spanish, *University of
New Mexico Bulletin, Language Series* 5.1–69 (1934).

266 KESSLER, HEINRICH: Zur Mundart des Schanfigg, *Beiträge zur Geschichte der deutschen
Sprache und Literatur* 55.81–206 (1931).

267 KIMMERLE, MARJORIE M.: Norwegian-American Surnames, *Norwegian-American
Studies and Records* 12.1–32 (1941).

268 ——: Norwegian-American Surnames in Transition, *American Speech* 17.158–65 (1942).

269 KING, GWENDOLYN NOON: Musical Experiences to Aid Mexican Bilingual Children in
Correcting Speech Defects, *University of Arizona Record* 40 (1947), no. 1.

270 KIPARSKY, V[alentin]: *Fremdes im Baltendeutsch* (= *Mémoires de la Société Néo-Philologique de Helsingfors* 11), Helsinki, 1936.

271 ——: [Discussion of VOČADLO (596)], in INTERNATIONAL CONGRESS OF LINGUISTS,
4TH (229), 176.

272 ——: [Discussion of Question IV], in INTERNATIONAL CONGRESS OF LINGUISTS, 6TH
(231), 501–4.

273 °KLECZKOWSKI, ADAM: Wpływ języka polskiego na dyalekty prusko-niemieckie, *Pamiątkowa księga ... Józef Tretiak*, Cracow, 1913, 119–32.
274 KLEMENSIEWICZ, ZENON: Pan i obywatel, *Język polski* 26.33–42 (1946).
275 KLOSS, HEINZ: *Die Entwicklung neuer germanischer Kultursprachen von 1800 bis 1950*, Munich, 1952.
276 ——: Die niederländisch-deutsche Sprachgrenze, insbesondere in der Grafschaft Bentheim, *Deutsche Akademie, Mitteilungen* 1930, 96–109.
277 —: *Nebensprachen*, Vienna, 1929.
278 ——: Sprachtabellen als Grundlage für Sprachstatistik, Sprachenkarten und für eine allgemeine Soziologie der Sprachgemeinschaften, *Vierteljahrsschrift für Politik und Geschichte* I (7).103–17 (1929).
279 KOBER, ARTHUR: *My Dear Bella*, New York, 1946.
280 ——: Reconciliation in the Bronx, *The New Yorker*, September 1, 1951, 25–8.
281 KOCK, AXEL: *Om språkets förändring*, Göteborg, ³1925.
282 KOHN, HANS: *The Idea of Nationalism; a Study in Its Origin and Background*, New York, 1945.
283 KOLEHMAINEN, JOHN ILMARI: Finnish Surnames in America, *American Speech* 14.33–8 (1939).
284 ——: The Finnicization of English in America, *American Sociological Review* 2.62–6 (1937).
285 KRANZMEYER, EBERHARD: Deutsches Sprachgut jenseits der Sprachgrenze in den Alpen, mit besonderer Rücksicht auf das Rätoromanische des Grödnertales, *Deutsches Archiv für Landes- und Volksforschung* 1.273–86 (1937).
285a °——: Der Wert der Mehrsprachigkeit für die Etymologie grenzgelagerter Ortsnamen, *Third International Congress of Toponymy and Anthroponymy*, 1949, vol. 2–3, 1951.
286 ——: Zur Ortsnamenforschung im Grenzland, *Zeitschrift für Ortsnamenforschung* 10.105–48 (1934).
287 KROEBER, A. L.: *Anthropology*, New York, ²1948.
288 KROH, OSWALD: Zur Psychologie der Umvolkung, *Auslandsdeutsche Volksforschung* 1.386–97 (1937).
289 KUENZI, A[DOLF]: Pour la langue française, *Bieler Jahrbuch* I (1927), 89–106.
290 KUHN, WALTER: *Deutsche Sprachinselforschung*, Plauen, 1934.
291 ——: Die Bedeutung der geographischen Schutzlage für Kremnitz, Deutsch-Proben und andere deutsche Sprachinseln, *Geographischer Jahresbericht aus Österreich* 17.8–26 (1933).
292 LAFON, R.: [Discussion of Question IV], in INTERNATIONAL CONGRESS OF LINGUISTS, 6TH (231), 507f.
293 LAGARDE-QUOST, P. H. J.: The Bilingual Citizen, *Britain Today* 140 (Dec. 1947), 15–9; 141 (Jan. 1948), 13–7.
294 LANDAU, ALFRED: Di slavishe elementn un hashpoes in yidish, *Filologishe shriftn fun Yivo* II (1927), 199–214.
295 LARISH, R.: Yidish in erets-yisroeldikn hebreish, *Yivo-Bleter* 5.80–4 (1933).
296 LARRY, ETTA CYNTHIA: *A Study of the English Language As Spoken by Five Racial Groups in the Hawaiian Islands*, New York, 1942.
297 LAUFER, BERTHOLD: Loanwords in Tibetan, *T'oung Pao* 17.404–551 (1916).
298 LEE, D. D.: The Linguistic Aspects of Wintuʻ Acculturation, *American Anthropologist* n.s. 45.435–40 (1943).
299 LEHMANN, EMIL: Zur Grenzland-Volkskunde, *Deutsches Archiv für Landes- und Volksforschung* 2.529–42 (1938).
300 LEHRER, LEIBUSH: *Psikhologie un dertsiung*, New York, 1937.
301 LEISCHNER, ANTON: Über die Aphasie der Mehrsprachigen, *Archiv für Psychiatrie und Nervenkrankheiten* 180.731–75 (1948).
302 LENDL, EGON: Die Wandlung eines südslawischen Zadrugendorfes in ein deutsches Strassendorf, *Sudetendeutsche Zeitschrift für Volkskunde* 5.237–9 (1932).
303 LEOPOLD, WERNER F.: *Bibliography of Child Language*, Evanston (Ill.), 1952.

134 LANGUAGES IN CONTACT

304 ——: *Speech Development of a Bilingual Child*, 4 vols., Evanston (Ill.), 1939–50.

305 ——: The Study of Child Language and Infant Bilingualism, *Word* 4.1–17 (1948).

306 Leslau, Wolf: The Influence of Sidamo on the Ethiopic Languages of Gurage, *Language* 28.63–82 (1952).

307 Lessiak, P[rimus]: Alpendeutsche und Alpenslawen in ihren sprachlichen Beziehungen, *Germanisch-Romanische Monatsschrift* 2.274–88 (1910).

308 Lévy, Ernest-Henri: Langue d'homme et langue de femme en judéo-allemand, *Mélanges Andler*, Strasbourg, 1928.

309 Levy, John: Conflicts of Cultures and Children's Maladjustment, *Mental Hygiene* 17.41–50 (1933).

310 Lévy, Paul: *Histoire linguistique d'Alsace et de Lorraine*, 2 vols. Paris, 1929.

311 ——: Histoire linguistique de Thionville, *Revue des études historiques* 89.423–52 (1923).

312 Linton, Ralph (ed.): *Acculturation in Seven American Indian Tribes*, New York, 1940.

313 ——: Nativistic Movements, *American Anthropologist* n.s. 45.230–40 (1943).

314 Livingston, Arthur: La Merica Sanemagogna, *The Romanic Review* 9.206–26 (1918).

315 Loesch, K. C. von: Eingedeutschte, Entdeutschte und Renegaten, *Volk unter Völkern* (ed. Loesch), Breslau, 1925, 213–43.

316 ——: Volkstümer und Sprachwechsel, *Wörter und Sachen* 17.153–64 (1936).

317 Loewe, Richard: Die Dialektmischung im magdeburgischen Gebiete, *Jahrbuch des Vereins für niederdeutsche Sprachforschung* XIV (1888), 14–52.

318 ——: Zur Sprach- und Mundartenmischung, *Zeitschrift für Völkerpsychologie und Sprachwissenschaft* 20.261–305 (1890).

319 Loey, Adolphe van: *La langue néerlandaise en pays flamand*, Brussels, 1945.

320 °——: Phénomènes linguistiques frontaliers, Unpublished Paper Read at the Institut de Sociologie Solvay on October 18, 1949.

321 °Lommel, Hermann: Das Fremdwort im Volksmund, *Bayerische Hefte für Volkskunde* 4.169–87 (1917).

322 Lomtev, T. P.: Stalin o razvitii nacional'nyx jazykov, *Voprosy filosofii* 1949, no. 2, 131–41; condensed in English in *Current Digest of the Soviet Press* II/7, 3–6 (1950).

323 Lontos, Sotirios S.: American Greek, *American Speech* 1.307–10 (1926).

324 Lopez, Cecilio: *The Language Situation in the Philippine Islands*, Manila, 1931.

325 Lotz, John: Speech and Language, *Journal of the Acoustical Society of America* 22.712–7 (1950).

326 Lowie, Robert H.: A Case of Bilingualism, *Word* 1.249–59 (1945).

327 Łukasik, Stanislas: *Pologne et Roumanie; aux confins des deux peuples et des deux langues*, Paris—Warsaw, 1938.

328 Lurie, Walter A.: The Measurement of Prestige and Prestige-Suggestibility, *Journal of Social Psychology* 9.219–25 (1938).

329 Lynn, Klonda: Bilingualism in the Southwest, *Quarterly Journal of Speech* 31.175–80 (1945).

330 Lytkin, V. I.: Fonetika severnovelikorusskix govorov i zaimstvovanija iz russkogo v komijskij, *Materialy i issledovanija po russkoj dialektologii* 2.128–207 (1949).

331 Mackensen, Lutz: Heimat, Kolonie, Umvolk, *Folk* 1.24–55 (1937).

332 ——: Sprachmischung als Wortbildungsprinzip, *Zeitschrift für deutsche Philologie* 51.406–12 (1926).

333 Mackenzie, Fraser: *Les relations de l'Angleterre et de la France d'après le vocabulaire*, 2 vols., Paris, 1939.

334 Mak, Wilhelm: Zweisprachigkeit und Mischmundart im Oberschlesien, *Schlesisches Jahrbuch für deutsche Kulturarbeit* 7.41–52 (1935).

335 Malherbe, Ernest Gideon: *The Bilingual School; a Study of Bilingualism in South Africa*, Johannesburg, 1934; Afrikaans Edition, Capetown, 1943.

336 Malinowski, Bronislaw: *Dynamics of Culture Change*, New Haven, 1945.

337 Marckwardt, A. H.: An Experiment in Aural Perception, *English Journal* 33.212–4 (1944).

338 ——: Phonemic Structure and Aural Perception, *American Speech* 21.106–11 (1946).

339 MARK, YUDL: Yidishe anglitsizmen, *Yorbukh fun Amopteyl [fun Yivo]* I, Yiddish Scientific Institute, New York, 1938, 296–321.

340 MARTINET, ANDRÉ: Are There Areas of *affinité grammaticale* As Well As of *affinité phonologique* Cutting Across Genetic Language Families? INTERNATIONAL CONGRESS OF LINGUISTS, 7TH (**232**), 121–4.

341 ——: Description phonologique du parler franco-provençal d'Hauteville (Savoie), *Revue de linguistique romane* 15.1–86 (1939).

342 ——: Diffusion of Languages and Structural Linguistics, *Romance Philology* 6.5–13 (1952/53).

343 ——: Function, Structure, and Sound Change, *Word* 8.1–32 (1952).

344 ——: *Phonology as Functional Phonetics* (= *Publications of the Philological Society* 15), London, 1949.

345 ——: Structural Linguistics, in *Anthropology Today* (ed. A. L. Kroeber), Chicago, 1953, 574–86.

346 ——: The Unvoicing of Old Spanish Sibilants, *Romance Philology* 5.133–56 (1951/52).

347 MATHESIUS, VILÉM: Zur synchronischen Analyse fremden Sprachguts, *Englische Studien* 70.21–35 (1935/36).

348 MAYER, KURT: Cultural Pluralism and Linguistic Equilibrium in Switzerland, *American Sociological Review* 16.157–63 (1951).

349 MEICHING, L.: Umvolkung als psychologisches Problem, *Zeitschrift für angewandte Psychologie und Charakterkunde* 54.138–49 (1938).

350 MEILLET, ANTOINE: *Linguistique historique et linguistique générale* (= *Collection linguistique publiée par la Société de Linguistique de Paris* 8, 11), 2 vols., Paris, 1921, 1938.

350a ——: *La méthode comparative en linguistique historique* (= *Instituttet for sammenlignende kulturforskning, Publikationer*, A, 2), Oslo, 1925.

351 ——, and SAUVAGEOT, A.: Le bilinguisme des hommes cultivés, *Conférences de l'Institut de Linguistique*, Paris, 1934, 5–14.

352 —— (with TESNIÈRE, LUCIEN): *Les langues dans l'Europe nouvelle*, Paris, 1928.

353 MENARINI, ALBERTO: *Ai margini della lingua* (= *Biblioteca de Lingua Nostra* 8), Firenze, 1947.

354 ——: L'Italo-Americano degli Stati Uniti, *Lingua nostra* 1.152–60 (1939).

355 MENCKEN, H. L.: *The American Language*, New York, ⁴1937.

356 MENDE, G. VON: Die willkürliche russische Beeinflussung des Tatarischen als Folge der Sowjetsprachenpolitik, *Wörter und Sachen* n.s. 1.297–303 (1938).

357 MERIAM, JUNIUS LATHROP: Learning English Incidentally (= *U. S. Department of Interior, Office of Education, Bulletin 1937*, 15), Washington, 1938.

358 MICHAELIS, A.: Der psychologische Einfluss des Auslandsmilieus auf die deutschen Jugendlichen, *Zeitschrift für pädagogische Psychologie* 34.212–33 (1933).

359 MICHEL, LOUIS: Réalités psycho-sociales et degrés du bilinguisme, in INTERNATIONAL CONGRESS OF LINGUISTS, 5TH (**230**), 32f.

360 MICHOV, D. M.: Die Anwendung des bestimmten Artikels im Rumänischen, verglichen mit der im Albanesischen und Bulgarischen, *Jahresbericht des Instituts für rumänische Sprache zu Leipzig* 14.1–111 (1908).

361 MIGLIORINI, BRUNO: Discontinuità linguistica e prestito morfologico, *Studj romanzi* 21.39–52 (1931).

362 MILKE, WILHELM: The Quantitative Distribution of Cultural Similarities and Their Cartographic Representation, *American Anthropologist* n.s. 51.237–52 (1949).

363 MILLER, GEORGE A.: *Language and Communication*, New York, 1951.

364 MINER, HORACE: *St. Denis, a French-Canadian Parish*, Chicago, 1939.

365 MINKOWSKI, M[IECZYSLAW]: Klinischer Beitrag zur Aphasie bei Polyglotten, speziell im Hinblick aufs Schweizerdeutsche, *Archives suisses de neurologie et de psychiatrie* 21.43–72 (1927).

366 °——: in *Comptes rendus du Congrès des Médecins et Neurologues de France*, 1949.

367 ——: Sur un cas d'aphasie chez un polyglotte, *Revue neurologique* 35.361–6 (1928).

368 MITZKA, WALTHER: Doppelsprachträger, *Zeitschrift für deutsche Mundarten* 1921, 143–51.

369 ——: *Grundzüge nordostdeutscher Sprachgeschichte*, Halle, 1937.

370 ——: *Studien zum baltischen Deutsch* (= *Deutsche Dialektgeographie* 17), Marburg, 1923.

371 °MLADENOV, STEFAN: Zu den bulgarisch-albanesischen Sprachbeziehungen, *Sofia University, Istoriko-filologičeski fakultet, Godišnik* XXIII (1923).

372 MÖCKLI, TH.: Le bilinguisme dans le canton de Berne, in BUREAU INTERNATIONAL D'ÉDUCATION (86), 62–8.

373 MÖHL, F. GEO.: Le mécanisme grammatical peut-il s'emprunter? *Mémoires de la Société de Linguistique de Paris* 7.196 (1892).

374 MØLLER, CHRISTEN: *Zur Methodik der Fremdwortkunde* (= *Acta Jutlandica* 5), Aarhus, 1933.

375 MORDINOV, A. JE.: O razvitii jazykov socialističeskix nacij S.S.S.R., *Voprosy filosofii* 1950, no. 3; reprinted in *Voprosy dialektičeskogo i istoričeskogo materializma v trude I. V. Stalina "Marksizm i voprosy jazykoznanija,"* Moscow, ¹1951, 151–72.

376 ——, and SANŽEJEV, G.: Nekotoryje voprosy razvitija mladopismennyx jazykov S.S.S.R., *Bol'ševik* 1951, no. 8, 38–48.

377 MORRIS, CHARLES: *Signs, Language, and Behavior*, New York, 1946.

378 MULCH, RUDOLF: Seelische Bedingungen im Leben der Wörter, *Indogermanische Forschungen* 51.1–73 (1933).

379 MÜLLER, FRIEDRICH [MAX]: *Grundriss der Sprachwissenschaft*, Vienna, 1879.

380 MÜLLER, KÄTHE: *Die Psyche des Oberschlesiers im Lichte des Zweisprachen-Problems*, Bonn, 1934.

381 MUÑIZ SOUFFRONT, LUIS: El problema de bilingüismo, *Revista de la Asociación de Maestros de Puerto Rico* 6, no. 6 (1947).

381a ——: *El problema del idioma en Puerto Rico; esfuerzos de la Asociación de Maestros de Puerto Rico para alcanzar la solución del problema*, San Juan (P.R.), 1950.

382 NAUMANN, HANS: Über das sprachliche Verhältnis von Ober- zu Unterschicht, *Jahrbuch für Philologie* I (1925), 57–69.

383 NEUMANN, J. H.: Notes on American Yiddish, *Journal of English and Germanic Philology* 37.403–21 (1938).

384 NEW EDUCATION FELLOWSHIP, SIXTH WORLD CONFERENCE: *A New World in the Making*, London, 1933.

385 NEWMAN, EDWIN B.: Pattern of Vowels and Consonants in Various Languages, *American Journal of Psychology* 64.369–79 (1951).

386 NIKOL'SKIJ, N. M.: Ob ispol'zovanii grammatičeskix parallelej iz rodnogo jazyka pri obučenii russkomu jazyku v nerusskix školax, *Russkij jazyk v škole* 8, no. 5, 63–7 (1947).

387 OFTEDAL, MAGNE: The Vowel System of a Norwegian Dialect in Wisconsin, *Language* 25.261–7 (1949).

388 ÖHMANN, EMIL: Zur Frage nach der Ursache der Entlehnung von Wörtern, *Mémoires de la Société Néo-Philologique de Helsingfors* 7.281–9 (1924).

389 °OLIJF, FRANÇOIS: *La question des langues en Belgique*, 2 vols., 1940–47.

390 ORTOZ, CARMELIA LOUISE: English Influence on the Spanish of Tampa [Florida], *Hispania* 32.300–4 (1949).

391 OSGOOD, CHARLES E.: A Psycholinguistic Analysis of Decoding and Encoding; I. Development in Normal Human Communication, Unpublished Paper Presented to the Conference of Anthropologists and Linguists, Bloomington, (Ind.), July 21–31, 1952.

392 ——: Ease of Individual Judgment-Processes in Relation to Polarization of Attitudes in the Culture, *Journal of Social Psychology* 14.403–18 (1941).

393 ——, and STAGNER, ROSS: Analysis of a Prestige Frame of Reference by a Gradient Technique, *Journal of Applied Psychology* 25.275–90 (1941).

394 PAGE, EUGENE R.: English in the Pennsylvania German Area, *American Speech* 12.203–6 (1931).

395 PAP, LEO: *Portuguese-American Speech*, New York, 1949.

396 PAPAHAGI, PER[ICLE]: Parallele Ausdrücke und Redensarten im Rumänischen, Albanesischen, Neugriechischen und Bulgarischen, *Jahresbericht des Instituts für rumänische Sprache zu Leipzig* 14.113–70 (1908).

397 PAUL, HERMANN: *Prinzipien der Sprachgeschichte*, Halle, ⁵1920.

398 PAULY, WILLY: *L'expertise en écritures chez les sujets bilingues*, Strasbourg, 1929.

399 PAVLOVITCH, MILIVOÏE: *Le langage enfantin; acquisition du serbe et du français par un enfant serbe*, Paris, 1920.

400 °PARLANGELI, O.: Fenomeni di simbiosi linguistica nel dialetto neogreco del Salento, *Annali della Facoltà di Filosofia e Lettere dell'Università Statale di Milano* I (1948), 335–55.

401 °PERERA, H. S.: *Sinhalese Pronunciation of English*, Colombo, 1923.

402 PETROVICI, ÉMILE: Bilinguisme, mots d'emprunt et calques linguistiques d'après l'Atlas linguistique roumain, in INTERNATIONAL CONGRESS OF LINGUISTS, 5TH (230), 35f.

403 PFAUNDLER, RICHARD VON: Das deutsche Sprachgebiet in Südungarn, *Deutsche Erde* 13 (1914/15); map is opposite p. 204.

404 °PICK, A.: Zur Erklärung gewisser Ausnahmen von der sogenannten Ribotschen Regel, *Abhandlungen aus der Neurologie, Psychiatrie, Psychologie und ihren Grenzgebieter* (= *Beiheft 13 zur Monatsschrift für Psychiatrie und Neurologie*, 1921), 151ff.

405 °——: Aphasie, *Archives suisses de neurologie et psychiatrie* 12.105–35 (1923).

406 PIERIS, RALPH: Bilingualism and Cultural Marginality, *British Journal of Sociology* 2.328–39 (1951).

407 PIHLBLAD, C. TERENCE: The Kansas Swedes, *The Southwestern Social Science Quarterly* 13.34–47 (1932).

408 PINTNER, R[UDOLF], and ARSENIAN, SETH: The Relation of Bilingualism to Verbal Intelligence and School Adjustment, *Journal of Educational Psychology* 51.255–63 (1937).

409 PISANI, V.: [Reply to Question IV], in INTERNATIONAL CONGRESS OF LINGUISTS, 6TH (231), 332f.

410 PITRES, A.: Étude sur l'aphasie chez les polyglottes, *Revue de médecine* 15.857–99 (1895).

411 POIRIER, PASCAL: *Le parler franco-acadien et ses origines*, [Quebec, 1928].

412 POKORNY, JULIUS: Substrattheorie und Urheimat der Indogermanen, *Mitteilungen der anthropologischen Gesellschaft in Wien* 66.89–91 (1936).

413 POLIVANOV, EVGENIJ: La perception des sons d'une langue étrangère, *Travaux du Cercle Linguistique de Prague* 4.79–96 (1931).

414 POST, P.: *Bilinguisme in Nederland; een beschouwing over de wenselijkheid van een fries-nederlandse school in Friesland* (= *Paedagogische Monographieën* 1), Groningen —Batavia, 1949.

415 PÖTZL, O.: Aphasie und Mehrsprachigkeit, *Zeitschrift für die gesamte Neurologie und Psychiatrie* 124.145–62 (1930).

416 ——: Über die parietal bedingte Aphasie und ihren Einfluss auf das Sprechen mehrerer Sprachen, *Zeitschrift für die gesamte Neurologie und Psychiatrie* 96.100ff. (1925).

417 POUND, LOUISE: On the Linguistics of Dreams, *American Speech* 9.175–80 (1934).

418 POUSLAND, EDWARD: *Étude sémantique de l'anglicisme dans le parler franco-américain de Salem (Nouvelle Angleterre)*, Paris, 1933.

419 POWERS, FRANCIS F., and HETZLER, MARJORIE: *Successful Methods of Teaching English to Bilingual Children in Seattle Public Schools* (= *U. S. Department of Interior, Office of Education, Pamphlet 76*), Washington, 1937.

420 PRAGUE LINGUISTIC CIRCLE: [Reply to Question III], in INTERNATIONAL CONGRESS OF LINGUISTS, 6TH (231), 274f.

421 PREZZOLINI, GIUSEPPE: La lingua della "giobba," *Lingua nostra* 1.122f. (1935).

138   LANGUAGES IN CONTACT

422 Pritzwald, Kurt Stegmann von: Sprachwissenschaftliche Minderheitenforschung; ein Arbeitsplan und eine Statistik, *Wörter und Sachen* n.s. 1.52–72 (1938).

423 *La querelle du bilinguisme; trois documents capitaux*, Montreal, [1941].

424 Racoviţă, C.: Notes sur le bilinguisme, *Faculté des Lettres de Bucarest, Bulletin linguistique* 6.238–42 (1938).

425 Räsänen, Martti: Wortgeschichtliches zu den Sprachen der Wolgavölker, *Finnisch-ugrische Forschungen* 26.125–43 (1940).

426 Raubicheck, Letitia: The Psychology of Multilingualism, *Volta Review* 36.17–20, 57f. (1934).

427 Raun, A[lo]: *Notes on Some Characteristic Errors in the Use of Russian by Finno-Ugrians and Turco-Tatars* (= *Contributions of the Baltic University* 36), Pinneberg, 1947.

428 Read, A[llan] W[alker]: Bilingualism in the Middle Colonies, 1725–1775, *American Speech* 12.93–100 (1937).

429 Read, William A.: *Louisiana French* (= *Louisiana State University Studies* 5), Baton Rouge (La.), 1931.

430 ——: Some Louisiana-French Words, *Zeitschrift für französische Sprache und Literatur* 61.62–84 (1938).

431 Récatas, B.: *L'état actuel du bilinguisme chez les macédo-roumains du Pinde et le rôle de la femme dans le langage*, Paris, 1934.

432 Redfield, Robert; Linton, Ralph, and Herskovits, Melville J.: Outline for the Study of Acculturation, in Herskovits (216).

433 Redlich, Friedrich A.: *Gemischtsprachige Dichtung im Baltikum* (= *Veröffentlichungen der volkskundlichen Forschungsstelle am Herderinstitut zu Riga* 6), Riga, 1937.

434 ——: Kinderspiel und Schülersprache des baltendeutschen Stammes in ihrer fremd-völkischen Beeinflussung, *Auslandsdeutsche Volksforschung* 1.305–8 (1937).

435 Reed, Carroll E.: The Adaptation of English to Pennsylvania German Morphology, *American Speech* 23.239–49 (1948).

436 ——: The Gender of English Loan Words in Pennsylvania German, *American Speech* 17.25–9 (1940).

437 Reed, David W.; Lado, Robert, and Shen, Yao: The Importance of the Native Language in Foreign Language Learning, *Language Learning* I (1), 17–23 (1948).

438 Reed, David W. and Spicer, John L.: Correlation Methods of Comparing Idiolects in a Transitional Area, *Language* 28.348–59 (1952).

439 Rees, W. H.: *Le bilinguisme des pays celtiques*, Rennes, 1939.

440 Reinecke, John E.: Personal Names in Hawaii, *American Speech* 15.345–52 (1940).

441 ——: Trade Jargons and Creole Dialects as Marginal Languages, *Social Forces* 17.107–18 (1938).

442 ——, and Tokimasa, Aiko: The English Dialect of Hawaii, *American Speech* 9.48–58, 122–31 (1934).

443 °Remacle, L.: Bilinguisme et orthophonie, *Bulletin de la Commission Royale de Toponymie et Dialectologie* 17.115–36 (1943).

444 Reynold, Gonzague de: Sur le bilinguisme, *Bieler Jahrbuch* II (1928), 101–16.

445 Rhodes, Willard: Acculturation in North American Indian Music, in International Congress of Americanists, 29th (228), 127–32.

446 Richter, Elise: *Fremdwortkunde*, Leipzig, 1919.

447 Riegler, R.: Italienisch-spanische Sprachmischung, *Neuere Sprachen* 29.218–21 (1921).

448 Ries, Nicolas: Le bilinguisme et le caractère luxembourgeois, in Bureau International d'Éducation (86), 16–25.

449 ——: Le dualisme linguistique et psychique du peuple luxembourgeois, *Programm [des] grossherzoglichen Gymnasium zu Diekirch* 1910/11.

450 Roberts, Murat H.: The Problem of the Hybrid Language, *Journal of English and Germanic Philology* 38.23–41 (1939).

451 Ronjat, Jules: *Le développement du langage observé chez un enfant bilingue*, Paris, 1913.

452 ROSARIO, RUBEN DEL: Bilingüismo, *Isla* 2.4f. (1940).

453 ROSENQUIST, CARL M.: Linguistic Changes in the Acculturation of the Swedes of Texas, *Sociology and Social Research* 16.221–31 (1931–32).

454 ROSETTI, AL.: Langue mixte et mélange des langues, *Acta Linguistica* 5.73–9 (1945/49).

455 ROTHENBERG, JULIUS G.: The English of *Aufbau*, *American Speech* 19.97–102 (1944).

456 ROTTENBERG, MICHEL: L'argot franco-turc du lycée de Galatasaray, *Le français moderne* 5.161–70 (1937).

457 RUBIN, ISRAEL: Vegn der virkung fun yidish oyfn geredtn hebreish in erets-yisroel, *Yivo-Bleter* 25.303–9 (1945).

458 RUDNYĆKYJ, JAROSLAU: Die Lage der ukrainischen Sprache in der Sowjetunion, *Wörter und Sachen* n.s. 1.284–97 (1938).

459 SADLO, JOSEPH: *Influences phonétiques françaises sur le langage des enfants polonais en France*, Paris, 1935.

460 SAER, D. J.: The Effect of Bilingualism On Intelligence, *British Journal of Psychology* 14.25–38 (1923).

461 ——; SMITH, F., and HUGHES, J.: *The Bilingual Problem; a Study Based on Experiments and Observations in Wales*, Aberyswyth, 1928.

462 SAER, HYWELLA A.: Experimental Inquiry Into the Education of Bilingual Peoples, *Education in a Changing Commonwealth*, London, 1931, 116–21.

463 °SANDER, FRIEDRICH: Einfluss der Zweisprachigkeit auf die geistige Entwicklung, *Bericht über den 5. Kongress für Heilpädagogik*, Cologne, 1930.

464 ——: Seelische Struktur und Sprache; Strukturpsychologisches zum Zweisprachenproblem, *Neue psychologische Studien* 12.59 (1934).

465 SANDFELD(-JENSEN), KR[ISTIAN]: Der Schwund des Infinitivs im Rumänischen und den Balkansprachen, *Jahresbericht des Instituts für rumänische Sprache zu Leipzig* 9.75–131 (1902).

466 ——: Les interférences linguistiques, in INTERNATIONAL CONGRESS OF LINGUISTS, 4TH (229), 60–5.

467 ——: *Linguistique balkanique*, Paris, 1930.

468 ——: Note de syntaxe comparée des langues balkaniques, *Revue internationale des études balkaniques* 1.100–9 (1934).

469 ——: Notes sur les calques linguistiques, *Festschrift Vilhelm Thomsen*, Leipzig, 1912, 166–73.

470 ——, and SKOK, P.: Langues balkaniques, *Revue internationale des études balkaniques* 2.465–81 (1936).

471 SAPIR, EDWARD: Language, in *Encyclopedia of the Social Sciences*, IX, 155–69; reprinted in *Selected Writings* (ed. D. G. Mandelbaum), Berkeley—Los Angeles, 1949, 7–32.

472 ——: *Language*, New York, 1927.

473 ——: *Time Perspective in Aboriginal American Culture; a Study in Method* (= *Canada, Department of Mines, Geological Survey, Memoir 90; Anthropological Series 13*), Ottawa, 1916; reprinted in *Selected Writings of Edward Sapir* (ed. D. G. Mandelbaum), Berkeley—Los Angeles, 1949, 389–462.

474 SAUVAGEOT, A.: [Discussion of Question IV], in INTERNATIONAL CONGRESS OF LINGUISTS, 6TH (231), 497–501.

475 SAVICKIJ, P. N.: Les problèmes de la géographie linguistique du point de vue de géographe, *Travaux du Cercle Linguistique de Prague* 1.145–56 (1929).

476 ŠČERBA, L[EV] V.: Očerednyje problemy jazykovedenija, *U.S.S.R. Academy of Sciences, Izvestija, Section of Literature and Language* IV (5), 1945, 173–86.

477 ——: Sur la notion de mélange des langues, *Jafetičeskij sbornik* IV (1926), 1–19.

478 SCHACH, PAUL: Hybrid Compounds in Pennsylvania German, *American Speech* 23.121–34 (1948).

479 ——: Semantic Borrowing in Pennsylvania German, *American Speech* 26.257–67 (1951).

480 ——: The Formation of Hybrid Derivatives in Pennsylvania German, *Symposium* 3.114–29 (1949).

481 SCHÄCHTER, MORDCHE: Aktionen im Jiddischen; ein sprachwissenschaftlicher Beitrag

zur vergleichenden Bedeutungslehre des Verbums, Unpublished Dissertation, Vienna, 1951.

482 ——: Di tushteygers in der yidisher shprakh, *Yidishe shprakh* 12.11–7, 83–7 (1952).

483 Scheludko, D.: Rumänische Elemente im Ukrainischen, *Balkan-Archiv* 1.113–46 (1926).

484 °Scheuermann, Friedrich: *Sprachenfreiheit und Sprachzwang in Belgien*, 1942.

485 Schliebe, Georg: Schrifttumsschau zur Psychologie der Zweisprachigkeit, *Deutsches Archiv für Landes- und Volksforschung* 3.475–88 (1939).

486 ——: Stand und Aufgaben der Zweisprachigkeitsforschung, *Auslandsdeutsche Volksforschung* 1.182–7 (1937).

487 Schmidt, Max, and Neumann, Walter: Eine Karte der steirischen Sprachgrenze, *Deutsches Archiv für Landes- und Volksforschung* 1.720–33 (1937).

488 Schmidt-Rohr, Georg: *Die Sprache als Bildnerin der Völker*, Jena, 1932. [Original edition of 490.]

489 ——: Die Sprache als raumüberwindende Macht, *Raumüberwindende Mächte* (ed. K. Haushofer), Leipzig—Berlin, 1934, 202–32.

490 ——: *Mutter Sprache*, Munich, 1932.

491 ——: Methodisches und Logisches zum Problem der Umvolkung, *Auslandsdeutsche Volksforschung* 2.373–81 (1938).

492 °——: Stufen der Entfremdung; ein Beitrag zur Frage der Assimilation von Sprachgruppen, *Volksspiegel* 1.75–82 (1934).

493 ——: Zur Frage der Zweisprachigkeit, *Deutsche Arbeit* 36.408–11 (1936).

494 Schneerson [Shneyerson], F.: *Lapsikhologia shel du-haleshoniut baarets*, reprinted from *Hakhinukh* 12, no. 1 (1939).

495 Schneeweiss, E.: Allgemeines über das Folklore auf dem Balkan, *Revue internationale des études balkaniques* 1.518–22 (1936).

496 Schuchardt, Hugo: *Dem Herrn Franz von Miklosich zum 20. November 1883: Slawodeutsches und Slawo-italienisches*, Graz, 1884.

497 [——]: *Hugo Schuchardt-Brevier* (ed. L. Spitzer), Halle, ²1928.

498 ——: Sprachverwandschaft, *Sitzungsberichte der königlich-preussischen Akademie der Wissenschaften* 37.518–29 (1917).

499 Schultze, Ernst: Sklaven- und Dienersprachen (sog. Handelssprachen); ein Beitrag zur Sprach- und Wanderungssoziologie, *Sociologus* 9.377–418 (1933).

500 Schumann, P.: *Der Sachse als Zweisprachler*, Dresden, 1904.

501 Schwartz, William Leonard: American Speech and Haitian French, *American Speech* 24.282–5 (1949).

502 Schwarz, Ernst: *Die Ortsnamen der Sudetenländer als Geschichtsquelle* (= *Forschungen zum Deutschtum der Ostmarken* II/2), Munich—Berlin, 1931.

503 Segerstedt, Torgny T.: *Die Macht des Wortes; eine Sprachsoziologie*, Zurich, 1947.

504 Seidel, Eugen: Linguistische Beobachtungen in der Ukraine, *Faculté des Lettres de Bucarest, Bulletin linguistique* °10.91ff. (1942), 11.73–111 (1943).

505 ——: Studie zur Sprachtypologie; rumäno-russische Kriterien, *Faculté des Lettres de Bucarest, Bulletin linguistique* 13.53–96 (1945).

506 Seifert, Lester W. J.: The Problem of Speech Mixture in the German Spoken in Northwestern Dane County, Wisconsin, *Transactions of the Wisconsin Academy of Sciences, Arts, and Letters* 39.127–39 (1947–49).

507 Seiler, Friedrich: *Die Entwicklung der deutschen Kultur im Spiegel des deutschen Lehnworts*, 8 vols., Halle, ⁴1923–24.

508 Seliščev, A.: Des traits linguistiques communs aux langues balkaniques, *Revue des études slaves* 5.38–57 (1925).

509 ——: Russkije govory kazanskogo kraja i russkij jazyk čuvaš i čeremis, *R.A.N.I.I.O.N.*, *Institut jazyka i literatury, Učenyje zapiski* 1.36–72 (1927).

510 ——: Russkij jazyk u inorodcev Povolžja, *Slavia* 4.26–43 (1925/26).

511 ——: Sokanje i šokanje v slavjanskix jazykax, *Slavia* 10.718–41 (1931).

512 SELK, PAUL: Die Dynamik des Sprachenwechsels in Schleswig, *Volkwerdung und Volkstumwandel*, Leipzig, 1943, 21–40.

513 ——: Mehrsprachigkeit in Schleswig; ein Beitrag zur Methode der Mehrsprachigkeitsforschung, [*Auslandsdeutsche*] *Volksforschung* 5.226–34 (1941).

514 SENN, ALFRED: Einiges aus der Sprache der Amerika-Litauer, *Studi Baltici* 2.35–58 (1932).

515 SHKLYAR, H.: Yidish-vaysrusishe shprakhlekhe paraleln, *Vaysrusishe visnshaft-akademie (Minsk), Institut far yidisher proletarisher kultur, Lingvistishe zamlung* I (1933), 65–80.

516 SHOEMAKER, HENRY W.: The Language of the Pennsylvania German Gypsies, *American Speech* 1.584–6 (1926).

517 SIDARITSCH, MARIAN: Begleitwort zu den Sprachenkarten, *Kartographische und schulgeographische Zeitschrift* 9.147f. (1921).

518 SIEGER, ROBERT: Sprachenkarte und Bevölkerungskarte, *Kartographische und schulgeographische Zeitschrift* 9.142–7 (1921).

519 SIMONYI, S.: Slavisches in der ungarischen Syntax, *Finnisch-ugrische Forschungen* 12.19–25 (1912).

520 SISSONS, CHARLES B.: *Bi-lingual Schools in Canada*, London, 1917.

521 SJŒSTEDT, M[ARIE] L[OUISE]: L'influence de la langue anglaise sur un parler local irlandais, *Étrennes de linguistique offertes ... à Émile Benveniste*, Paris, 1928, 81–122.

522 SKOK, P.: Restes de la langue turque dans les Balkans, *Revue internationale des études balkaniques* 1.585–98 (1936).

523 ——, and BUDIMIR, M.: But et signification des études balkaniques, *Revue internationale des études balkaniques* 1.1–28 (1934).

524 SKWARCZYŃSKA, STEFANIA: Estetyka makaronizmów, *Prace ofiarowane Kazimierzowi Wóycickiemu (= Z zagadnień poetyki* 5), Vilna, 1937, 337–70.

525 °SMAL'-STOCKYJ, R.: *Ukrain'ska mova v sovetskyji Ukrainy*, Warsaw, 1936.

526 SMITH, CHRISTINA A.: *Mental Testing of Hebridean Children in Gaelic and English*, London, 1948.

527 SMITH, HARLEY and PHILLIPS, HOSEA: The Influence of English on Louisiana "Cajun" French in Evangeline Parish, *American Speech* 14.198–201 (1939).

528 SMITH, (JAMES) MAPHEUS: An Empirical Scale of Prestige Status of Occupations, *American Sociological Review* 8.185–92 (1943).

529 SMITH, MADORAH E.: A Study of Five Bilingual Children From the Same Family, *Child Development* 2.184–7 (1931).

530 ——: A Study of the Speech of Eight Bilingual Children of the Same Family, *Child Development* 6.19–25 (1935).

531 ——: Some Light on the Problem of Bilingualism as Found From a Study of the Progress in Mastery of English Among Pre-School Children of Non-American Ancestry in Hawaii, *Genetic Psychology Monographs* 21.119–284 (1939).

532 °SOEDERHEIM, HENNING: *Finskt och svenskt i Finland; en orientering i språk- och nationalitets-frågorna*, Stockholm, 1935.

533 SOMMERFELT, ALF: Sur la propagation des changements phonétiques, *Norsk tidskrift for sprogvidenskab* 4.76–128 (1930).

534 ——: Un cas de mélange de grammaires, *Avhandlinger i det norske Videnskaps-Akademi (hist.-fil. Kl.)*, II, no. 4, Oslo, 1925.

535 *The Soviet Linguistic Controversy*, New York, 1951.

536 SPICER, EDWARD H.: Linguistic Aspects of Yaqui Acculturation, *American Anthropologist* n.s. 45.410–26 (1943).

537 SPITZER, LEO: Ein Fall von Sprachmischung, *Revue internationale des études balkaniques* 2.123–9 (1935).

538 ——: Confusion Schmooshun, *Journal of English and Germanic Philology* 51.226–33 (1952).

539 SPOERL, DOROTHY TILDEN: Bilinguality and Emotional Adjustment, *Journal of Abnormal and Social Psychology* 38.37–57 (1946).

540 ——: The Academic and Verbal Adjustment of College Age Bilingual Students, *Journal of Genetic Psychology* 64.139–57 (1944).

541 SPRINGER, OTTO: The Study of Pennsylvania German, *Journal of English and Germanic Philology* 42.1–39 (1943).

542 STAMMLER, WOLFGANG: Das "Halbdeutsch" der Esten, *Zeitschrift für deutsche Mundarten* 1922, 160–72.

543 STAVRULLI, M.: K voprosu o dvujazyčii, *Prosveščenije nacional'nostej* 1935, no. 4, 38–46.

544 °ST. DENIS, HENRI: Bilingual education, *Canadian School Journal* 12.213–7, 246 (1934).

545 STECKER, HUBERT: Erfahrungen und Studien über Zweisprachigkeit in Ibero-Amerika, *International Education Review* 1.598–608 (1932–33).

546 STEINER, E[MIL]: *Die französischen Lehnwörter in den alemannischen Mundarten der Schweiz; kulturhistorisch-linguistische Untersuchung mit etymologischem Wörterbuch*, Vienna—Basle, 1921.

547 STEINMETZ, ALEXANDER: Schrift- und Volkssprache in Griechenland, *Deutsche Akademie, Mitteilungen* 1936, 370–9.

548 STENGEL, E., and ZELMANOWICZ, J.: Über polyglotte motorische Aphasie, *Zeitschrift für die gesamte Neurologie und Psychiatrie* 149.292–311 (1933).

549 STERN C[LARA] and W[ILLIAM]: *Kindersprache*, Leipzig, ⁴1928.

550 STERN, WILLIAM: Die Erlernung und Beherrschung fremder Sprachen, *Zeitschrift für pädagogische Psychologie* 20.104–8 (1919).

551 ——: Über Zweisprachigkeit in der frühen Kindheit, *Zeitschrift für angewandte Psychologie* 30.168–72 (1923).

552 STRAUS, OLIVER H.: The Relation of Phonetics and Linguistics to Communication Theory, *Journal of the Acoustical Society of America* 6.709–11 (1950).

552a STRUBLE, GEORGE G.: The English of the Pennsylvania Germans, *American Speech* 10.163–72 (1935).

553 STUTCHKOFF, NAHUM: Der oytser fun der yidisher shprakh (ed. M. Weinreich), New York, 1950.

554 ŠUFFLAY, MILAN: *Srbi i Arbanasi* (= *Biblioteka arhiva za arbanasku starinu, jezik i etnologiju, istoriska serija* 1), Belgrade, 1925.

555 SULI (Σούλη), CHRISTO J.: Ta Bukuraïka . . ., 'Ηπειρωτικά χρονικά 3.310–20 (1928).

556 SWADESH, MORRIS: Observations of Pattern Impact on the Phonetics of Bilinguals, *Language, Culture, and Personality*, Menasha (Wis.), 1941, 59–65.

557 ——: Lexico-Statistic Dating of Prehistoric Ethnic Contacts, With Speical Reference to North American Indians and Eskimos, *Proceedings of the American Philosophical Society* 96.452–63 (1952).

558 ——: Sociologic Notes on Obsolescent Languages, *International Journal of American Linguistics* 14.226–35 (1948).

559 SYLVAIN, SUZANNE: *Le créole haïtien; morphologie et syntaxe*, Wetteren (Belgium), 1936.

560 SYMONDS, PERCIVAL M.: The Effect of Attendance at Chinese Language Schools on Ability With English Language, *Journal of Applied Psychology* 8.411–23 (1924).

561 SZADROWSKY, MANFRED: *Rätoromanisches im Bündnerdeutschen* (= *Beilage zum Programm der Bündnerischen Kantonsschule* 1930/31), Chur, 1931.

562 TAGLIAVINI, CARLO: Modificazioni del linguaggio nella parlata delle donne, *Scritti in onore di Alfredo Trombetti*, Milano, 1936, 82–146.

563 TAPPOLET, E[RNST]: *Die alemannischen Lehnwörter in den Mundarten der französcischen Schweiz; eine kulturhistorisch-linguistische Untersuchung*, Basle, 1913–16.

564 TAUTE, BEN: *Die bepaling van die mondelinge beheer van skoolkinders vor die tweede taal en van die korrelasies tussen hierdie beheer en sekere bekwaamhede faktore; 'n voorlopige ondersoek* (=*Annale van die Universiteit van Stellenbosch* XXIV/B, 1), Capetown, 1948.

565 TAYLOR, DOUGLAS: Structural Outline of Caribbean Creole: I. Morphology, *Word* 7.43–61 (1951).

566 TERKELSEN, FREDE: Kirke og Skole, *Haandbog i det slesvigske Spørgsmaals Historie*, 1900–1937 (ed. Franz v. Jessen), Copenhagen, 1938, III, 121–72.

567 TERRACHER, A.-L.: *Les aires morphologiques dans les parlers populaires du nord-ouest de l'angoumois (1800–1900); atlas*, Paris, 1914.

568 TESNIÈRE, LUCIEN: La lutte des langues en Prusse Orientale, *La Pologne et la Prusse Orientale* (= *Problèmes politiques de la Pologne contemporaine* 4), Paris, 1933, 45–96.

569 ——: Le *ü* du dialecte alsacien, *Études germaniques* 3.147–56 (1948).

570 ——: Phonologie et mélange de langues, *Travaux du Cercle Linguistique de Prague* 8.83–93 (1939).

571 THOMAS, C. K.: Jewish Dialect and New York Dialect, *American Speech* 7.321–6 (1931/32), 8.80f. (1932/33).

572 THURNWALD, RICHARD: The Psychology of Acculturation, *American Anthropologist* n.s. 34.557–69 (1932).

573 TIREMAN, LLOYD S.: *Spanish Vocabulary of Four Native Spanish Speaking Pre-I-Grade Children* (= *University of New Mexico Publications in Education* 2), Albuquerque (N.M.), 1948.

573a ——: *Teaching Spanish-Speaking Children*, Albuquerque (N.M.), 1948.

574 TITS, DESIRÉ: *Le mécanisme de l'acquisition d'une langue se substituant à la langue maternelle chez une enfant espagnole âgée de six ans*, Brussels, 1948.

575 TOUSSAINT, N.: *Bilinguisme et éducation*, Brussels, 1935.

576 TRAGER, GEORGE L.: Spanish and English Loanwords in Taos, *International Journal of American Linguistics* 10.144–60 (1944).

577 ——, and SMITH, HENRY LEE, JR.: *An Outline of English Structure* (= *Studies in Linguistics, Occasional Papers* 3), Norman (Okla.), 1951.

578 ——, and VALDEZ, GENEVIEVE: English Loans in Colorado Spanish, *American Speech* 12.34–44 (1937).

579 TRAVIS, L. E.; JOHNSON, W., and SHOVER, J.: The Relation of Bilingualism to Stuttering, *Journal of Speech Disorders* 2.185–9 (1937).

580 TREML, LAJOS: Der dynamische Wortakzent der ungarischen Lehnwörter im Rumänischen, *Faculté des Lettres de Bucarest, Bulletin linguistique* 2.34–65 (1934).

581 °TROST, P.: K dvojjazyčnosti Vojny a míru, *Pocta Trávníčkovi a Wollmanovi*, Brno, 1948, 405–13.

582 TROUBETZKOY, N.: [Proposal 16] in First International Congress of Linguists, *Actes*, Leiden, 1928, 17f.

583 ——: *Principes de phonologie*, Paris, 1949.

584 TURNER, LORENZO D.: *Africanisms in the Gullah Dialect*, Chicago, 1949.

585 ULLMAN, STEPHEN: *Words and Their Use*, New York, 1951.

586 UNBEGAUN, BORIS: Le calque dans les langues slaves littéraires, *Revue des études slaves* 12.19–48 (1932).

587 UNITED STATES, DEPARTMENT OF COMMERCE, BUREAU OF THE CENSUS: *Sixteenth Census of the United States, 1940; Population, Nativity, and Parentage of the White Population; Mother Tongue*, Washington, 1943.

588 VALKHOFF, MARIUS: *Geschiedenis en actualitet der Frans-Nederlandse taalgrens*, Amsterdam, 1950.

589 °——: *Superstrats germanique et slave*, Groningen, 1947.

590 VASTERLING, CHRISTIAN: *Entdeutschungsgefahren im Jugendalter; zur Psychologie der Umvolkung Jugendlicher*, Berlin, 1936.

591 VAUGHAN, HERBERT H.: Italian and Its Dialects as Spoken in the United States, *American Speech* 1.431–5 (1926), 2.138 (1926).

592 VELIKOVSKY, IMMANUEL: Can a Newly Acquired Language Become the Speech of the Unconscious? Word-Plays in the Dreams of Hebrew Thinking Persons, *Psychoanalytic Review* 21.329–35 (1934).

593 VELLEMAN, A.: Influenzas estras i 'l ladin, *Annalas della Società Retorumantscha* 45.87–116 (1931).

594 VENDRYES, J.: *Le langage*, Paris, 1921.

595 VIATTE, L.: La germanisation du Jura, *Actes de la Société Jurassienne d'Émulation* 2ᵉ série) 15.61–77 (1908).

596 VOČADLO, OTAKAR: Some Observations on Mixed Languages, in INTERNATIONAL CONGRESS OF LINGUISTS, 4TH (229), 169–76.

597 VOEGELIN, C. F.: Influence of Area in American Indian Linguistics, *Word* 1.54–8 (1945).

598 ——, and HARRIS, ZELIG S.: Methods for Determining Intelligibility Among Dialects of Natural Languages, *Proceedings of the American Philosophical Society* 95.322–9 (1951).

599 VOGT, HANS: Dans quelles conditions et dans quelles limites peut s'exercer sur le système morphologique d'une langue l'action du système morphologique d'une autre langue? in INTERNATIONAL CONGRESS OF LINGUISTS, 6TH (231), 31–45.

600 ——: Substrat et convergence dans l'évolution linguistique; remarques sur l'évolution et la structure de l'arménien, du géorgien, de l'ossète, et du turc, *Studia septentrionalia* 2.213–28 (1945).

601 VOLKMER, AUGUST: Die Zweisprachigkeit im Lichte der neueren Seelenkunde, *Der Obserschlesier* II (1936).

602 °VOOYS, C. G. N. DE: *Duitse invloed op de nederlandsche woordvoorraad*, Amsterdam, 1946.

603 VOSSLER, KARL: Sprache und Nationalgefühl, in his *Geist und Kultur der Sprache*, Heidelberg, 1925, 130–48.

604 WACKERNAGEL, J[AKOB]: Sprachtausch und Sprachmischung, *Nachrichten der königlichen Gesellschaft der Wissenschaften zu Göttingen; geschäftliche Mitteilungen* 1904, 90–111.

605 WAGNER, GEOFFREY: The Use of Lallans for Prose, *Journal of English and Germanic Philology* 51.212–25 (1952).

606 WALTERSHAUSEN, A. SARTORIUS FREIHERR VON: Die Germanisierung der Rätoromanen in der Schweiz; volkswirtschaftliche und nationalpolitische Studien, *Forschungen zur deutschen Landes- und Volkskunde* 12.365–474 (1899/1900).

607 WARTBURG, W[ALTHER] VON: Merkwürdigkeiten der Sprachgrenzen in der Schweiz, *Schweizer Geograph* 20.155–62 (1943).

608 WATERMAN, RICHARD ALAN: African Influence on the Music of the Americas, in INTERNATIONAL CONGRESS OF AMERICANISTS, 29TH (228), 207–18.

609 WECHSSLER, EDUARD: Gibt es Lautgesetze? *Forschungen zur romanischen Philologie* 1900, 349–538.

610 °WEIDLEIN, J.: Die Mundarten der deutschen Streusiedlungen in Ostungarn, *Südostdeutsche Forschungen* 2.139–51 (1937).

611 WEIGAND, GUSTAV: Vorwort, *Balkan-Archiv* 1.v–xv (1925).

612 WEIGHTMAN, J. G.: *On Language and Writing*, London, 1947.

613 WEIGOLD, HERMANN: *Untersuchungen zur Sprachgrenze am Nordufer des Bielersees auf Grund der lokalen Orts- und Flurnamen* (= *Romanica Helvetica* 24), Berne, 1948.

614 °WEIJNEN, ANTONIUS ANGELUS: *Tweetaligheid* (= *Opvoedkundige Brochurenreeks* 139), Tilburg, 1944.

615 WEIMAN, RALPH WILLIAM: *Native and Foreign Elements in a Language; a Study in General Linguistics Applied to Modern Hebrew*, Philadelphia, 1950.

616 WEINREICH, MAX: Di problem fun tsveyshprakhikayt, *Yivo-Bleter* 1.114–29 (1931).

617 ——: English un di imigrantn-shprakhn in Amerike, *Yivo-Bleter* 3.79–84 (1932).

618 ——: Tsveyshprakhikayt: mutershprakh un tsveyte shprakh, *Yivo-Bleter* 1.301–16 (1931).

619 ——: Yidishkayt and Yiddish; on the Impact of Religion on Language in Ashkenazic Jewry, *Mordecai M. Kaplan Jubilee Volume*, New York, 1953.

620 WEINREICH, URIEL: Di forshung fun mishshprakhike folkslider, *Yivo-Bleter* 34.282–8 (1950).

621 ——: Di shveytser romantshn arbetn farn kiyem fun zeyer shprakh, *Bleter far yidisher dertsiung* 5 (1953).

622 ——: Di velshishe shprakh in kamf far ir kiyem, *Yivo-Bleter* 23.225–48 (1944).

623 ——: Present-Day Approaches to the Study of Bilingualism, Unpublished M.A. Thesis, Columbia University, 1949.

624 ——: Research Problems in Bilingualism, With Special Reference to Switzerland, Unpublished Dissertation, Columbia University, 1951; available on microfilm; summary in *Dissertation Abstracts* 12.418f. (1952).

624a ——: *Sábesdiker Losn* in Yiddish: A Problem of Linguistic Affinity, *Slavic Word* 1 (1952).

625 ——: Tsurik tsu aspektn, *Yidishe shprakh* 12.97–103 (195?).

626 WEISENBURG, THEODORE H. and McBRIDE, KATHERINE E.: *Aphasia, a Clinical and Psychological Study*, New York, 1935; 97, 160–82.

627 WEISGERBER, LEO: Zweisprachigkeit, *Schaffen und Schauen* 9 (1933).

628 WEISS, A[NDREAS] VON: Review of GEISSLER (163), *Wörter und Sachen* n.s. 3.311–4 (1938).

629 ——: Zweisprachigkeit und Sprachtheorie, *Auslandsdeutsche Volksforschung* 1.256–66 (1937).

630 WEISS, RICHARD: Die Brünig-Napf-Reuss-Linie als Kulturgrenze zwischen Ost- und Westschweiz auf volkskundlichen Karten, *Geographica Helvetica* 21.153–75 (1947).

631 °——: Sprachgrenzen und Konfessionsgrenzen als Kongruenzen, *Laos* 1.96–110 (1951).

632 WERNER, GERHARD: Das Deutschtum des Übermurgebietes, *Geographischer Jahresbericht aus Österreich* 17.76–87 (1933).

633 ——: Sprache und Volkstum in der Untersteiermark, *Forschungen zur deutschen Landes- und Volkskunde* 31.111–285 (1936).

634 WERNER, W. L.: English Words in the Pennsylvania German Dialect, *American Speech* 6.123f. (1930).

635 WEST, MICHAEL: *Bilingualism (With Special Reference to Bengal)*, Calcutta, 1926.

636 °WEYHER, ERNST: *Die Grundschule im Zweisprachengebiet; methodische Gedanken*, Breslau, 1922.

637 WHITNEY, W[ILLIAM] D[WIGHT]: On Mixture in Language, *Transactions of the American Philological Association* 12.1–26 (1881).

638 WIESER, STEFAN: Die Deutschkenntnis der Sathmarer Schwaben, *Nation und Staat* 3.161–76 (1929/30).

639 WIJK, N[ICOLAS] VAN: L'étude diachronique des phénomènes phonologiques et extra-phonologiques, *Travaux du Cercle Linguistique de Prague* 8.297–318 (1939).

640 WILLEMS, EMILIO: *A aculturação dos alemães no Brasil; estudo antropológico dos imigrantes alemães e seus descendentes no Brasil* (= *Brasiliana* 250), São Paulo, 1946.

641 ——: *Aspectos da aculturação dos japoneses no Estado do São Paulo* (= *Universidade de São Paulo, Faculdade de Filosofia, Ciências e Letras, Boletim* 82 [*Antropologia* 3]), São Paulo, 1948.

642 ——: Linguistic Changes in German-Brazilian Communities, *Acta Americana* 1.448–63 (1943).

643 WILLIAMS, JAMES G.: *Mother-Tongue and Other-Tongue; or a Study in Bilingual Teaching*, Bangor, 1915.

644 WILSON, ARTHUR HERMAN: English Spoken by Pennsylvania Germans in Snyder County, Penna., *American Speech* 23.236–8 (1948).

645 WINDISCH, E.: Zur Theorie der Mischsprachen und Lehnwörter, *Berichte über die Verhandlungen der sächsischen Gesellschaft der Wissenschaften zu Leipzig* (phil.-hist. Kl.) 49.101–26 (1897).

646 WINTELER, J.: *Die Kerenzer Mundart des Kanton Glarus, in ihren Grundzügen dargestellt*, Leipzig—Heidelberg, 1876.

647 WINTER, EDUARD, ed.: *Die Deutschen in der Slowakei und in Karpathorussland* (= *Deutschtum im Ausland* 1), Münster (Westfalen), 1926.

648 WOLFF, HANS: Partial Comparison of the Sound Systems of English and Puerto-Rican Spanish, *Language Learning* 3.38–40 (1950).

649 WOLFLE, DAEL LEE: *The Relation Between Linguistic Structure and Associative Interference in Artificial Linguistic Meterial* (= *Language Monographs* 11), Baltimore, 1932.

650 WONDERLY, WILLIAM L.: Phonemic Acculturation in Zoque, *International Journal of American Linguistics* 12.92–5 (1946).

651 WREDE, FERDINAND, ed.: *Deutsche Dialektgeographie*, 1–40 (1908–41).

652 °WUTTE, MARTIN: *Deutsch-Windisch-Slowenisch* [?].

653 ——: *Die utraquistische Volksschule in Kärnten*, Klagenfurt, 1919.

654 XAJRULLA, ABDULAJEV: K voprosu o russkix predlogax i ix ekvivalentax v uzbekskom jazyke, *Russkij jazyk v škole* 8, no. 6, 66–8 (1947).

655 ZALLIO, A. S.: The Piedmontese Dialects in the United States, *American Speech* 2.501–4 (1927).

656 ZIEKURSCH, IRENE: Angelsachsentum und Keltentum im heutigen Schottland, *Anglia* 65.303–27 (1941).

657 ZIMMERLI, JACOB: *Die deutsch-französische Sprachgrenze in der Schweiz*, 3 vols., Darmstadt, 1891–99.

658 ZVEGINCEV, V. A.: K ponjatju vnutrennix zakonov razvitija jazyka, *U.S.S.R. Academy of Sciences, Izvestija, Section of Literature and Language* 10.319–35 (1951).

Index to the Bibliography

In the listing which follows, the bibliographical references are classified according to certain specialized topics. Only languages that have been influenced are indexed; thus, a study on the impact of German on French appears only under 'French'.

147

ERRATA

Page	Line (– From Bottom)	Reads	Should Read
x	– 11	James	Johannes
8	24	of	or
15	21	Vowels	Stressed vowels
19	15	two	three
22	7	[еве]	[ebe]
31	27	morphemes	forms
33	13	42	4.2
36	– 7	*t-l-g-r-f*	*t-l-gr-f*
40	22	*on,*	*on-,*
41	4	Albanian, and Modern Greek;	and Albanian;
41	15	*habēo*	*habeō*
57	1	Volga	Volga region
85	1	but practically	but there are practically
89	4	intermediate	overlapping
98	23	ranking two mother- tongue groups	ranking mother-tongue groups
98	27	4.36	4.32(8)
99	– 11	aggressive purposes.	political aggression.
113	24	I ettish	Lettish
117	– 11	Group Identification	Identification With a Group

Page	Item in Bibliography	Reads	Should Read
134	308	d'homme de femme 1928	des hommes des femmes 1924
136	366	*Médecins et Neuro- logues de France*	*Médecins Aliénistes et Neurologistes, 12-18 sept.*
137	421	1935	1939
139	472	1927	1921
142	557	Speical	Special
146	649	*Meterial*	*Material*

Add to Index:

147   Cheremis, 509
        Chuvash, 509